MISSOURI'S WAR

THE CIVIL WAR IN THE GREAT INTERIOR

Series Editors
Martin J. Hershock and Christine Dee

Ohio's War: The Civil War in Documents, edited by Christine Dee
Missouri's War: The Civil War in Documents, edited by Silvana R. Siddali
Indiana's War: The Civil War in Documents, edited by Richard F. Nation and
  Stephen E. Towne

FORTHCOMING:

Kansas's War: The Civil War in Documents, edited by Pearl T. Ponce
Michigan's War: The Civil War in Documents, edited by John W. Quist
Wisconsin's War: The Civil War in Documents, edited by Chandra Manning

MISSOURI'S WAR

The Civil War in Documents

~

EDITED BY SILVANA R. SIDDALI

Ohio University Press

Athens

Ohio University Press, Athens, Ohio 45701

www.ohioswallow.com

© 2009 by Ohio University Press

All rights reserved

To obtain permission to quote, reprint, or otherwise reproduce or distribute
material from Ohio University Press publications, please contact our rights and
permissions department at (740) 593-1154 or (740) 593-4536 (fax).

16 15 14 13 12 11 10 09   5 4 3 2 1

Cover art: *Order No. 11,* by George Caleb Bingham. Courtesy Cincinnati Art
Museum, The Edwin and Virginia Irwin Memorial

Library of Congress Cataloging-in-Publication Data
Missouri's war : the Civil War in documents / edited by Silvana R. Siddali.
   p. cm. — (The Civil War in the great interior)
   Includes bibliographical references and index.
   ISBN 978-0-8214-1732-4 (pbk. : alk. paper)
   1. Missouri—History—Civil War, 1861–1865—Sources. 2. Missouri—History—
Civil War, 1861–1865—Social aspects—Sources. 3. Missouri—Politics and
government—1861–1865—Sources. 4. Slavery—Missouri—History—19th
century—Sources. 5. Slavery—Political aspects—Missouri—History—19th
century—Sources. 6. African Americans—Missouri—History—19th century—
Sources. 7. African Americans—Missouri—Social conditions—19th century—
Sources. I. Siddali, Silvana R.
   E517.M576 2009
   977.8'03—dc22

                                                    2009024626

Dedicated to my brothers, Wolff, Raphael, and Steve.

Contents

One

Slavery in Missouri   6

Two

Missouri Divides   31

Three

Missourians Confront War 58

Four

Missouri's Battles 84

Five

Civilians Cope with War   121

Six

Bushwhackers, Jayhawkers, and Prisoners   155

Seven

First Steps toward Emancipation   190

Eight

Illustrations

Series Editors' Preface

The Civil War in the Great Interior series focuses on the Middle West, as the complex region has come to be known, during the most critical era of American history. In his Annual Message to Congress in December of 1862, Abraham Lincoln identified "the great interior region" as the area between the Alleghenies and the Rocky Mountains, south of Canada and north of the "culture of cotton." Lincoln included in this region the states of Ohio, Indiana, Michigan, Wisconsin, Illinois, Missouri, Kansas, Iowa, Minnesota, and Kentucky; the area that would become West Virginia; and parts of Tennessee and the Dakota, Nebraska, and Colorado territories. This area, Lincoln maintained, was critical to the "great body of the republic" not only because it bound together the North, South, and West but also because its people would not assent to the division of the Union.

This series examines what was, to Lincoln and other Americans in the mid-nineteenth century, the most powerful, influential, and critical area of the country. It considers how the people of the Middle West experienced the Civil War and the role they played in preserving and redefining the nation. These collections of historical sources—many of which have never been published—explore significant issues raised by the sectional conflict, the Civil War, and Reconstruction. The series underscores what was unique to particular states and their residents while recognizing the values and experiences that individuals in the Middle West shared with other Northerners and, in some cases, with Southerners.

Within these volumes are the voices of a diverse cross-section of nineteenth-century Americans. These include African Americans, European immigrants, Native Americans, and women. Editors have gathered evidence from farms and factories, rural and urban areas, and communities throughout each state to examine the relationships of individuals, their communities, the political culture, and events on the battlefields. The volumes present readers with layers of evidence that can be combined in a multitude of patterns to yield new conclusions and raise questions about prevailing interpretations of the past.

The editor of each volume provides a narrative framework through brief chapter introductions and background information for each document, as well as a timeline. As these volumes cannot address all aspects of the Civil War experience for each state, they include selected bibliographies to guide readers in further research. Documents were chosen for what they reveal about the past, but each also speaks to the subjective nature of history and the decisions that historians face when weighing the merits and limits of each piece of evidence they uncover. The diverse documents included in these volumes also expose readers to the craft of history and to the variety of source materials historians utilize as they explore the past.

Much of the material in these works will raise questions, spark debates, and generate discussion. Whether read with an eye toward the history of the Union war effort, a particular state or region, or the Civil War's implications for race, class, and gender in America, the volumes in The Civil War in the Great Interior help us consider—and reconsider—the evidence from the past.

Martin J. Hershock
Christine Dee

Preface

As early as November 1861, the *Missouri Republican* published reports of blasted farms, gangs of horse thieves, and a "war amongst neighbors and brothers."[1] More than any other border state, Missouri suffered criss-crossing raids by guerrilla fighters, invasions by soldiers of both armies, and bitter internal violence. Indeed, for many Missourians, civil warfare began years before the battle of Fort Sumter. Through primary source documents, *Missouri's War* seeks to capture the experience of the people who lived through the war: soldiers and their families; slaves and their owners; politicians, newspaper editors, and businessmen. Although the reader will find some familiar texts, such as General John C. Frémont's famous proclamation of martial law and Dred Scott's petition for freedom, many of the documents have never been published before: letters, diary entries, newspaper editorials, official correspondence, songs, and pamphlets.

The book begins with Missourians' early commitment to slavery and the conflicts with antislavery forces in neighboring Kansas. These divisions provide the context for the continuing struggles in the state throughout the Civil War and Reconstruction. Chapter 1 reveals the lives of people in bondage and the important role they played in Missouri's economy. Their daily existence was hard, and many of them suffered terrible losses as family members were sold away. Most Missourians, however, adamantly maintained that slavery was a permanent part of the state's way of life and that the U.S. Constitution protected their right to own slaves. The settlers' commitment to the institution of slavery led to terrible conflicts across the border in the Kansas Territory—conflicts that continued to plague Missourians throughout the Civil War. The antislavery settlers in Kansas, most of whom had come from New England, clashed violently with the pro-Southern Missouri farmers, who feared that a free Kansas would lure their slaves to escape.

The story continues in chapter 2, as Missourians fought over secession. Would the state remain in the Union or join the Confederacy? The secession struggle reveals once again how Missouri's internal disagreements erupted into violence that only escalated in the ensuing years. During the secession crisis, problems were often exacerbated by stubborn U.S. military and political commanders like General Nathaniel Lyon, who refused to try to conciliate among conflicting elements. But they were also caused by disloyal men like Governor Claiborne Jackson, who made secret deals with Confederate president Jefferson Davis.

Chapter 3 reveals how Missourians coped with the outbreak of warfare. The first battle in Missouri was, in truth, a civilian massacre and can be blamed at least in part on the ethnic divisions that were especially evident in St. Louis. The so-called

Battle of Camp Jackson symbolized the difficulties that continued to plague the city and the state. The documents that follow show not only the efforts of Missourians (especially women loyal to their respective sides) to support their war effort but also the ways in which soldiers and officers struggled with military discipline, loneliness, and hardship.

The documents in chapter 4 portray the battles and military movements in Missouri in the first two years of the war, most of which revolved around control over cities, armories, and transportation routes. Those targets included Jefferson City, the state capital; St. Louis, an economically vital port city and the site of military installations like the arsenal and Jefferson Barracks. Perhaps most important was the Mississippi River itself, for both the Union and Confederate armies. In 1861, soldiers were still writing home about the "first rate" times they had in their tents, and both sides were mobilizing: building armies, supplying gunboats, and strengthening rail connections. The earlier internal divisions continued to cause serious problems on the home front. The major battles in and near Missouri included Wilson's Creek in 1861 and Pea Ridge in 1862, after which the Confederacy lost hope of taking control of the state.

Chapter 5 takes the story to 1862 and deals with the troubles of civilians caught between the two warring armies. Those who took sides could expect reprisals. But even those who did not, or who attempted to keep their opinions to themselves, were often at the mercy of soldiers or guerrillas who simply did not care about their allegiances. Many civilians suffered attacks and raids by both sides, and some were caught in horrific massacres by bushwhackers. Women's service as nurses soon became more crucial, because the state and federal governments were unprepared to cope with battlefield casualties, especially in the trans-Mississippi theater of the war. This collection includes several excerpts from the memoirs of women who volunteered in army hospitals, as well as from soldiers who recuperated in them.

As the war dragged on and the rebel forces were gradually pushed out of the state, the federal army was troubled chiefly by vigilante violence, gang warfare, and bushwhackers. Chapter 6 begins with General Thomas Ewing's notorious Order No. 11 and shows how soldiers and officers attempted to control guerrilla warfare. As recruitment slowed during this period, the federal government began enlisting black soldiers. The officers of both sides continued to be troubled by a lack of funding, manpower, and adequate training. In the meantime, Missouri residents were often pressed into service by both sides. No man was safe. Missourians like Cyrus Russell and George Cruzen were forced to leave their families. Russell was captured by the Confederates, Cruzen by the federals, and both eventually managed to make their escape.

By late 1862, Missouri Republicans were ready to move ahead on emancipation. As the violence within the state and along its borders grew out of control,

Republicans felt that the only way to win the war was to free the slaves. Chapter 7 contains documents that reveal the first steps toward emancipation in the state, as well as the growing acrimony between the pro- and antiemancipation factions. As Republicans increased their call for emancipation, the proslavery forces in the state worried about the prospect of living among freed black people and losing millions of dollars of investment in their human property.

The last chapter brings the story of the war to a close. The end of the war in Missouri brought new problems and divisions but also some promise for the freed slaves and reconciliation among former enemies. Of course, some of the bitterness took a long time to die down; but in the end, rebel soldiers (and even some criminals, like Frank James) were able to regain their standing in the community. The situation for freed slaves was harder to gauge. Radical Republicans, who gained considerable power for about five years after the end of the war, ensured the early passage of a state constitutional amendment that freed the slaves and by 1866 had secured basic political rights for black people. In the end, however, many lost their savings when the Freedman's Bank collapsed and the state government returned to policies of segregation and discrimination. Some Missourians achieved reconciliation and made their peace; for others, the decades after the war brought disappointment and more struggle.

A note on the sources. In order to preserve the original meaning of these documents, I have edited them as sparingly as possible. Any changes are indicated by ellipses or square brackets. In rare cases, I have clarified punctuation in manuscript letters.

Acknowledgments

I thank Christine Dee most of all, not only for giving me the opportunity to work on this project but also for all her constant support, friendship, and guidance. This book would not have been possible without her excellent commentaries. I'm also grateful to Gillian Berchowitz for her patient and cheerful help in shepherding the project through to completion. I am grateful to Rick Huard for his extraordinary care and patience. His comments and corrections improved the book beyond measure.

I've received a great deal of assistance from scholars, librarians, and friends throughout the time I worked on this book. I'm particularly grateful to Diane Mutti Burke, Louis Gerteis, and Christopher Phillips for their collegiality and generosity. I also thank Major Douglas L. Gifford, whose outstanding staff rides and publications helped me understand the military history of our state. I'm grateful to friends and colleagues who read drafts or helped hunt down documents and facts, including Frank Aufmuth, Randy Baehr, Doug Harding, Victoria Harrison, Deborah Hyland, Chandra Manning, Pearl Ponce, and Jen Popiel. Charles Hoskins read and commented on the entire book—thanks, Charles! Dennis Boman has been a supportive friend throughout this process, lending books, discussing details of Missouri history, and always ready to answer questions. I thank Cindy Stachecki for all of her assistance. She is a resourceful, dedicated young scholar. Amy Wallhermfechtel created the excellent map of Missouri. Cathy Champion graciously donated her time in tracking down genealogical information. Of course, all errors are my own responsibility.

Archivist Dennis Northcott of the Missouri Historical Society in St. Louis has been of incalculable help to me. His collection guide to Civil War documents is a priceless resource. I also thank the librarians and archivists at the Western Historical Manuscripts Collections at the University of Missouri, both in St. Louis and in Columbia; the St. Louis Mercantile Library; the Abraham Lincoln Presidential Library in Springfield; the Midwest Jesuit Archives; and the Missouri State Archives at Jefferson City. I am grateful to Ranger John Sutton of the Wilson's Creek National Battlefield for his assistance in obtaining the meeting minutes of the Missouri rebel legislature.

Thanks go also to Anna Allen and Vivian Murphy for their kindness and friendship. Thanks go especially to Patrick McAllister, who is always in my corner, no matter which side of the Civil War I happen to support.

Athens
Kirksville
Missouri
Mississippi
Liberty
Kansas City Lexington Glasgow Centralia
Lawrence Independence
Westport Boonville
Lone Jack Jefferson City Saint Louis
Pottawatomie River River
Kansas Osage River
Osceola Rolla
Fort Davidson
Carthage Springfield Hartville Fredericktown
Silver Creek Cape Girardeau
Neosho Wilson's Creek Belmont
Newtonia New Madrid
Pea Ridge Arkansas

"Little Dixie"
★ battles
● major cities

The Civil War in Missouri. *Map by Amy Wallhermfechtel*

Introduction

*I*N EARLY JANUARY 1856, the Kickapoo Rangers, a group of proslavery Missourians, left their homes to cross the border into the Kansas Territory. They had heard that the first election under the new antislavery constitution was shortly to be held near Leavenworth, and the rangers were determined to prevent the hated abolitionists from gaining ground in the neighboring territory. On January 15, the election went off peacefully enough at the private home of a Mr. Minard, who had agreed (with the help of armed antislavery, or free-state, men) to host the election. After sunset, however, about thirty Kickapoo Rangers surrounded his house, demanded the ballot box, and in the ensuing scuffle killed one man and wounded two others. When the news reached St. Louis several days later, the editor of a Republican newspaper expressed profound anxiety about the violence. He feared that the flames ignited in the feud between Kansas and Missouri would soon be "fanned into a wide-spread civil war."[1]

Why, in 1856, did residents of Missouri fear the outbreak of civil warfare? What in the state's history caused these people to anticipate the imminent outbreak of a war that did not, in fact, begin for another five years? Why did the residents of such a prosperous and thriving state, one replete with natural resources and a diverse and growing population, have to cope with unparalleled suffering and even starvation during the war years? Finally, why did a state that traditionally yearned for moderation come to experience the bitterest internal violence of any border state during the Civil War? The answers to some of these questions, paradoxically, lie in Missouri's rich land, wide rivers, and varied past. From its earliest days, Missouri has stood at the crossroads of America. Bordering both southern and western states, Missouri was a place where diverse economic interests, political views, and during the Civil War, military forces clashed. The results were passionate, violent, and lasting. Throughout the years of conflict, Missourians desperately sought out moderation and neutrality, but they were unable to achieve either. The violence in Missouri—a distinctive feature of the nineteenth-century West—helped immortalize the images of hardened western soldiers, fiercely independent states-rights settlers, and frontier outlaws and ruffians. Their troubled history also demonstrated that in Civil War–era Missouri, there were *many* sides. Men and women, federals and rebels, slave and freeborn, immigrants and natives, pro- and antislavery residents all faced complex choices within a state that experienced the bloodiest guerrilla fighting of the Civil War. No other state suffered as much from internal division during the conflict. This documentary history, therefore, emphasizes Missouri's distinctive situation—a state caught in the crossroads between East and West, North and South, slave and free, order and chaos.

The region's mighty rivers drew Native Americans, explorers, traders, and in the late eighteenth century, settlers to the land that would become Missouri. In the early nineteenth century, farmers from Kentucky, Tennessee, and Virginia crossed the Mississippi River into the Missouri Territory, eager to profit from Missouri's waterways and western trails for transportation and commerce. The earliest settlements clustered along the rivers. In the north-central part of the state, along the Missouri River, these upland Southerners found a fertile land for their hemp and tobacco crops. The central counties along the Missouri River—called "Boon's Lick" after the attempt by Daniel Boone and his sons to start a salt-refining business there—included the prosperous slaveholding counties: Boone, Callaway, Howard, Monroe, and Randolph. (Today these counties are called "Little Dixie.") The southeastern bootheel section of the state that juts into Arkansas and Tennessee was home to ardently pro-Southern settlers who grew cotton and traded along the Mississippi. Farther north, across the river from Illinois, the first French and Spanish pioneers had founded St. Louis—soon to become the most important city in the American West. That city, which still retained some of its French ambience in the middle of the nineteenth century, drew a more diverse population of traders and merchants, shipbuilders and steamboat captains, European immigrants and travelers. It drew aspiring businessmen, including an unusually high number of lawyers, who were lured by land speculation and the concomitant land title business.[2] St. Louis served briefly as the state capital, after which the honor went to St. Charles, the "last civilized settlement" visited by the Lewis and Clark expedition. But in keeping with western ideas about democracy, the state legislature founded a new capital city in the very center of the state, a sign of their faith that the entire territory would soon be settled. According to historian William Parrish, the naming of the state capital in honor of Thomas Jefferson reflected the heritage of the many Missourians whose ancestors had originally come from Virginia.[3]

The southwestern part of the state, along the Arkansas border and in the rocky Ozark region, was less populated and harder to farm; the people who set down roots there relied on subsistence farming, hunting, and fishing for their survival and retained a fierce independence throughout the war. Settlements like Independence, not far from modern-day Kansas City, served as jumping-off points for settlers journeying to Oregon and California. Missouri also attracted European immigrants, including Germans who settled in the central region and in St Louis.

Most of the early settlers were subsistence farmers who grew their own food, as well as lead miners, fur trappers, and traders. Though few settlers outside of the central Missouri counties brought slaves with them, the majority did bring a commitment to the ideas that opportunity for white males rested on the possibility of owning slave labor and that their independence was preserved by the system of slavery. As early as 1830, there were at least a few slaves living in every county in Missouri, though the majority were concentrated in the north-central Boon's Lick area. Though slaves constituted a little less than 10 percent of the population, politicians had to pay attention to the powerful and influential slaveholding interests in the state, particularly the wealthy Boon's Lick aristocracy, whose social and political influence dominated the state until the Civil War. Because of their commitment to the institution of human bondage, these people supported the extension of slavery into the new western territories and strongly resented any threat of interference.[4]

As a result of their support for slavery, most Missourians voted Democratic throughout the decades before the outbreak of the Civil War. After the war with Mexico, as new territories were brought into the Union, the political lines in Missouri became more sharply drawn. Proslavery Democrats firmly believed that they could not survive without slave labor; they also believed that if new neighboring territories (like Kansas) came into the Union as free states, their own right to slave property would be endangered. The powerful Central Clique of the Boon's Lick area, composed of prominent slaveholders with a great deal of political pull, was able to bring an end to the career of longtime senator Thomas Hart Benton when he publicly voiced his opposition to the extension of slavery. On the other hand, the old Whigs in the state soon joined with Free Soil Democrats (that is, Democrats who opposed the extension of slavery into new territories and states). Whigs and Free Soil Democrats were more numerous in urban areas such as St. Louis.[5]

The state's growing ethnic diversity also influenced political debates over the expansion of slavery into the federal territories. Before the early 1830s, German immigrants had brought their families to the central region of Missouri, whose rolling hills reminded them of the wine-growing regions of their homeland. This group differed sharply from the so-called Forty-eighters, German immigrants who escaped the failed democratic revolutions in Europe and moved into Missouri in the late 1840s and early 1850s. The earlier settlers considered themselves more cultured and aristocratic than the newcomers, and they had a much more tolerant attitude toward the institution of slavery. Those fiercely outspoken Germans who had fled political persecution in their homeland allied themselves with the new Republican Party. Their loyalty to the Union and their antislavery sentiments brought them into direct conflict with pro-Southern, proslavery groups. Both groups disliked and despised the Irish immigrants who had fled famine and poverty and who settled Missouri around the same time. These differences played out in politics as well. The earlier, more prosperous immigrants voted Democratic, because of their inclinations toward slavery and because the Whigs and later the new Republican Party expressed antiforeigner sentiments. The state as a whole remained solidly Democratic, but as new immigrants came in, they were able to change the political climate in the areas in which they settled, particularly in St.

Louis. In the momentous 1860 presidential election, the state voted for the most
pro-Union Democratic candidate, Stephen A. Douglas, if only by a bare majority. The fact that so many Missourians voted for Douglas demonstrated only that
they remained committed to the Union, not that they were changing their minds
about slavery. The fact that most of the Boon's Lick slaveholders cast their ballots
for John Bell, the candidate of the new Constitutional Union Party, indicated that
the wealthy planters believed their interests—that is, slavery—were best served
by a platform that favored the status quo but that they remained uncomfortable
with Douglas's staunch support of a permanent Union. Both choices indicate a
consistent desire for moderation, even as Missourians themselves participated in
mounting violence throughout the state. But the ethnic and political divisions in
the state only grew as the pro-Union element gained in strength and influence and
as threats against the institution of slavery grew.

From the early 1850s through the mid-1870s, almost every community in Missouri suffered terrible internal divisions. As Missouri's neighbors—free states to
the north and east, slave states to the south and east, and federal territories to the
south and west, including troubled Kansas—quarreled among themselves over the
era's most controversial issues, some Missourians' commitment to moderation
began to falter as well. Missourians took up arms in defense of their communities, for
and against slavery, for and against the Union, and ultimately against each other. While
shipping and trade bound the state's economic interests firmly to the Union, probably at least one-third of its residents either actively opposed the Union or were
uncommitted to any national government, favoring their own personal independence over all. Civilian commitment to the Confederacy, combined with a background of border violence, rendered life nearly unsustainable for many Missouri
families caught between opposing forces. The civilians who found themselves in
the path of partisan warfare, the contending armies, and even the enmity of their
neighbors lived in a state of bitterness and violence that outlasted even the war.

Missouri contained within itself elements so antagonistic that it became home
to two wartime governments: the Union administration at Jefferson City and the
pro-Southern one in exile in Texas. Unlike recruits from virtually every other state
in the Great Interior, Missourians fought in significant numbers in both armies:
110,000 enrolled on the side of Union, and 30,000 joined the rebels. An additional
10,000 to 14,000 fought in the Missouri State Guard, an organization that was
formed from the Missouri state militia in 1861 and, while never officially a part
of the Confederate armies, usually fought against the federals. Thousands more
battled illegally as "bushwhackers," or guerrillas, or found their way into other partisan groups. From its troubled and violent place at the crossroads of the nation,
Missouri's war was distinctive, yet it also reflected issues and experiences touching
all Americans of the era, Northern and Southern, white and black.

Not the least of these was the issue of emancipation. The end of slavery did not come swiftly or easily in Missouri, but the process revealed dramatic swings in public opinion in the border state. Before the secession crisis and into the first two years of the war, voters had supported a moderate proslavery stance. Yet the state was one of the first to emancipate slaves and took a progressive line on black people's civil and political rights in the later years of the war. This change can be attributed in part to weariness with guerrilla violence and in part to the rise of the radical Republicans in state politics, but it still represented a significant shift in popular opinion, especially considering the polarized population. When the war ended, most Missourians were able to bury old enmities and even some of their prejudices, but they held on to others. The radical Republicans who governed Missouri's state and national politics ensured that at least until the early 1870s, black men had some voting rights. Unfortunately, many of their progressive reforms were rescinded by the early 1870s with the revival of the Democratic Party and the defeat of the radical Republicans. On the issues of social and political equality for black people, real change would take more than a century.

ONE

~

Slavery in Missouri

*I*N 1820, Missouri's white settlers wanted their territory to enter the Union as a slave state, even though most of them did not own slaves. They had come from the Upper South states of Kentucky, North Carolina, Tennessee, and Virginia and brought with them a firm commitment to the institution of slavery. When these settlers first decided to move westward, they chose the Missouri Territory rather than the Old Northwest states and territories, where slavery was prohibited. During the early years of settlement, the Kentuckians and Tennesseans who had moved to Missouri (most of whose families were descended from Virginians) found the older French community sympathetic to their views on slavery. Even those who owned no slaves were convinced that slave labor was necessary to grow cash crops like tobacco and hemp. Whenever extra farm labor was needed, those who did not own slaves hired them from those who did.[1]

They came by the thousands, drawn by the rich soil, great rivers, and sympathy for their institutions. By 1818, the territory had a population of more than 66,000. But Missouri's application for admission into the Union caused a firestorm of hard feelings between pro- and antislavery politicians in the rest of the nation. The battles over this slaveholding western territory brought about the first threats of secession in Congress and even hinted warnings of civil warfare. During the congressional debates, Tennessee representative Francis Jones explained that if Missouri were kept out of the Union because of her commitment to slavery, then "her name will be written in characters of blood."[2] The debates revolved around the problem of restrictions on slavery in the new state: Should the institution of human bondage be placed on a gradual path of extinction? Should Missouri slaves be emancipated when they reached adulthood? Missourians—both those who owned slaves and most of those who did not—vehemently opposed any federal interference in their rights to their human property, and they refused to consider coming into the Union with any restrictions on slavery. Historian William Parrish has explained that if proslavery forces had evinced greater willingness to bring Missouri into the Union with some restrictions, such as gradual emancipation, they might have helped resolve the problem without bloodshed. The end of slavery would certainly have been better for the slaves themselves.[3] But slave labor

6

was an important aspect of the economy in Missouri, producing hemp, tobacco, and grains that were shipped to the North and even to Europe. By 1850, the Boon's Lick planters had established powerful economic links with St. Louis and New Orleans through the river trade.[4]

Like settlers in other midwestern territories, most Missourians belonged to the Democratic Party; and because slavery had already gained a foothold in the territory, most of them were willing to enter the Union as residents of a slave state. But when the Missouri Territory applied for membership in the Union in 1818, Northern representatives and senators feared that the addition of another slave state would cause an imbalance in Congress. Moreover, they wanted the western territories to remain open for free labor. They worried that a growing slave interest would make it impossible for white Northerners to find good land west of the Mississippi. New York representative Henry Tallmadge decided to make Missouri's admission to the Union a test case. He proposed that in exchange for coming in as a slave state, Missouri would have to agree to a gradual emancipation scheme, which would free every slave as soon as she or he reached the age of twenty-five. Furthermore, his amendment to the admission bill forbade the importation of more slaves into Missouri. The amendment passed the House in 1819 but was defeated in the Senate.

After lengthy congressional debates, Illinois senator Jesse B. Thomas carefully crafted a compromise that, for the moment, seemed to defuse the worst disputes. Kentucky representative Henry Clay worked hard to ensure the passage of this compromise in the House, by which Missouri would come in as a slave state, and a new free state—Maine—would be carved from northern lands owned by Massachusetts. But the most significant and potentially explosive aspect of the compromise was the establishment of a line to divide the nation between slave and free. It probably seemed like a fair and equitable way of arranging the growing nation's fundamental differences; but in reality, the Missouri Compromise line, drawn across 36° 30' north latitude from the East Coast to the western border of the Louisiana Purchase, exacerbated a deep rift between the sections.

Proslavery politicians were up in arms about Tallmadge's amendment because they felt that it threatened the existence of slavery everywhere. In the congressional debates, Southerners emphasized the dangers of federal interference with slavery in the states.[5] They also feared that emancipating some slaves would lead to discontent among those left in bondage—slave insurrections in Virginia and South Carolina had left slaveholders everywhere anxious. The proslavery Boon's Lick politician Duff Green, who had been born in Kentucky, argued that Missouri ought to come in without any restriction. Claiming that the Union was dear to Missourians, he declared, however, that "Liberty was dearer."[6] Missourians were enraged at the thought of congressional interference with their slave property, but the statehood debate ignited anger throughout the entire South.

In the bitter political fights over the future of slavery in Missouri, the concerns of the people in bondage were often forgotten. The lives of slaves in Missouri differed somewhat from those of their counterparts on great plantations in the Deep South. Although Missouri's bondspeople faced many of the same restrictions on their liberty, as well as the heartbreak of the sale of family members, they also had greater hope of achieving their freedom through lawsuits. Historian Diane Mutti Burke has suggested that because they lived and worked more closely with their owners, Missouri's slaves may have experienced somewhat better treatment than those who were enslaved on large southern plantations. Missouri's slaves, both men and women, labored in the fields; they also worked in the houses as servants and as skilled craftsmen. They worked at all tasks associated with farming, usually alongside the white family members, since gang labor was virtually unknown in the territory. Their lives were as arduous as those of any agricultural workers in Missouri, but they had much less freedom, especially as the bonds of slavery tightened in the state.[7]

By the turn of the nineteenth century, territorial laws forbade slaves to assemble in crowds, to leave their masters' property without a pass, or to own weapons without express permission from their owner and the local justice of the peace. Slaves could not own property, engage in business, or visit relatives on other farms without permission. Punishments for such acts ranged from branding, whipping, and imprisonment to death. The point of these laws was to limit the slaves' ability to meet with one another to plan insurrections or escapes. Indeed, as the national conflict over slavery grew, Missouri slave owners became increasingly worried about their human property and urged their territorial legislature to pass strict laws further limiting the freedom of black people, both free and enslaved. In 1845, for example, Missouri passed a law that barred free black people from establishing schools or churches and even from living in the state without posting a prohibitively high bond. Such laws had become increasingly common throughout the South, in response to increased antislavery agitation.

Slaves could sometimes fight their way free from bondage in Missouri. In 1824, the state legislature reenacted an earlier (1807) territorial law that allowed persons held in slavery to sue for their freedom if they could prove that they were wrongfully held in bondage. The territorial law had been instituted to clarify the doubtful status of black persons who claimed their liberty by virtue of having spent time in a free state or territory. The 1824 statute became a road to freedom for many slaves who had been taken to the states and territories initially organized under the Northwest Ordinance, such as Illinois, Indiana, Ohio, and the Wisconsin Territory. More than three hundred slaves won their liberty under the 1824 freedom law, which remained valid until the institution of slavery finally ended in Missouri in 1865.

The law established a precedent for one of the most famous freedom suits in American history: the *Dred Scott* case. Dred Scott, a Missouri slave, had lived for some years in the free state of Illinois and the free territory of Wisconsin with his family. When his owner brought him back to Missouri, Scott sued for his freedom on the grounds that because slavery was illegal in Illinois and Wisconsin under the Northwest Ordinance, he deserved to be set at liberty. Unfortunately for Scott, the Missouri Supreme Court denied his petition in 1852, after an earlier 1847 decision in St. Louis that had upheld his claim. *Scott v. Sandford* reached the Supreme Court in 1856, and Chief Justice Roger B. Taney issued his famous decision in February 1857. Taney's declaration that black people were not American citizens and had no right to sue for their liberty caused repercussions, which would resound even after the institution of slavery ended.[8]

Stringent restrictions on property ownership and other rights induced more than half of Missouri's free black people to live in cities, especially in St. Louis and in Jefferson City, where they could more easily find work and housing. Nevertheless, they endured severe limitations on their liberties and often experienced racial prejudice and discrimination. The Free Negro and Mulatto Law, passed in 1845 and strengthened in 1847, stripped free black people in Missouri of nearly all their rights. Free black people living in Missouri had to acquire a license from their county court, the fee for which could range from $100 to $500. At that time, $500 would pay a year's rent on a house in a respectable section of St. Louis and was a sum out of the reach of most free blacks. Such laws were extremely common in midwestern states, such as Indiana and Illinois, whose legislatures feared the in-migration of free black families as black codes became more stringent in the antebellum South. Even within the restrictions of Missouri's laws, however, some black families were able to build decent lives for themselves; according to a free black man named Cyprian Clamorgan, there was a "colored aristocracy" in St. Louis whose combined wealth probably reached the "millions of dollars." Moreover, free black people in Missouri could own property and initiate lawsuits. But they could not vote, nor were they permitted to testify against white people in court. Some of the less prosperous free black people in St. Louis ran boardinghouses and grocery shops, or they worked on the dockyards, steamboats, or barges on the Mississippi River.[9] Those whose labors brought them within reach of the Mississippi River probably had more freedom and suffered fewer restrictions than those who worked in town. Their work was necessary to the important transportation networks that brought goods into and out of the state. But the situation of free black people in Missouri, even those who lived in cities, was always constrained both by law and by prejudice.

A PROSLAVERY SPEECH ON THE ADMISSION OF MISSOURI

Tennessee shared a border with the Missouri Territory, whose inhabitants were clamoring for admission to the Union. But because territorial delegates did not have the right to address Congress (they could testify, but could not make motions or vote) John Scott, Missouri's delegate, could not speak in favor of Missouri's admission. The proslavery faction had to rely on speeches by their colleagues, such as Tennessee representative Francis Jones. Congressional speeches were not officially transcribed in Congress but were included in The Debates and Proceedings in the Congress of the United States *(informally known today as the* Annals of Congress*), a compilation of debates published in newspapers between 1834 and 1856.*

EXCERPTS FROM A SPEECH OF MR. FRANCIS JONES OF TENNESSEE, HOUSE OF REPRESENTATIVES, ON THURSDAY, FEBRUARY 24, 1820

I said, sir, that this question was a momentous one; . . . one geographical half of the Union is arrayed against the other; and . . . we see a disposition manifested to proceed at all hazards; . . . a determination is avowed to sever the people of Missouri; to drive a line through the centre of her population, and to say to those on the right, you shall enjoy your property, and to those on the left, you shall not; and to both, that neither of you shall come into the Union. . . . Freedom and slavery, we are told, are the parties now before us, and we are reminded of the blessings of liberty, of the voice of humanity and religion, and of the miseries of slavery; and, indeed, it would seem, by the use, or rather abuse, of those broad and comprehensive terms, that by some revolution in human affairs, or rather by some beneficent dispensation of Divine Providence, an opportunity had been afforded to this nation to make all men equal, or at least to make all men free. Would to Heaven this were the fact. . . .

To say that slavery is an evil, that it is contrary to the laws of nature and of nature's God, does not prove that the Constitution has not recognised its existence; neither does it prove that the power to remedy the evil has, by the States, been surrendered to the General Government, believing themselves (as they must have done) incompetent to the management of their slaves, or to their emancipation. . . .

It ought to be remembered that the same instrument by which Congress have acquired a right to make rules and regulations for the Territory, has guarantied to the master a right to his slave; and if your rule or regulation be inconsistent with, or is calculated even in its effects to deprive him of this right, your rule or regulation is unconstitutional. . . .

It will not be denied that, when Congress is under no obligations other than those imposed by the Constitution, it may admit or reject a State, as in the case of a new State formed out of an old State, where there has been no contract, either express or implied, between Congress and such new State, as to its admission. But I deny that Congress can impose this restriction, or any other, upon a State, as a condition upon which it shall be admitted. . . .

But, sir, suppose we yield to gentlemen the Constitutional power—the question will then arise, ought it now, under existing circumstances, to be exercised? I put this question to those who contend for restriction. Is it possible for you to effect your object? Suppose you have in this House a majority of votes—what then? Do not the Journals of the Senate show us what there has been the fate of this measure? If you persevere in your present course, Maine and Missouri both must sink. What then will you have effected? Will you have prevented, as you propose to do, the extension of slavery? No, Missouri will still be left open for the reception of slaves. She will continue rapidly to increase every description of her population. And do gentlemen suppose that she is to be kept in a state of vassalage forever, because she will not submit to the imperial dictates of their consciences? Sir, we have been asked, during this debate, what will Missouri do, if we refuse to admit her; will she resist the Government? Sir, gentlemen ought to remember, that, although Missouri be an infant, she reposes upon the laps of eleven mothers. And, let me tell you, sir, that, if ever Missouri subscribes to this humiliating condition, her name will be written in characters of blood.

Sir, I hope Missouri, let her fate be what it may, will continue to act (as she has heretofore done) with moderation. I know, sir, that she will not, driven by anger or despair, appeal to the last resort of men or nations. She will not, she cannot war with you. But, sir, push these measures; convince her that upon this condition alone can she be received, and with all the calmness, but with all the majesty, of insulted justice, she may tell you that she will govern herself.

Annals of the Congress of the United States, 16th Cong., 1st sess., 1460–62.

A GIRL NAMED MOURNING

John Sappington was a wealthy slave owner and a successful medical doctor. He wrote the first medical text to be published west of the Mississippi and was known for his use of quinine to cure malarial fevers. His patent medicines brought him enormous wealth and influence. Claiborne Fox Jackson, the rebel governor of Missouri, married three of Sappington's daughters in succession. Upon his death, Sappington he left most of his wealth to the care and education of poor children. In 1821, he purchased an adolescent girl.

Know all men, I Shimey Merritt of Williamson County Tennessee for & in consideration of the sum of Five hundred Dollar, to me in hand paid and acknowleged to have been received here and by these presents do bargain sell & convey to John Sappington of the State of Missouri a negro Girl named Mourning aged thirteen or fourteen, his heirs & assigns forever warranting & defending the right & title of said girl & that she is healthy and sound & sensible. Witness my hand & seal the 1ⁿᵗʰ of May 1821

test

V. Breathitt   Shimmey Merritt

Wm. H. Eaton

B. 1, f. 1, Sappington-Marmaduke Papers, 1810–21, Western Historical Manuscripts Collection, University of Missouri, Columbia.

THE FREEDOM LAW, 1824

The 1824 freedom law passed by the Missouri Assembly provided the basis for slaves' suits against their owners.

AN ACT TO ENABLE PERSONS HELD IN SLAVERY TO SUE FOR THEIR FREEDOM.

SEC 1. *Be it enacted by the General Assembly of the state of Missouri,* That it shall be lawful for any person held in slavery to petition the circuit court, or the judge thereof in vacation, praying that such person may be permitted to sue as a poor person, and stating the ground upon which his or her claim to freedom is founded; and if, in the opinion of the court or judge, the petition contains sufficient matter to authorize the commencement of a suit, such court or judge may make an order that such person be permitted to sue as a poor person to establish his or her freedom, and assign the petitioner counsel,—which order shall be endorsed on the petition. And the court or judge shall, moreover, make an order that the petitioner have reasonable liberty to attend his or her counsel and the court, when occasion may require; and that the petitioner shall not be taken or removed out of the jurisdiction of the court, nor be subject to any severity because of his or her application for freedom,—which order, if made in vacation, shall be endorsed on the petition, and a copy thereof endorsed on the writ and served on the defendant.

SEC 2. *Be it further enacted,* That if the court, or the judge thereof in vacation, shall be satisfied, at the time of the presenting the petition, or at any time during the pendency of any suit instituted under the provisions of this act, that any petitioner hath been or is about to be restrained by any person from reasonable liberty of attending his or her counsel or the court, or that the petitioner is about to be removed out of the jurisdiction of the court, or that he or she hath been or is about to be subjected to any severity because of his or her application for freedom, or that any order made by the court or judge in the premises as a aforesaid has been or is about to be violated, then and in every such case, the court, or the judge thereof in vacation, may cause the petitioner to be brought before him or them by a writ of *habeas corpus;* and shall cause the defendant, or the person in whose possession the petitioner may be found, his or their agent, to enter into a recognizance, with a sufficient security, conditioned that the petitioner shall at all time during the pendency of the suit have reasonable liberty of attending his or her counsel, and that such petitioner shall not be removed out of the jurisdiction of the court wherein the action is to be brought or is pending, and that he or she shall not be subjected to any severity because of his or her application for freedom,—which recognizance shall be recorded or filed among the records of the court, and be deemed and taken to all intents and purposes to be a record of such court. But if the party required to enter into a recognizance as aforesaid shall refuse so to do, the court or judge shall make an order that the sheriff take possession of the petitioner and hire him or her out to the best advantage, from time to time, during the pendency of the suit; and that he take a bond from the person hiring the petitioner, in such penalty as the court shall in such order direct, and with such security as the sheriff shall approve, conditioned as directed in the recognizance of the defendant, and moreover that he will pay the hire to the sheriff at the time stipulated, and return the petitioner at the end of the time for which he or she is hired, or sooner if the action shall sooner be determined; and the sheriff shall proceed accordingly, and pay the money received for hire to the party in whose favor the suit shall be determined.

Sec. 3. *Be it further enacted,* That all actions to be commenced and prosecuted under the provisions of this act, shall be in form, trespass, assault and battery, and false imprisonment, in the name of the petitioner, against the person holding him or her in slavery, or claiming him or her as a slave. And whenever any court of judge shall make an order as aforesaid, permitting any such suit to be brought, the clerk shall issue the necessary process, without charge to the petitioner: the declaration shall be in the common form of a declaration for assault and battery and false imprisonment, except that the plaintiff shall aver that before and at the time of the committing the grievances he or she was and still is a free person, and that the defendant held and detained him or her and still holds and detains in slavery,—upon which declaration the plaintiff may give in evidence any special matter; and the defendant may plead as many pleas as he may think is necessary for his defence, or he may plead the general issue, and give the special matters in evidence. And such actions shall be conducted in other respects in the same manner as the like actions between other persons, and the plaintiff may recover damages as in other cases.

SEC. 4. *Be it further enacted,* That in all actions instituted under the provisions of this act, the petitioner, if he or she be a negro or mulatto, shall be held and required to prove his or her right to freedom; but regard shall be had not only to the written evidence of his or her claim to freedom, but to such other proofs, either at law or in equity, as the very right and justice of the case may require. And if the issue be determined in favor of the petitioner, the court shall render a judgment of liberation from the defendant or defendants, and all persons claiming from, through or under him, her or them.

SEC. 5. *Be it further enacted,* That if any party to a suit instituted under the provisions of this act, shall feel him or herself aggrieved by the judgment of the circuit court, he or she may have and prosecute an appeal or writ of error to the supreme court, as in other cases; *Provided,* That if the petitioner appeal or prosecute a writ of error, he or she shall not be required to enter into a recognizance, but such appeal or writ of error shall operate as a *supersedeas* without such recognizance.

This act shall take effect and be in force from and after the fourth day of July next.

[*Approved, December 30, 1824.*]

1825 Missouri Laws 404.

"YESTERDAY WAS THE . . . SALE OF MY DARKEYS"

A. A. Edwards was a slave owner who resided in Saline County, Missouri. Edwards wrote to his uncle Lewis G. Harvey in Virginia about the recent sale of several slaves. Around the time Edwards wrote this letter, there were about 700 slaves in Saline County. A decade later, that number had more than doubled to 1,615.

Lewis G. Harvey Esq.,
W[illegible] Church in Northumberland Co., VA
Saline County Missouri
February 12th, 1834

Dear Uncle,

. . . Yesterday was the day of my sale in the Sale of my darkeys. I did not sell the whole of them as I had advertised, but only sold two, reserving the Woman and three children, as they were valuable negroes and bore a fairer character than any negroes in the country[.] I sold a girl about fifteen—badly grown for $800 also the boy Griffin very badly grown, and a very crooked unlikely negro for $1225[.] I would not have sold either of them had they pleased me, but I think I can do better in Virginia with the same money or even less. Negroes here are very high—likely negro men [worth] anything from $1400 to $1500, but I would not like to tell every body of the high prices of negroes until I buy one or two in Virginia myself[.] If you see a chance where you can purchase a likely Negro man on moderate terms, before I get there I wish you would do so for me. I can pay the cash or what is pretty much the same thing, I can do so in four months from date, as that is the time upon which I sold my Negroes. I would also like to have a good stout woman if I could get one cheap—I think I can spare the money to buy.

. . .

Yours truly & affectionately

A. A. Edwards

Harvey Family Papers, 1834–49, Western Historical Manuscripts Collection, University of Missouri, Columbia.

"THE GIRL I SHALL NOT WARRANT SOUND"

Nothing is known about the writer of this letter, because—as he explains to the sheriff of Howard County, Missouri—he preferred to remain anonymous. The recipient, Newton G. Elliott, was a slave owner and justice of the peace from 1837 to 1852 in Howard County, Missouri. While slave dealers would typically take slaves out of the state or "down river," most local slave sales in Missouri were handled by sheriffs. The descriptive word "likely," when applied to slaves, usually referred to their good looks, health, and disposition. [10]

Saline County Mo.

Sunday

N. Elliot Esq.

Dr Sir

I caused some advertisements to be put up stating that you would offer for sale a likely negro man, woman, girl & child on Monday the first of December. I have concluded to postpone the sale till New Years day 1ˢᵗ Jany thinking it would be a better time to sell. There was an advertisement put up in Fayette, I should like to have it altered so as to make the time 1ˢᵗ next Jany—not wishing my negroes to know of my intention to sell lest they might slip off or be out of the way when wanted you will see the reason that no name was attached to the advertisements nor to this, . . . lest they might hear of it. The negro man cannot be surpassed by any, is a stout likely fellow—the woman is a good cook and washer and of a very fine disposition & her child likely. The girl I shall not warrant sound as I did not purchase her for a sound negro.

Yours Respectfully

[no signature]

Newton G. Elliott Papers, Missouri Historical Society, St. Louis.

"RACHEL IS FREE"

In 1834 a slave named Rachel sued her owner, William Walker, for her freedom under the 1824 freedom statute. Rachel's previous owner, a U.S. Army officer named T. B. W. Stockton, had taken her to Prairie du Chien in the Michigan Territory, where he was stationed with his family. Stockton subsequently sold Rachel to Walker. Because Stockton had been sent to the territory (which was at that time governed by the Northwest Ordinance) under military orders, the St. Louis Circuit Court ruled that he had had no choice in residing there and therefore denied Rachel's suit for freedom. In 1836 Rachel's case was brought on appeal before Missouri Supreme Court justice Mathias McGirk, who favored a strict reading of the 1824 act and granted Rachel her liberty. After McGirk's retirement in 1841, proslavery supreme court justices were less likely to find in favor of slaves who sued for their freedom.

Rachel)   Sup Court June Term 1836
  vs)
Walker)

Rachel sued Walker for her freedom in the St[.] Louis Circuit Court & at the last March Term there was a trial & judgment for Walker, from which Rachel appeals, according to the Bill of exceptions the facts are that one Stockton an officer in the United States army then stationed at St[.] Peters, wishing to obtain a slave to live with him at that place, sent to St[.] Louis & purchased Rachel from Maj. Brant & took her to St[.] Peters where he kept her as a slave in his family for a year he was afterward stationed at Prairie du Chien on the east side of the Mississippi in Michigan Territory whither he removed & resided with his family there still holding Rachel in slavery & held her then near two years when he sold her. During all this time she was employed entirely in immediate attendance on his family—Rachel is free

See act of Congress of March 6th, 1820 Story's U.S. Laws page 1762 Sec. 8 which forbids slavery North of 36 degrees 30 minutes. Also the Ordinance of 1787 for Government of Territory North West of Ohio 1 Vol. L, U.S. 475. . . .

J. Spalding
for appellant

Rachel, a woman of color v. Walker, William, November 1834, Circuit Court Case Files, Office of the Circuit Clerk, St. Louis, Missouri State Archives–St. Louis.

"ALL HANDS AT WORK AT THE PEACHES"

Virginia native Thomas W. Conyers was a landowner, merchant, and politician who moved to Missouri in 1822. In 1836 Conyers brought his family to Monroe

County, Missouri. He farmed, using the labor of three or four slaves, and ran a general store at Paris. His diary details activities on his farm, including the task system of slavery, which was more common in Missouri than the gang system that was prevalent in the lower South. Ironweed is a native purplish-blue wildflower with tough, thick stems.

Friday, 22 Aug. [1845?] Sam hauling rock for underpinning the house & filling up a pass way in the drian [drain]
George & Harriott Mary & the two boys cutting up the Ironweed & bushes in the pasture at Town

23 Saturd Sam hauling rock & putting in the drian
George Harriott Mary & Clay cut'g Iron weeds & Bushes in the pasture at town
I wrote to I. S. C. by Bro H Thomas in relation to the costs of the Suit Conyers & McBride vs. Gains

24 Sunday. In the night Br.° A Wilson brought me a letter from I. S. C. informing me I would have to pay half the costs in the case . . . . also that W. S. had bought 11 mules and that he was gone to Colon. Williams' to see his mules.

25 Mondy Sam & George went up to the home place and brought a load of Oats 570 Bundles left the stack broke and it rained hard this night
Harriott Mary & Clay cutting Iron weed [at] Paris

26 Tuesd Sam & Clay hauling Rock to make cross way
George Harriott & Mary cutg. Ironweed &c. at Paris . . .

27 Wedn.y Sam & George went up and brought the balance of the stack of Oats 404 Bundles and shocks of hay to make out the Loads
Harriott & Mary with Clay cutting Iron weeds . . .

28 Thursd. Sam & George cut & hauled a Load of wood to Mr. Nise and brought home a load of Slabs for crib floor
Harriott Mary & Clay cutting Iron weeds

29 Friday Sam & George hauled hay from home place
Harriott Mary & Clay cutg. Ironweeds

30 Satu.y Sam & George hauled hay from home place
Harriott Mary & Clay cut.g Iron weeds at home
Mr. Slaughter started home and is to return next Tuesday with his wife to see the place or wednesday.
Mr. Minor came and agrees if I sell to give possession

Sept. 1 Monday Sam & Clay hauled a Load of Oats 465 Bundles from home

Harriott & George & Mary finished cut.g Iron weeds

Began to peal peaches to dry & 20 [illegible] to preserve

2 Tuesday W. S. had the 80 Acres by Miles' surveyed

Sam & George hauled a Load of Oats from Minors and found the Steer Bull[,] put him in Mr. Miles' stubble field brought the load home then he and Clay went and with W. S. brought the steer down and put him in the pasture at the Rogers place.

Mr. & Mrs. Slaughter came this evening

Sept. 3 Wednesday Sam & George hauled a Load of hay from big Meadow

W. S. went up and divided the hay with Jn.° Vaughn

Eliza & myself went up with Mr. & Mrs. Slaughter to the home place & sold it to them for $1500 payable in 4 yearly payments, . . .

4 Thursday Sam & George haul'g hay

Harriott helping about drying peaches

Mrs. D. C. M. Parsons her 2 Children and F Parsons came out yesterday evening. Mr. & Mrs. Jones spend the day here

Mr. & Mrs. Jn.° Parsons came out this evening

5 Friday Sam & George haulg hay

Levy Smith called to see us a while this morning

I. S. C. & P came down he on his way to St. Louis

E. W. McB & Julian came out this evening

6 Sat. Sam & George hauled a Load of hay

I. S. C. & W. S. started to St. Louis this morning

All hands at work at the peaches

8 Mondy Sam & George hauled a Load of hay

Paulina came out yesterday even'g with Mr. Maupin

Bro. & Sis. Smozer & Arabell spent the day here

9 Tuesday Mrs. D. C. M. Parsons, her 2 Children Frank Parsons and Ann Eliza came out staid until evening Ann went back with them

Sam & George hauled a Load of hay to day

Mrs. Maupin came out & took Paulina in

Mrs. Heitz came out yesterday staid a while.

10 Wedn'y Sam & George hauled a Load of hay . . .

Thomas W. Conyers, diary, f. 2, Conyers Papers, 1817–1903,C755, Western Historical Manuscripts Collection, University of Missouri, Columbia.

STATUTORY RESTRICTIONS ON THE RIGHTS
AND LIBERTIES OF FREE BLACK PEOPLE

In 1845 and 1847, the Missouri General Assembly enacted two new laws that circumscribed the rights of free blacks in the state. Such laws were extremely common in the midwestern states, whose legislatures feared the in-migration of free black families as black codes became more stringent in the antebellum South. Indiana and Illinois, for example, passed laws as well as state constitutional amendments that prevented free black people from entering their states or forced them to pay exorbitant fines if they entered without permission.

NEGROES AND MULATTOES
AN ACT RESPECTING SLAVES, FREE NEGROES AND MULATTOES.

Be it enacted by the General Assembly of the State of Missouri, as follows:

1. No person shall keep or teach any school for the instruction of negroes or mulattoes, in reading or writing in this State.

2. No meeting or assemblage of negroes or mulattoes, for the purpose of religious worship, or preaching, shall be held or permitted where the services are performed or conducted by negroes or mulattoes, unless some sheriff, constable, marshal, police officer, or justice of the peace, shall be present during all the time of such meeting or assemblage, in order to prevent all seditious speeches, and disorderly and unlawful conduct of every kind.

3. All meetings of negroes or mulattoes, for the purposes mentioned in the two preceding sections, shall be considered unlawful assemblages, and shall be suppressed by sheriffs, constables, and other public officers.

4. No free negro or mulatto shall, under any pretext, emigrate to this State, from any other State or territory.

5. If any person shall violate the provisions of this act, he shall, for every such offence, be indicted and punished by fine not exceeding five hundred dollars, or by imprisonment not exceeding six months, or by both such fine and imprisonment.

6. Free negroes and mulattoes, who are under the age of twenty-one years, and who would not be entitled to receive from the county court a license to remain in this State, if they were twenty-one years old, shall not be bound out as apprentices in this State.

Approved February 16, 1847.

AN ACT "TO AMEND AN ACT CONCERNING FREE NEGROES AND MULATTOES," APPROVED MARCH 26, 1845.

Be it enacted by the General Assembly of the State of Missouri, as follows:

1. Whenever any free negro or mulatto, duly licensed to reside in this State, shall remove from the county in which such license is granted, to any other county in this State, he shall give bond in the county to which he shall so remove, in the manner required by the 10th section of the act to which this is an amendment, no free negro or mulatto shall be permitted to reside in any county in this State, to which he shall so remove, unless such free negro or mulatto shall first give bond as above required.

2. It shall be the duty of every sheriff, constable, coroner or marshal, whenever he shall know or have cause to believe, that there is any free negro or mulatto in his county who has not complied with the provisions in the first section of this act, or the nineteenth section of the act, to which this is an amendment, to apprehend such negro or mulatto, and take him before some justice of the peace of said county, and if it appear to such justice that such free negro or mulatto has not complied with the provisions of this act and the act to which this is an amend- ment, to sentence such free negro or mulatto to pay a fine of ten dollars, and to leave such county forthwith.

3. If any free negro or mulatto shall fail or refuse to comply with the sentence of said justice, it shall be the duty of the sheriff, constable, or other officer to commit him to the county jail until the sentence of the justice is complied with, or such free negro or mulatto shall consent to leave such county.

This act to take effect from and after its passage.

Approved February 16, 1847.

1847 Missouri Laws 103.

CHARLES PEABODY DESCRIBES SLAVERY IN LEXINGTON, MISSOURI

The Reverend Charles Peabody, a district secretary for the American Tract Society, kept a travel diary from May 21, 1846, to September 11, 1846, while journeying through the western states and territories. Peabody visited Illinois, Iowa, Kentucky, Michigan, and Missouri in order to observe and write about church communities in the Midwest. Lexington was a lively river trade town not far from Kansas City.

June 22nd Lexington—

. . . Most of the people in this part of Mo. are from Ky. Tenn. and Ga. Hence here flourished the "patriarchal institution" there is no Ohio River, as a terror to all slave holders,—a Rubicon beyond which their human property so often passes on a returnless journey towards a north star. One half of the 18 hundred people of Lexington are slaves! But here is slavery in its mildness. I have seen no cruelty—no ill usage—no whipping—nothing but contentment and happiness among the whole black population.—There is the family of Rev. Mr. Yantes, - pres. Minister in L. Harry is a tough good looking fellow and has the entire management of his farm and affairs. The farm horses are Harry's horses—when anybody wants one of them to ride, he must go to Harry and if Harry says no he must go elsewhere for a pony—Jane, his wife is queen of the kitchen and, assisted by another old woman some 60 years old, has the entire management of the household affairs. Her three or four black urchins look healthy and hearty and are destined to bring a good price when they are old enough for market. These "niggers" all have their own way and do very much as they please. So it is with all the families I saw—a slave calls his master's horse his horse, his master's wagon, his wagon—and whatever he has charge of he denominates in intercourse with others as mine—If you ask a slave whom you meet, whose is that fine horse he is riding, he will say "Mine Sir". I saw nothing while at L. but comfort and happiness and perfect contentment among these poor wretches, they know not the Sweet consciousness of self ownership.

Diary of Charles Peabody's Western Trip, from New York through the Ohio and Mississippi Valleys, May 21–September 11, 1846, Western Historical Manuscripts Collection, University of Missouri, St. Louis (transcript copy, original in the Historical and Philosophical Society of Ohio, Cincinnati).

DRED SCOTT SUES FOR HIS FREEDOM

Dred Sott filed his initial suit on April 6, 1846, under the Missouri statute that provided a legal avenue through which persons who believed that they were wrongfully held in slavery could petition for their freedom. The Old St. Louis Courthouse, in which Scott's suit was decided in his favor, still stands as a landmark to his struggle for freedom. Although such suits were routine, and although hundreds of people gained their freedom in this way, Dred Scott's case became a touchstone for proslavery forces in the state and eventually resulted in a Supreme Court decision that sent Scott back into slavery and denied citizenship to black Americans until the ratification of the Thirteenth Amendment.

Dred Scott, 1857.
Courtesy of Missouri Historical Society

To the Hon. John M. Krum, Judge of the St. Louis Circuit Court.

Dred Scott, a man of color, respectfully states to your honor, that he is claimed as a slave by one Irene Emerson, of the County of St. Louis, State of Missouri, widow of the late Dr. John Emerson, who at the time of his death was a surgeon in the United States army. That the said Dr. John Emerson purchased your petitioner in the city of St. Louis, about nine years ago, he then being a slave, from one Peter Blow now deceased, and took petitioner with him to Rock Island in the State of Illinois, and then kept petitioner to labor and service, in attendance upon said Emerson, for about two years and six months, he the said Emerson being attached to the United States troops there stationed as surgeon. That after remaining at the place last named for about the period aforesaid, said Emerson was removed from the garrison at Rock Island aforesaid, to Fort Snelling on the St. Peters river in the territory of Iowa, and took petitioner with him, at which latter place the petitioner continued to remain in attendance upon Dr. John Emerson doing labor and service, for a period of about five years. That after the lapse of the period last named, said Emerson was ordered to Florida, and proceeding there left petitioner at Jefferson Barracks in the County of St. Louis aforesaid in charge of one Capt. Bainbridge, to whom said Emerson hired Petitioner—that said Emerson is now dead, and his widow the said Irene claims petitioners services as a slave, and as his owner, but believing that under this state of fact, that he is entitled to his freedom, he prays your honor to allow him to sue said Irene Emerson in said Court, in order to establish his right to freedom + he will pray be.

his
Dred X Scott
mark

[reverse side]
     State of Missouri)
     St. Louis County Ss)   Dred Scott being sworn
says that the facts set forth in the forgoing petition are true
     Sworn to submitted)   his
     the 6th Day of Apl 1846)   Dred X of Color
     before the undersigned)   mark
        justice of the peace)
        [illegible] Bullen JP.)

The Judge of the St. Louis Circuit Court grants this petitioner leave to sue etc. as prayed for, and orders: First. That the petitioner Dred Scott be allowed to sue, on giving security satisfactory to the Clerk, for all costs that may be adjudged against him.

Second. That said Dred Scott have reasonable liberty to attend his counsel and the Court, as occasion may require: and that he be not removed out of the jurisdiction of the Court, and that he be not subject to any severity on account of his application for freedom.

St. Louis April 6. 1846

John M Krum
Judge St. Louis Circuit Court

Scott, Dred, a man of color v. Emerson, Irene, November 1846, Circuit Court Case Files, Office of the Circuit
Clerk, St. Louis, Missouri State Archives–St. Louis.

BOND FOR A FREE BLACK WOMAN

A free black St. Louis woman named Marie Louise Alexander filed a petition for a
license in 1846, the same year in which Dred Scott first sued for his freedom. Marie
was about twenty-one or twenty-two years old when she filed her petition. Little
is known about her surety, Paul L. Chouteau, other than that he was listed as a
slaveholder in the 1811 St. Louis census.

Know All Men by these Presents, That We, Marie Louise Alexander as principal, and Paul L Chouteau as securities, are held and firmly bound unto the State
of Missouri in the just and full sum of one hundred Dollars, lawful money of the
United States, for the payment of which we bind ourselves, our heirs, executors
and administrators, firmly by these presents, sealed with our seals, and dated this
24th day of December A.D. 1846.

The condition of the above obligation is such, that whereas the said Marie Louise
Alexander has applied to the County Court of St. Louis County for and obtained
a license to reside in the State of Missouri, during good behavior: Now, if the said
applicant shall be of good character during her residence in the State of Missouri,
then this obligation to be void, else of full force and virtue.

her
X
Marie Louise Alexander
mark
P. L. Chouteau

Dexter Tiffany Collection, series 14, subseries A, Free Negro Bonds, December 24–31, 1846, Slavery Papers,
Missouri Historical Society, St. Louis.

WILLIAM WELLS BROWN REMEMBERS HIS LIFE AS A SLAVE

William Wells Brown was born a slave in Kentucky. After he escaped from slavery
at age nineteen, he lived in Ohio, New York, and London. He became active as an
abolitionist and author, publishing his autobiographical narrative in 1847. Brown
also wrote works of fiction, including Clotel; or, the President's Daughter *(1853),*
a novel that used the fictional characters of Thomas Jefferson's slave daughters to

critize slavery and racism, as well as The Black Man, His Antecedents, His
Genius, and His Achievements *(1863), which documented African American
contributions to American society. The following excerpt from the autobiography
describes a period of Brown's childhood in St. Louis.*

[My] master removed to the city of St. Louis, and purchased a farm four miles
from there, which he placed under the charge of an overseer by the name of
Friend Haskell. He was a regular Yankee from New England. The Yankees are
noted for making the most cruel overseers.

My mother was hired out in the city, and I was also hired out there to Major
Freeland, who kept a public house. He was formerly from Virginia, and was a horse-
racer, cock-fighter, gambler, and withal an inveterate drunkard. There were ten or
twelve servants in the house, and when he was present, it was cut and slash—knock
down and drag out. In his fits of anger, he would take up a chair, and throw it at
a servant; and in his more rational moments, when he wished to chastise one, he
would tie them up in the smoke-house, and whip them; after which, he would cause
a fire to be made of tobacco stems, and smoke them. This he called *"Virginia play."*

I complained to my master of the treatment which I received from Major Freeland; but it made no difference. He cared nothing about it, so long as he received
the money for my labor. After living with Major Freeland five or six months, I
ran away, and went into the woods back of the city; and when night came on, I
made my way to my master's farm, but was afraid to be seen, knowing that if Mr.
Haskell, the overseer, should discover me, I should be again carried back to Major
Freeland; so I kept in the woods. One day, while in the woods, I heard the barking
and howling of dogs, and in a short time they came so near that I knew them to
be the bloodhounds of Major Benjamin O'Fallon. He kept five or six, to hunt
runaway slaves with.

As soon as I was convinced that it was them, I knew there was no chance of
escape. I took refuge in the top of a tree, and the hounds were soon at its base, and
there remained until the hunters came up in a half or three quarters of an hour
afterwards. There were two men with the dogs, who, as soon as they came up,
ordered me to descend. I came down, was tied, and taken to St. Louis jail. Major
Freeland soon made his appearance, and took me out, and ordered me to follow
him, which I did. After we returned home, I was tied up in the smoke-house, and
was very severely whipped. After the major had flogged me to his satisfaction, he
sent out his son Robert, a young man eighteen or twenty years of age, to see that
I was well smoked. He made a fire of tobacco stems, which soon set me to cough-
ing and sneezing. This, Robert told me, was the way his father used to do to his
slaves in Virginia. After giving me what they conceived to be a decent smoking, I
was untied and again set to work.

Robert Freeland was a "chip of the old block." Though quite young, it was not unfrequently that he came home in a state of intoxication. He is now, I believe, a popular commander of a steamboat on the Mississippi river. Major Freeland soon after failed in business, and I was put on board the steamboat Missouri, which plied between St. Louis and Galena. The commander of the boat was William B. Culver. I remained on her during the sailing season, which was the most pleasant time for me that I had ever experienced. At the close of navigation I was hired to Mr. John Colburn, keeper of the Missouri Hotel. He was from one of the free states; but a more inveterate hater of the negro I do not believe ever walked God's green earth. This hotel was at that time one of the largest in the city, and there were employed in it twenty or thirty servants, mostly slaves.

Mr. Colburn was very abusive, not only to the servants, but to his wife also, who was an excellent woman, and one from whom I never knew a servant to receive a harsh word; but never did I know a kind one to a servant from her husband. Among the slaves employed in the hotel was one by the name of Aaron, who belonged to Mr. John F. Darby, a lawyer. Aaron was the knife-cleaner. One day, one of the knives was put on the table, not as clean as it might have been. Mr. Colburn, for this offence, tied Aaron up in the wood-house, and gave him over fifty lashes on the bare back with a cow-hide, after which, he made me wash him down with rum. This seemed to put him into more agony than the whipping. After being untied he went home to his master, and complained of the treatment which he had received. Mr. Darby would give no heed to anything he had to say, but sent him directly back. Colburn, learning that he had been to his master with complaints, tied him up again, and gave him a more severe whipping than before. The poor fellow's back was literally cut to pieces; so much so, that he was not able to work for ten or twelve days.

There was, also, among the servants, a girl whose master resided in the country. Her name was Patsey. Mr. Colburn tied her up one evening, and whipped her until several of the boarders came out and begged him to desist. The reason for whipping her was this. She was engaged to be married to a man belonging to Major William Christy, who resided four or five miles north of the city. Mr. Colburn had forbid her to see John Christy. The reason of this was said to be the regard which he himself had for Patsey. She went to meeting that evening, and John returned home with her. Mr. Colburn had intended to flog John, if he came within the inclosure; but John knew too well the temper of his rival, and kept at a safe distance:—so he took vengeance on the poor girl. If all the slave-drivers had been called together, I do not think a more cruel man than John Colburn—and he too a northern man—could have been found among them.

While living at the Missouri hotel, a circumstance occurred which caused me great unhappiness. My master sold my mother, and all her children, except myself. They were sold to different persons in the city of St. Louis. . . .

I was soon after taken from Mr. Colburn's, and hired to Elijah P. Lovejoy, who was at that time publisher and editor of the "St. Louis Times." My work, while with him, was mainly in the printing office, waiting on the hands, working the press, &c. Mr. Lovejoy was a very good man, and decidedly the best master that I had ever had. I am chiefly indebted to him, and to my employment in the printing office, for what little learning I obtained while in slavery.

Though slavery is thought, by some, to be mild in Missouri, when compared with the cotton, sugar and rice growing states, yet no part of our slave-holding country is more noted for the barbarity of its inhabitants than St. Louis. It was here that Col. Harney, a United States officer, whipped a slave woman to death. It was here that Francis McIntosh, a free colored man from Pittsburg, was taken from the steamboat Flora and burned at the stake. During a residence of eight years in this city, numerous cases of extreme cruelty came under my own observation; to record them all would occupy more space than could possibly be allowed in this little volume. I shall, therefore, give but a few more in addition to what I have already related.

From William Wells Brown, *Narrative of William W. Brown, An American Slave. Written by Himself.* London: Charles Gilpin, 1850.

"EMANCIPATION . . . WOULD CONVERT THIS VAST REGION . . . INTO A HOWLING WILDERNESS"

After passage of the Kansas-Nebraska Act and in the wake of efforts to secure Kansas for free labor, a group of prominent Missouri slaveholders and proslavery activists met in Lexington in 1855 to encourage one another in resisting the antislavery factions that threatened the survival of the institution in Kansas. In this speech, Irish-born educator and Baptist preacher James Shannon defends slavery. Shannon had served as president of several Missouri colleges, including the University of Missouri, Columbia, from 1850 to 1856.

AN ADDRESS DELIVERED BEFORE THE PRO-SLAVERY CONVENTION OF THE STATE OF MISSOURI, . . . 1855.

. . . [I]t is manifest, that the Union must be preserved, if it would exert any influence whatever for the accomplishment of this sublime result. In my deliberate judgment, however, the Union is placed in jeopardy by the persevering aggressions of anti-slavery fanaticism on the Constitutional rights of the South; and no created power can save it many years, unless those aggressions are successfully *resisted* and *arrested,* and a proper regard paid to the Constitutional rights of the slaveholding States. How, then, can this be accomplished, fanaticism converted or beaten back, and the Union saved, to fulfil its high destiny in the regeneration of a ruined world?

I am free to confess, that I can conceive of no better means for the accomplishment of these sublime results than to *cure* or *kill free-soil fanaticism,* the only hydra by which, at present, our country is in danger of being destroyed. And I am unable even to imagine a better method for correcting this fanaticism, than to enlighten the public mind on the subject of slavery in its various aspects. Hence I feel impelled alike by patriotism, and the highest regard for the salvation of a lost world, to enlighten my fellow-men to the utmost of my ability on this absorbing topic. . . .

Slavery is found in our midst. It was forced on the South by the combined efforts of old England and New England, now also leagued together for selfish ends, in an unholy alliance, for its extermination. The present generation of slaveholders are in no shape responsible for its existence. They had no agency in its introduction; and, therefore, although its existence were admitted to be their *misfortune,* it can never be proved to be their *fault.* Its abolition, under existing circumstances, is believed to be morally impossible. In 1850, according to the census of the United States, there were in the slave States, including the District of Columbia, three million one hundred and ninety-five thousand nine hundred and fifty-one slaves. The average value of an ordinary lot of slaves is generally estimated at one-half the price of a prime field hand. Such a slave will now readily sell for 1,200 dollars. Taking $600, then, as the average, it will give us 1,917,570,600 dollars as the total value of the slaves in 1850. The natural increase, since that time, makes it reasonable to estimate their present value, in round numbers, at two thousand millions of dollars. At six per cent., the annual interest on that sum will amount to one hundred and twenty millions.

Strike out of existence at once this vast amount of productive capital, and it is not in the power of human arithmetic to compute, or of human language to express, the amount of financial ruin that would result, not merely to the slaveholding, but also to the non-slaveholding States, and to the civilized world. Besides, it should not be forgotten that negro slaves alone are constitutionally adapted to labor in those climates where the great staples of cotton, rice and sugar can be produced. Emancipation, therefore, would convert this vast region, the abode of wealth, civilization and refinement of the highest order, into a howling wilderness. The loss of productive property in land, houses, machinery, and improvements of various kinds, thus rendered valueless, can hardly be estimated. . . .

But the financial ruin is by no means the most important item in this account of prospective abolitionism. Look to St. Domingo and the British West Indies. In short, look where you please, all history attests that emancipation would be the greatest calamity that could be inflicted on the blacks themselves; that American slavery has elevated their character, and ameliorated their condition, in all respects; and that wherever fanaticism or misguided philanthropy has cut them loose from the guardianship of the white race, they have not merely degenerated, but have retrograded with rapid strides towards a savage, and even a brutal state. Facts innumerable and well authenticated might be produced to sustain this position, did time permit. Again, the blacks form about one-third of the whole population included in the slave States: what disposition could be made of them, if emancipated? The free States, although rabid to steal them—when, in so doing, they are compelled to commit perjury, murder, and the most unblushing and indubitable nullification of the Constitution and laws of the United States—would not consent to receive even a moiety of them, if they could be had honorably and without committing these crimes.

They could not be sent to Africa. Even if benevolence presented no barrier to their expulsion, the resources of the Union—impoverished, as it would be, by their emancipation—would be inadequate to transport them to Africa, or to any foreign land.

They could not remain in our midst. It needs no argument to prove that the two races, in numbers so nearly equal, *especially under a republican form of government,* could not possibly coëxist on a footing of social and political equality. Self-preservation, the first law of Nature, would compel one race to expel, exterminate, or enslave the other. The foregoing difficulties exist in their full magnitude even on the hypothesis that emancipation could be effected peaceably. But who that is not absolutely insane, or idiotic, can imagine for a single moment that this is at all possible? Who can imagine that more than six millions of American citizens, inhabiting fifteen States of this Union, would consent to be robbed of property to the extent of two thousand millions, to which their rights are as clearly recognized, and as sacredly guarded, in the Constitution, and in the Bible, as to any other species of property? Would they not rather, in view of the inevitable and utter ruin that emancipation must bring in its train, appeal to the God of battles, buckle on their armor, meet the fanatical invader on the outposts of the Constitution with fire and faggot, and, if need be, perish bravely in the defence of their altars and their firesides, rather than meanly live to drag out a wretched existence, and in the end to suffer a more wretched and intolerable doom. In view of such appalling results, even supposing them to be barely probable, who but a madman, a traitor, or a fiend, could give countenance to that reckless anti-slavery fanaticism, which is rushing madly forward—through perjury, theft and murder, and over the prostrate, mangled, bleeding Constitution—to rob six millions of their fellow-citizens of two thousand millions of property; at the imminent peril, too, of dissolving the Union, or lighting up the torch of civil, perhaps servile war; baptizing our happy land in a sea of fraternal blood, and plunging in an abyss of rayless gloom this last, this best, this only hope for the regeneration of a debased and ruined world?

To all this, however, it may be objected, that slavery is a moral wrong; that our obligation to do right is paramount to all others; and that it never can be justifiable to do wrong from an apprehension of any evils, whether real or imaginary, that may be anticipated to result from doing right. . . .

All who are well informed on the subject know, that, if the Bible sanctions any thing, it sanctions slaveholding. The most candid and prominent of the anti-slavery leaders (whether religious or *infidel*) have, within the last ten years, totally abandoned the Bible argument; and many of the latter class may now be heard blaspheming the God of the Bible in terms so malignant and fiendish, as might well make demons shudder. . . .

The master of a slave knows and feels, that he is bound to protect that slave from all possible harm, to supply all his reasonable wants while living, and to bury him decently when dead; and that his whole estate, even if he be a millionaire, together with his own personal energies, are legally as well as morally bound for the faithful performance of these duties, although that slave should never be able to render him compensation to the value of a single cent. The slave knows this, and that, if he have a good master, he need not be troubled about these things, but attend faithfully, when able, to the performance of reasonable service, and his necessary wants will all be supplied.

It must not be forgotten or overlooked, that the relations of master and slave are correlative, and the duties of these relations reciprocal. Both legally and morally, the master as truly belongs to the slave for the performance of a master's duties, as the slave belongs to the master for the performance (*when able*) of a slave's duties. In this respect, each may with equal propriety be said to own the other. Hence, in decrepitude from sickness or old age, the slave can say, "I have all things and abound." "I own a master, whose whole estate, and whose own personal energies are pledged for my support." The slave is, therefore, independent and happy.

Not so the poor hireling, who is wholly dependent on his daily labor for his daily bread. In sickness or old age, and *often* at other times, his only prospect is starvation, or the repulsive charity of a selfish and often heartless world. . . .

In this enlightened age, among those whose opinions are entitled to consideration, there is but little, if any, difference with respect to the fundamental principles of the social compact. All admit, that human government is, in its very nature, an abridgment of natural liberty, and can be justified only on the ground of its necessity; but, at the same time, it is universally conceded that human government is indispensably necessary to protect its subjects from the wrongs which self-willed man is constantly liable to commit on the person, property and character of his brother man. . . .

The [abolitionist] fanatics have already driven us to the very brink of the precipice; and if they persist in the execution of their unholy and treasonable designs, and are not speedily crushed by the intelligence and patriotism of the free States, *where alone it can be done,* who so blind as not to see, that the Union will inevitably and speedily be dissolved! And who in the South so craven, so lost to manly impulse, so very a traitor, as to advise or desire, that the slave States should take no vigorous measures of even *necessary self-defence,* until they are completely wound up in the anaconda folds of this deadly serpent, and crushed, without the power of even a feeble resistance! The free States, if they choose, can elect an abolition President. The legislative balance of power in the Senate has been lost by the introduction of California as a free State, while it is obvious, that the salvation of the Union may depend on its restoration; and if the intelligence and patriotism of the North are not brought to the rescue in this fearful crisis, what have the fifteen slave States, with more than six millions of free citizens, to depend on, but their own brave hearts, and strong arms?

Thank Heaven, [the slave-holding states] *have all the courage, more than twice the numbers, and at least twenty times the resources,* that our revolutionary sires had, when they defied the haughty tyrant George the Third, and, after a protracted struggle, drove his menial cohorts off the soil, that had been polluted by their unholy tread.

It is, therefore, vain to imagine, it is suicidal to hope, that such a people will submit to a worse tyranny in that government, which they themselves created for the *"common defence,"* and which they could not have been induced to create at all, and CAN NOT NOW BE FORCED TO TOLERATE, FOR ANY OTHER PURPOSE.

Let us then, fellow-citizens, be united, be vigilant. Let us husband our resources, concentrate our energies, and exhaust all peaceable means to protect our rights, and save the Union, if possible, from the Vandal assaults of abolition traitors and nullifiers. Let us hope for the best, and prepare for the worst; and then, *having done all that men can do to save the Union,* if a dissolution is forced upon us by domestic traitors, instigated thereto by the decrepid monarchies of the Old World, then I, for one, say, in the language of a distinguished Georgia statesman and patriot, *"having exhausted the argument, we will stand to our arms;"* our motto this, "God will defend the right!" and our consolation, that, *if Rome must fall,* we are innocent.

An Address Delivered before the Pro-Slavery Convention of the State of Missouri, Held in Lexington, July 13, 1855, on Domestic Slavery, as Examined in the Light of Scripture, of Natural Rights, of Civil Government, and the Constitutional Power of Congress. Published by the order of the Convention. St. Louis, MO. Printed at the Republican Book and Job Office, 1855.

TWO

~

Missouri Divides

*T*HE NEW STATE OF MISSOURI proved to be a roaring success. Settlers farmed the fertile lands along the rivers, hunted furs, mined lead, and generally found prosperity in the 1820s and 1830s. Barges, flatboats, and steamboats navigating the Missouri and Mississippi rivers carried tobacco, hemp, and furs to the rest of the nation and to ships that crossed the Atlantic. The river trade and hundreds of miles of new railroads brought goods, travelers, and news through the state. During those years, Missouri's popular senator Thomas Hart Benton continued to voice the old-fashioned Democratic doctrine of hard money and readily available land for westward migration.

The state's economic growth and prosperity came with a cost, however. Missouri's population doubled and then doubled again in the 1830s and 1840s. In 1830, more than 140,000 people lived in the state; by 1860, the population had reached more than a million.[1] Immigration from Europe, especially Germany, played a significant role in this growth, especially in St. Louis. In 1840, St. Louis had a population of about 20,000; by 1850, that number had increased to 75,000 and, within another decade to about 160,000.[2] Two-thirds of St. Louisans were foreign born. German immigrants' ideas, beliefs, and customs differed sharply from those of the more established Missourians, especially those who hailed from the slave states. These new Germans changed the political climate of cities like St. Louis and the state capital, Jefferson City. Many of them were political refugees who had been driven from their homeland because of their radical democratic and anticlerical views, and they never hesitated to express their opinions. This new population had a profound influence on St. Louis as it began to lose its French colonial character and as public opinion began to reflect the views and customs of the newer German citizens.

The Democratic Party, which had long ruled the state, was not always able to keep pace with the changes. As Missouri grew and changed, it remained at the crossroads of regions, labor systems, and politics. Missourians struggled mightily over national issues and conflicts—especially over the expansion of slavery into the western territories. While Missouri did not have a strong antislavery contingent, some opponents of slavery were beginning to reach the limits of their tolerance. When new western territories clamored to join the Union after the war with Mexico, Senator

31

Benton feared that agitation over slavery would endanger the Union and warned that slaves should be kept out of the new territories. His position earned him a great deal of enmity with the powerful Boon's Lick party leaders and brought about the end of his twenty-year Senate career. Benton was a nationalist committed to keeping slavery out of the territories, and by 1850, Missouri's Democrats were bitterly divided: some agreed with Benton, while others denied that Congress possessed the power to legislate on slavery in the territories. Whigs capitalized on this division, particularly in St. Louis and Jefferson City, and made gains throughout the decade, even as old Whigs from Virginia supported both slavery and some of the more modern improvements, such as railroads, educational reform, and banks.[3]

After the passage of the Compromise of 1850, many Missourians hailed what they considered to be its most beneficial provision: the Fugitive Slave Act. Because the state bordered free territories, slave owners lived with the constant risk that their slaves might escape into freedom. The compromise quelled sectional tensions for a time, until Iowa senator Augustus C. Dodge introduced a bill organizing the Nebraska and Kansas territories in 1853. Illinois senator Stephen A. Douglas, who chaired the Committee on Territories, took over the bill and proposed that the slavery question be decided by the settlers themselves or, as he called it, by "popular sovereignty." Because both territories were located north of the 36° 30' line, the bill effectively repealed the Missouri Compromise of 1820. Congress passed the law and President Franklin Pierce signed it in 1854. The Kansas-Nebraska Act caused a firestorm of protest among Northerners but was applauded in the South. In Missouri, it exacerbated an already volatile situation. Missourians, along with settlers from the Upper South, had already been crossing into the Kansas Territory for some time—illegally, because the territory had not yet been opened for settlement. Passage of the act galvanized Missourians to defend their interests. For Missourians, the addition of new western states was cause for concern. A slaveholding Kansas would intensify antislavery sentiment in Missouri, but a free Kansas would undermine the institution of slavery in the state as bondsmen gained another path to freedom. Fights broke out over boundaries and property lines as well as over the issue of slavery. In the absence of a functioning government in Kansas Territory, it was nearly impossible to control the fighting.

Missourians watched with anxiety as abolitionists from the North took an interest in the settlement of Kansas. Abolitionists such as Henry Ward Beecher and Eli Thayer organized the New England Emigrant Aid Company in 1855, which outfitted and armed more than twelve hundred antislavery settlers from Massachusetts and sent them to create a free territory in Kansas. Proslavery men from Missouri and other Southern states suspected a vast Northern conspiracy to deprive them of the right to bring their human property into the Kansas Territory. By the end of the year, thousands of proslavery Missourians known as "border ruffians" had swarmed across the border to vote—illegally, of course—for a proslavery constitution and a congressional delegate. Because of this fraud, the proslavery forces swept the elections. In response, the New England free-staters who had settled in the territory set up a rival legislature at Topeka. Although a congressional delegation investigated the elections and deemed them fraudulent, the Pierce administration, reflecting the president's Southern sympathies, continued to support the proslavery Kansas legislature and constitution. With presidential support, it was relatively easy for proslavery forces to expel or silence their opponents. The illegally elected proslavery politicians enacted a harsh Kansas Code designed to force antislavery men and ideas out of the territory.[4]

The violence in Kansas overflowed into Missouri and raged back again: the border ruffians' interference in Kansas politics served only to increase anger and political divisions in Missouri. The violence also contributed to a climate of lawlessness that became ever more dangerous—especially for families living near the western border of Missouri—and increasingly difficult to control. Missouri senator David Atchison, one of the most outspoken and most popular proponents of the proslavery point of view, became deeply involved in the Kansas struggle. His fiery rhetoric exhorted proslavery Kansans and Missourians to defend slavery "with the *bayonet* and with *blood*" and, if necessary, "to kill every God-damned abolitionist in the district."[5]

This tense political situation exploded into violence. A grand jury in Lecompton indicted the free-staters, including Senator James Lane and several newspaper editors, for treason, and the men were promptly arrested. Proslavery Kansans and Missourians decided to carry out the sentence themselves without observing legal niceties. A vigilante posse of eight hundred armed men rode to Lawrence, where they arrested the free-staters and proceeded to sack and loot the town.[6] They set fire to the Eldridge Hotel (known to house free-state sympathizers), a printing press, a grocer, and several other businesses; in all, they destroyed property worth more than $100,000. The violence in Kansas continued to escalate through the end of the decade as proslavery and antislavery forces clashed near the border. When abolitionist John Brown initiated a brutal massacre of proslavery settlers at Pottawattomie Creek, revenge came quickly. Four hundred proslavery Missourians raided the town of Osawatomie in August 1856. Brown fought back hard against the attackers; his son Frederick died in the assault, and most of the settlement was destroyed by fire.

Some of the lawlessness on the Kansas-Missouri border was for political reasons, some of it for revenge, and much of it simply for plunder. The criminal aspect intensified—and soon included mass murder. Georgia native Charles Hamilton conducted a raid through Kansas in early spring 1858, during which he murdered several unarmed free-state settlers before crossing the border into Missouri. On

May 19, 1858, near Marais des Cygnes, Hamilton and his gang captured eleven men, some of whom were former friends and neighbors, shot them in cold blood, and left them for dead. This ugly incident horrified the nation. Poet John Greenleaf Whittier wrote a bitter poem about it, calling the murderers "foul human vultures" and "wolves of the Border."[7] Further massacres occurred even after the new territorial governor took office, and in the end, nearly sixty people died in the violence that became known as "Bleeding Kansas." After the 1860 presidential election, law and order would be restored in Kansas, making it possible for the free-state majority to assert itself. Kansas would enter the Union in 1861 as a free state, but even that failed to assuage the bitterness between pro- and antislavery forces along the border.

In 1857, as violence escalated in Kansas and overflowed into Missouri, U.S. Supreme Court justice Roger B. Taney issued his famous opinion in the *Dred Scott* case, which declared that black people (both free and enslaved) could never be citizens and would never be entitled under the Constitution to any rights that a "white man was bound to respect."[8] Because this decision declared the 1820 Missouri Compromise unconstitutional, it essentially nationalized slavery by giving slave owners the right to bring their bondspeople into the free states with impunity. The fact that the Supreme Court could set aside a national political compromise (albeit one already negated by the Kansas-Nebraska Act) convinced many abolitionists that slavery had forced its way into the free states: no one was safe from the encroachments of the institution of human bondage. Northerners reasoned that the South would continue to push its institutions into free states and territories until it gained supremacy in Congress. For their part, Southerners were convinced of a Northern conspiracy to incite slave insurrections and to abolish the institution. John Brown's raid on the federal arsenal at Harpers Ferry in 1859 inflamed Southern public opinion. Many Southerners had heard that New Englanders had helped fund the raid. One by one, the "fire-eaters" (passionate secessionists in the South) declared that if Abraham Lincoln won the 1860 presidential contest, their states would leave the Union.

In 1860, Missourians faced two crucially important political decisions. The first, the gubernatorial election, would determine the role of the state in what most already knew would soon become a national conflict. The second was the presidential election. Missourians believed that newly elected Kentucky-born governor Claiborne F. Jackson would see them safely through the dangers ahead. He had publicly supported Stephen A. Douglas for the presidency and appeared to be a moderate Democrat. What most Missourians did not know, however, was that Jackson had voted (illegally) in the Kansas elections and was already preparing to support the pro-Southern candidate John C. Breckinridge for president in November 1860.[9]

Claiborne Fox Jackson. *Courtesy of Missouri Historical Society*

In a Democratic state like Missouri, Abraham Lincoln had little chance of winning. He represented the new Republican Party, which had not yet garnered many adherents in the state, at least not outside German-dominated St. Louis. The party opposed the extension of slavery but did not advocate interference with the institution where it already existed. Still, for slaveholders, both in Missouri and in other slave states, that position seemed dangerously close to abolitionism. Lincoln should have been easy to defeat. Both within the state and across the national, however, the Democratic Party was in trouble. At their nominating convention, Southern Democrats had walked out rather than endorse Stephen A. Douglas because he was a moderate and a staunch Unionist.

Douglas barely won the general election in Missouri with 58,801 popular votes and garnered the state's nine electoral votes. Close behind him was John Bell, of Tennessee, who ran on the ticket of the new Constitutional Union Party and polled 58,372 votes. The Constitutional Union Party espoused a moderate pro-Union, pro-Constitution platform and was composed of former Whigs and Know-Nothings, who disliked the radicalism of both the Democrats and the Republicans. Proslavery Missourians supported Vice President John C. Breckinridge, of Kentucky, who later fought in the Confederate army. Breckinridge received 31,317 votes, most of them in the northwestern slaveholding counties. Lincoln won the national election with a large majority of electoral votes (180 to Douglas's 12, Breckenridge's 72, and Bell's 39). But Lincoln won only 39.8 percent of the popular vote nationwide. In Missouri, he made a poor showing but carried St. Louis with 9,483 votes. Douglas came in second in the city with 8,538 votes. Only 4,533 St. Louisans voted for Bell, and Breckinridge came in a distant fourth with only 544 votes. The outcome of the election in St. Louis and, more generally, throughout the state revealed Missourians' commitment to moderation. As the election results showed, the secessionists were in the minority. The election also highlighted divisions within the state, especially between St. Louis and the rest of the state.[10]

In the Deep South states, Lincoln's victory was a clarion call to secession. In Missouri, much to the surprise of the moderates who had recently elected him, Governor Jackson made it clear that he had no intention of supporting Lincoln's fight to keep the Union together. When Lincoln issued his proclamation

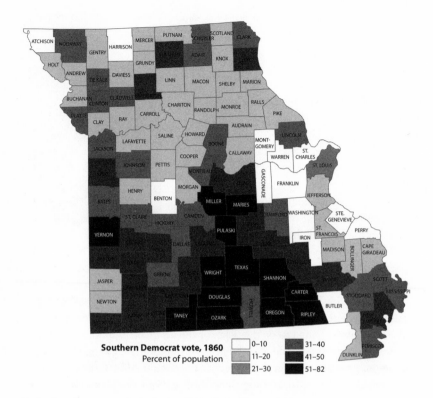

Southern Democrat vote, 1860
Percent of population

0–10	31–40
11–20	41–50
21–30	51–82

The Southern Democrat vote in the election of 1860. *Map by Margaret Pearce*

of April 15, 1861, requisitioning state militias for three months' service in the U.S. Army, Jackson indignantly refused. Jackson's sympathies were entirely with the seceding states; indeed, he hoped and expected that he would be able to lead his state out of the Union. But he had misread Missouri's public opinion. While few Missourians would have debated the right of their fellow citizens to hold human property, most of them remained loyal to the Union even after the states of the Lower South began to secede. Most Missourians believed that the government had no business interfering with slavery or any other internal state affairs, but they were far more dependent on their economic ties to the rest of the country than were the Deep South states. The Mississippi River trade connected the state not only with the East and the North but also with European trade partners. Even the planters in the Little Dixie counties depended on eastern markets, especially for sales of hemp, which had become one of the most important crops in Missouri. Missourians enjoyed lucrative navy contracts for hemp rope, and its planters could ill afford to jettison their alliance with the federal government.

During the secession crisis, Missourians faced difficult choices. They thought of themselves as westerners, but despite their economic ties to the North, they remained committed to slaveholding. Most of all, they cherished their independence. Those who were most sympathetic to the South and to slavery (like residents in the border states of Maryland, Kentucky, and Delaware) believed that the U.S. government should not coerce Southern states to remain in the Union, and they opposed any form of military action against the South. They were "conditional Union" men: they felt that they owed loyalty to the Union until and unless the government took unconstitutional steps. Others remained uncertain over the path the state should take and were easily influenced by harsh actions by either side.[11]

THE *SQUATTER SOVEREIGN* PROCLAIMS: "KANSAS DECLARED IN FAVOR OF SLAVERY"

A group of politically powerful Missourians, among whom were some of the staunchest defenders of slavery in the nation, founded the town of Atchison (named after Missouri senator David Rice Atchison) in the Kansas Territory in 1854. Proslavery Missourians not only crossed the border to settle and vote in Kansas but also maintained a vocal and visible presence. Dr. John H. Stringfellow and Robert S. Kelley founded a printing press and quickly established the Squatter Sovereign. *After 1857, antislavery Samuel C. Pomeroy bought the* Sovereign *and turned it into a free-state paper. The editorial mentions Kansas governor Andrew Horatio Reeder, a proslavery Southern sympathizer appointed by President Franklin Pierce in 1854. Reeder supported the Kansas-Nebraska bill and the principle of popular sovereignty, but when he spoke out against the electoral fraud in the territory, he was attacked in the press. After the fraudulently elected proslavery party began arresting free-state supporters, Reeder left Kansas.*

SUSTAIN US.

The election in this Territory having terminated with such disastrous results to the Abolitionists, and with such credit to the Southern citizens, the pro-slavery press in Kansas may with propriety come in for their share of the honor. As for ourselves, we want for our REWARD, the well-wishes and support of our pro-slavery friends. It is all important that we should have papers of the "right stripe" in the Territory; and it is evident that, for a year or two, they must be supported by the South. We then appeal to our friends for that material aid, which is so necessary to the success of a newspaper. We shall arrive to make the Squatter Sovereign what the true Southern man would wish it—an uncompromising pro-slavery print— and with this end in view, we appeal to our friends to sustain us. . . .

KANSAS ELECTION.

OUT WITH THE GUN.

"WE HAVE MET THE ENEMY, AND THEY ARE OURS!"

The entire forces of Abolitionism, Reederism, Free Soilism, and other isms combined, completely Routed. Kansas declared in favor of Slavery.

We have the satisfaction and pleasure of recording one of the most brilliant political victories ever accomplished by any party. Kansas has spoken in thunder-tones, and repudiated our Freesoil governor, and his allies. She has taken a noble stand in the Pro-Slavery ranks, and there she will remain forever! The combined forces of Abolitionism, Freesoilism, and Reederism made a desperate effort to carry the Territorial Legislature. But their exertions proved unavailing, against the true men of the South. We have battered down all opposition, and Kansas now stands pre-eminent as one of the Southern constellation. "We have met the enemy and they are ours!" And for that act, we deserve, and will no doubt receive, the heartfelt thanks of the entire South.

Squatter Sovereign, April 3, 1855.

A REPUBLICAN NEWSPAPER EDITOR COMMENTS
FAVORABLY ON THE HIGH PRICE OF MISSOURI SLAVES

Despite its rather misleading name, the St. Louis Globe-Democrat *subscribed to Republican principles. Nineteenth-century newspapers often published editorials or letters from rival publications, even those whose points of view differed sharply from their own. Here the* Globe-Democrat *prints a letter from an outspoken proslavery rival, the* Missouri Republican, *in order to discredit reports that free-state agitation threatened the security of the institution of slavery in Missouri. In the final paragraph, the writer refers to the troublesome 1856 contest for the Speakership of the House of Representatives, which greatly exacerbated party enmities within the national Congress.*

PRICE OF NEGROES IN MISSOURI

We copy the following from the Missouri Republican of yesterday. The Republican has been one of those papers which has been constantly representing that negro property among us is endangered and depreciated by the hostility of free States to the institution. And it has endeavored to arouse the animosity of slaveholders against Northern men, and the Northern States, by eternally harping upon this string. To show how false, and how wickedly foolish, this charge is, and to prove that the accusation is made with a design merely to create bad feelings between the States, for which there is no ground, we publish the following. It will be seen that in this region of Missouri, more exposed than any other, from its proximity to Northern Illinois and Chicago, the price is greater than it was ever known to be before, either in this or any other State; and is constantly advancing:

Prairieville, Pike County, Mo.,

January 2, 1855

Mr. Editor: There must be a California in North East Missouri, or the El Dorado is in the farmers' pockets. Negro men sold on yesterday at the following prices: $1,365, $1,542, $1,405, $1,215, $1,275. These men were common crop hands ranging from thirty to forty-five years of age. Women brought from eight to nine hundred dollars, and one went as high as $1,040, another as high as $1,753! These two last good house servants and seamstresses. The women bringing $800 and $900 were over middle age. All of these sales were for cash, or for bonds bearing six per cent interest from date. They were bona fide sales, and the negroes were all purchased by citizens of the surrounding counties, for farming purposes. The rise in the prices of agricultural products, is now telling in the value of labor, and our farmers seem to think that the "peculiar institution" is still of some account.

While negroes sold for these prices, they hired at corresponding rates. Common farm hands, young and likely, hired for $220 and $232; boys of fifteen and seventeen years of age, or thereabouts, hired for $140 and $150—in every instance the individual hiring, and not the owner, paying all charges of every description.

These items may be of interest to many of your readers.—They may serve to show that the people in the country still think that matters are by no means desperate, though Congress can't elect a Speaker.

Very respectfully yours, etc., P.C.

St. Louis Globe-Democrat, January 7, 1856.

A ST. LOUIS NEWSPAPER LAMENTS THE "FRATRICIDAL STRIFE ON THE SOIL OF KANSAS"

By the mid-1850s, the St. Louis Globe-Democrat *proclaimed strong antislavery views and published a prophetic opinion piece on the Kansas troubles, highlighting the border violence between Kansas and Missouri. Benjamin F. Stringfellow was famous as a lawyer and firebrand orator who sometimes defended his proslavery opinions with physical violence.*

RENEWAL OF THE CIVIL WAR IN KANSAS.

The subjoined telegraphic dispatch received by us last evening, from an authentic source, speaks for itself, and dismally heralds the renewal of fratricidal strife on the soil of Kansas. Already the news that comes from that virgin territory is written in blood. From the character of the dispatch, and from what we know of the designs secretly entertained by the banditti of Atchison and Stringfellow, who hang upon the Missouri border like Zouaves, prepared to *"harry"* the settlements of the free settlers of Kansas at the first signal from their leader, we cannot but give it full and implicit credit. At the same time, we fully concur in the statement expressed therein that a true version of the origin of the difficulty cannot be looked for from the partisan press at Kickapoo. We have had too much reason already to know how the truth has been violated heretofore in regard to past difficulties, for the purpose of betraying our border population into a hasty and perhaps fatal interference in the affairs of Kansas, to place much reliance upon like inflammatory appeals again. While refraining, therefore, until better advised of the facts, from commenting upon the causes of this lamentable occurrence, we must, in common with every true friend of constitutional liberty and every zealous defender of the Union of the States, deeply deplore the evil consequences likely to flow from this border feud, if, as we fear it may, it be fanned into a wide-spread civil war.

[By the National Line.]

Weston, Jan. 18.

To the *Missouri Democrat:*

An extra from the *Pioneer* at Kickapoo, dated eight o'clock this morning, says that a battle took place last night at Kansas about 12 o'clock between the Abolitionists and pro-Slavery men; the former making the attack, one pro-Slavery man named Cook, was killed and several wounded. . . . Also that the Abolition company from Lawrence was on the ground, commanded by one Brown, who commenced the fight and is said to be urging them on to other acts of violence. The Kickapoo Rangers were brought to arms, and a large number of persons would leave that place for the seat of war in about twenty minutes. Such at least is the account . . . given by the Pioneer. Allowance should be made for its partisan zeal, in taking its say so.

The extra declares that the war has again commenced, and . . . inflammatory appeal to the people to rally at once. I think a serious difficulty has occurred, growing out of the Freesoil election the other day, and regard this as but another move to get up a civil war in Kansas. It is the last desperate game of the Atchisonites.

St. Louis *Globe-Democrat,* January 19, 1856.

WILLIAM B. NAPTON DEPLORES THE POSSIBILITY
OF EMANCIPATION IN MISSOURI

The fiery judge William B. Napton was one of the leading lights of the proslavery Democratic Party in Missouri. In his letter to Claiborne F. Jackson (who was then serving as state banking officer) he expressed his concern about the future of slavery in Missouri. By "great accessions" in the second paragraph he means "support."

October 3, 1857.
William B. Napton to Claiborne F. Jackson.

My Dear Sir,

. . . The subject of *emancipation* is the most important of these topics, *if* it should appear that serious danger threatens the security & stability of slavery. That a respectable organization now exists, whose avowed object is to convert our state into a second Illinois, is conceded—the question is, what prospects have they of success?

I have no fears of the fanatics—either the genuine ones—or the meek philanthropists, the Blairs, Browns & Bornsteins who for political purposes cheer them on. The danger lies in another direction. Without great accessions from other quarters, the handful of anti slavery agitators can effect nothing. Where then can they look for the necessary assistance?

The insatiable thirst for gain, that now pervades the body politic—the appetite for *plunder*—for getting rich without labor, or to use your forcible & homely illustration, the belief that a man can raise himself to the ceiling by taking hold of the seat of his breeches—this is the *real basis* of emancipation strength. It is by this notion that the little band of Yankee abolitionists & German radicals have gotten possession of Illinois & have made that place as thoroughly hostile to slavery as Chicago. From St. Louis the idea has crept up & down the rivers—has found location in the river towns—& gradually & slowly pervaded to a slight extent into the country. The idea is, that cities grow more rapidly— villages increase in number & population—town lots go up—commerce flourishes—manufactures increase—& every body has a chance to get rich out of nothing—where slavery has no foothold. Illinois is cited as the example & all the free states are appealed to.

Hard times will, I think, cure this disease—& we may safely rely, that the remedy is near at hand.

In what other quarters then shall we look for danger? The northern tier of counties through which the Hannibal & [illegible] road runs, after great accessions from northern emigration, is expected to cast in their lot with the Emancipationists. But all recent developements of sentiment in this quarter indicate a very different state of public sentiment—these counties, especially the Eastern end of the tier, seem to be sound & firm & during the seven years war with Benton, our principal & most reliable strength lay in this quarter. The South West is expected to join in this crusade—simply because she supported Benton & has few slaves—but the North West is filled up with Tennesseans & Kentuckians,

& although non slaveholders, I anticipate but little danger from them. The North West is also looked to, & I confess indications there are unfavorable. Their population is chiefly from Indiana, Ohio & Illinois—& they cannot be trusted— still, so long as the river counties maintain a firm posture, even with Illinois & the North West to contend against, we may consider ourselves safe. What then are the dangers in the Missouri River & upper & lower Mississippi counties? They have the wealth, the population[,] the intelligence & consequently the power—& until this power is turned against us, we may rest secure. . . .

I remain yours very truly
W. B. Napton

W. B. Napton to C. F. Jackson, October 3, 1857, Miscellaneous Manuscripts, Mss. 1879, Western Historical Manuscript Collections, University of Missouri, Columbia.

DEMOCRATIC AND CONSTITUTIONAL UNION
NEWSPAPER EDITORIALS ON THE 1860 PRESIDENTIAL ELECTION

In Missouri, only a few St. Louis newspapers endorsed the candidacy of Abraham Lincoln. Daily and weekly papers in the rest of the state supported one of the two Democratic presidential candidates, John C. Breckinridge and Stephen A. Douglas, or the Constitutional Union candidate, John Bell. While the Republican St. Louis Globe-Democrat crowed about the success of its candidate, reaction among Democratic papers was far more mixed.

The Western Journal of Commerce, *for example, had supported Douglas.*

WHAT WILL BE DONE.

Now that the election of Lincoln is conceded on all hands, the questions upon every tongue are, . . . will the south secede? will there be war? We have not yet received intelligence from sufficient scope of the country, and especially from down South, to enable us to state what is passing in that section. Consequently, we can give only our own opinions and the grounds upon which they are based.

Of course we do not believe that any *cause* of secession, of war, or even of a public commotion, exists. In fact nobody is talking of secession, or of trouble, except the recent supporters of Mr. Breckinridge. Even *they* are like the settlers in the early days of Indiana upon the "milk sick" question. Everywhere it was rumored that the State was full of it; but you could never find a community where it existed. No one would admit that they had "milk sickness" in *their* community, but over the next county, or just up the creek there "were lots of it." They will say *they* don't want the Union dissolved, but that down South, they are sure to do it. But down south, even, no *cause* of dissolution exists.

In '32, when South Carolina put on her hat to walk out of the Union, an act had actually been committed which that State *did* have some reason to regard as infringing upon her rights and interests; yet even *then* she was not [supported] by any of the other States, and not one of them could be found that would consent to cooperate with her. But treason thrives and grows upon a soil to which it is born, and especially does it obtain a rank growth when fed by the fires of a morbid and insane ambition. Now, in '60, when no act has been committed that affects her rights or her interests, but an act that may rightfully occur under the Constitution, she again talks and prepares to *act,* treason; for a renunciation of, and a war upon the constitution, while yet its provisions remain inviolate, *is* treason.

All admit that so long as the Constitution is maintained in good faith and its provisions enforced, we can all live together under it. When those provisions are disregarded or violated, then *all of us* are for resistance. But until then, he who would trample upon and spurn that Constitution, and "precipitate the Cotton States" or any other States, in a revolution, is a *traitor,* and should be treated as such. The election of Lincoln, then, is no cause of revolution, and those who would attempt to subvert the Constitution and dissolve the government without just cause, should be restrained by the power of the government and by all the appliances within its control, we care not whether they be nullifiers of the Fugitive Slave Law at the North, or nullifiers of the Constitution at the South.

We say nobody is talking of dissolution and war but the recent adherents to the disastrous political fortunes of Mr. Breckinridge; and nobody is to blame for this state of things, on account of which they threaten war, but they themselves. Nobody has contributed so much to Lincoln's election as they. Everybody knows that Lincoln never could have been elected but for the split in the Democratic party, and everybody knows that they made that split. Everybody knows that, had they remained in the Convention, Mr. Douglas could never have been nominated, and that some man would have been put in nomination whom all could have supported; Mr. Douglas' friends never talked nor dreamed of bolting. The Breckinridgeites have elected Lincoln—they have made their own bed; *now let them lie in it. . . .*

But will they attempt revolution now? We do not believe they will. They never were in a worse condition in the world, to attempt it. They have not enough bread-stuffs in all the Cotton States to feed them until spring; nor have they as heavy stocks of Sugar, rice and Cotton as usual to sell in order to enable them to buy from abroad and carry on a war besides. Political leaders may call conventions and declare hostilities, and they may find enough of the idle rabble, who have nothing at stake in the matter, to join their armies, but they can declare no war, nor effect any secession without the consent of the people, and this consent will never be given without greater provocation than they yet have. When it comes to stopping

their business and bearing all the heavy taxation necessary to sustain the new government and defray the expenses of war, and all for a political abstraction—for a
vague fear of what Lincoln *may* do in the future, the heavy planters and tradesmen
will object; they will prefer to wait until that time comes, in the hope, if nothing
else, of being in better condition to stand it than they now are. They would find,
like the newly married pair, that there were a great many little things to buy that they
had never dreamed of,—and they less able to buy than they ever were in their lives.

We believe there will be no secession—no one.

Western Journal of Commerce (Kansas City, Missouri), November 2, 1860.

The St. Louis Republican, another Democratic paper, had also supported Douglas.

Mr. Lincoln is elected President of the United States. . . . It was no fault of
ours that he was not beaten, for we took some pains to do it, and are only sorry
that equal success did not attend the exertions made in other quarters. The State
of Missouri, we think we may take upon ourselves to say, is the only State in the
Union that has stood by the regular nominees of the Democratic party—the only
one that has been true to the man who has done more, and suffered more, for the
south and the slave States than any living statesman. . . . For this good service, in
maintaining her integrity, and laying such a host of impudent pretenders to leader-
ship in the party on the shelf, the people, we repeat, are entitled to great credit.

Our correspondent from Washington tells us that Mr. LINCOLN, it is arranged,
will take an early occasion to declare the principles upon which he will administer
the Government. This may be done as a serenade to be given to him as soon as it is
ascertained that he has votes enough to make his election certain, and which will
hardly be postponed more than a week. We shall not wait for the declaration, but
will proceed to give expression to our views upon one or two questions brought
prominently forward by the result of his election.

We say, then, that Mr. LINCOLN has been elected President of the United States
according to all the forms of the constitution—that, on his induction into office on
the 4th of March next, he should be recognized by all good citizens as the President
of the Republic—and that there is no justification, in anything that has yet taken
place, for threats of Secession from the Union by any one or more States, or for any
demonstration of an intent to break up the Government. Now that the election is
over, and that men are able to realize the folly of which they have been guilty, we
assert that if the South is made to suffer at all by any act of Mr. LINCOLN, or of the
party to which he belongs, it is her own fault. Nothing can be clearer than that,
if the south acting under the instructions of Mr. BUCHANAN, had not opposed the
election of Mr. DOUGLAS after his nomination, he would have received two thirds
of the electoral vote, and been elected president. . . . But the representatives of
the South, intent on precipitating the cotton States into a revolution, refused to

second the nomination of Douglas—the only man who could, by any posibillity, carry a Northern State—and upon them rests the responsibility of Mr. Lincoln's election. In this dilemma, even if it were defensible on any grounds, we say that no good citizen of Missouri ought to take any step, nor do any act, which looks to the destruction of the Union. Let Mr. Lincoln go into the Presidential office. Let him show his hand. Let him say whether, under the solemn obligation which he must take in front of the Capitol, on the 4th of March, to support the Constitution, and see that the laws are faithfully executed, he will pledge himself to carry out the fugitive slave law, and to respect the rights of all sections of the Union alike, and if he refuses to do it, or should select such a Cabinet as would justify the belief that he does not intend to do it, it will then be time enough to adopt measures looking to a dissolution of the Union. We have no very high opinion of Mr. Lincoln's ability to administer the government. We think there are defects in his character which will lead him to confide in bad men, and to be controlled by bad men. The very auspices under which he is elected—the fact that Seward, Sumter, Greeley, Lovely, Wilson, Trumbull, . . . and many others of the same stamp, who have been chiefly instrumental in his election, will . . . control him—are all against an equitable, just and impartial treatment of fifteen States of the Union. But let us be right in this case, if a great outrage was committed in bringing out Breckinridge, and so conducting the campaign as to defeat Douglas; and then, in case of aggression upon the rights or the property of the South, there will be but one mind and one will in opposing resistance to the tyranny of the Government.

The country needs repose. It has suffered, and must continue to suffer, so long as this slavery agitation is pressed upon the people and their Representatives. It has been productive of an incredible amount of mischief already, and if continued it will destroy the best interests of the country. It is already well established that Lincoln can do no harm, even if he were so disposed, for he will have the Senate to pass upon his nominations, and an opposition House to check all dishonest or extravagant appropriations. . . . The spoils are in the hands of Lincoln and his men all over the country, and they will soon forget the means which they have taken to accomplish their object, if the South will only let them alone. The vote of Virginia, Kentucky, Tennessee, Missouri—all against Breckinridge—and the fact that, if he carries Louisiana, Alabama and other States, it can only be by a plurality vote, ought to satisfy the South that Secession will not be countenanced by the very States upon which they have hitherto relied for aid in the event of the adoption of the extreme measures by South Carolina. Again we say, let there be Peace between the North and the South, until Lincoln is guilty of some act of oppression justifying revolution, and, in that event, there will be but one voice heard in vindication of the rights of the South.

St. Louis Republican, November 8, 1860.

The Clay County Flag *was a Douglas paper. Clay County, birthplace of Frank and Jesse James, is in northwest Missouri, near the Kansas border.*

OUR COURSE.

We have been asked by many of our friends, and *tauntingly* by some of our ill-wishers, what course will you take now? Are you still DOUGLAS? What will be the course of the *Flag* in the present exigency? *Do you intend to support Lincoln's administration?*—Will you justify him in his "irrepressible conflict" doctrine against the rights of the South?

Our creed is a short one—THE UNION, ONE AND UNDIVIDED! We see nothing as yet, and we trust, that our eyes may be closed in the sleep that knows no waking, before we witness such a violation of the Constitution as will *justify* Secession. But what mean you by *Secession,* ask friends and enemies? We answer, the withdrawal of a State or States from the family compact which binds these United States into the glorious galaxy composing the UNION. But, say our querists—may not a State withdraw from the Union? We answer.

First premising that no cause has as yet occurred, which will justify the withdrawal of a sovereign State from the Union, we reply, that the original thirteen States surrendered certain rights and powers, when they entered into the compact with the Federal government, and under that compact their reserved rights were guaranteed to them. Apart from the doctrine of revolution, which is but the principle that "might makes right," the mere assertion of brute force—in other words, the right of the strongest—the States originally forming the Union (and the principle applies to all which have been since admitted,) by the terms of their compact—by the very letter of the Federal Constitution, appointed a tribunal to declare and determine their respective rights, to prevent and guard against their violation, and that tribunal is the *Supreme Court of the United States.* Has this tribunal been shorn of its power? Are not its decrees enforced? Will Mr. LINCOLN when duly and constitutionally inaugurated as President of these United States, obey the behests of this tribunal? Will he fail to enforce its decrees? Will he in violation of the oath which he solemnly takes as President, *fail to enforce the laws of the country,* and the provisions of the Federal Constitution?

"The devil, himself," says an old proverb, "is not quite as black as he is represented," and let President LINCOLN *when he becomes* President, be answerable for his official acts. Let us presume that he is innocent of any infraction of his official duties until we find him guilty of violating *our rights,* THE RIGHTS OF THE SOUTH. And then, what then, shall be our course? We answer, the moment ABRAHAM LINCOLN, the constitutionally elected President of these United States, prostitutes the high functions of his office to the advancement of the interests of *a wicked and sectional party* like the Black Republicans—the moment he avails himself of the power placed in his hands to trample upon the rights of not merely the SOUTH, but of any portion of this Confederacy; we then will go with you heart and hand in—not dissolving the Union—not in dividing our attachment to the memory of WASH-INGTON—not in forgetting that the rights and privileges we so cooly canvass and under estimate, were *gained,* WON and ENFORCED at the point of the bayonet, shoulder to shoulder, in the teeth of overpowering odds, with the help of a Righteous Providence, by not the NORTH or the SOUTH, but by the united, persistent, and self sacrificing arms of the whole Confederacy. *We will aid you in impeaching and punishing President* LINCOLN *in* ACCORDANCE WITH THE PROVISIONS OF THE CONSTITUTION, *for any dereliction of official duty.* We will help you depose him from his high office, and the example afforded by his punishment and deposition, will be fraught with a salutary lesson to every citizen of our Confederacy, so long as Providence in its wisdom, may permit this, the best and wisest form of government devised by man to exist.

But, we will be asked, are there no bounds to your submissions? Can no conceivable event arise in which you will sustain the slave-holding States in their secession from the Union? Our answer is that we cannot—we will not anticipate that any party, however wild and reckless, DARE *trample upon the spirit and letter of the Constitution . . . .* We will not anticipate evil; we will bear and forbear until forbearance *almost* ceases to be a virtue. But if the evil day must come, we will enter into the inevitable conflict with the honest conviction, that no act of ours has hurried the catastrophe; and then may "God save the Right!" . . .

Clay County Flag, November 14, 1860.

Marshall is a town in Saline County, Missouri. Its paper, the Democrat, *had supported John C. Breckinridge.*

THE PRESIDENTIAL ELECTION.

Sufficient returns of the late election have been received to indicate the election of Mr. Lincoln to the Presidency of the United States. How that result was brought about it is useless for us now to inquire, as our worst fears have been confirmed; and the only subject now to be discussed is the most feasible plan to avert the danger that is upon us. That Lincoln was elected upon purely sectional grounds, no one, we presume, will pretend to deny; and that his elevation to the Chief Magistracy of the nation will be fraught with imminent danger to the equality and well-being of the slave-holding States is patent to every one. The question now to be discussed is, what is the best course to pursue? It is useless to tell us that a Congress opposed to the Executive is a sufficient curb to his power when disposed to exercise it to the prejudice of one section of the country. Nearly one-third of the time Congress is not in session, and even when it is, the rules require two-thirds to act independent of the Executive. The South can expect nothing from the Administration of Lincoln but encroachment, against which she must look for defense within her own resources. It is the policy of Lincoln to put slavery in the course of ultimate extinction. The moral effect of his election alone, will have this tendency. The south cannot escape the issue, if she would. We cannot now foresee the result of things, but this Republican party must either be put down, the South subjugated by the infernal fanaticism and domination of their numerical strength, or physical resistance will produce disruption.

The question of this result of the election has been freely discussed in the South during the canvass, and the Southern mind is much better prepared to receive it than it would have been but for the course of events for the last few years. The matter was agitated in the canvass of '56; the Kansas troubles did much to place the Republican party in its true light before the people of the South, and their unmistakable sympathy for the fanatics engaged in the invasion of Virginia more than a year ago has roused the Southern people to a sense of their danger in the event of the domination of that party. What we have been discussing must now be looked squarely in the face, for the crisis is upon us without help or subterfuge. Already there are rumors rife that some of the Southern States have taken measures looking to a dissolution of the confederacy, and that their oft repeated declaration of never being willing to submit to the inauguration of a Black Republican President is now about to be practically applied. The Legislatures of nearly all the Southern States have been convened, and a very few weeks will inform us of the course that is to be pursued. The people of South Carolina have taken the initiatory step, and we are mistaken if the Southern States in a body do not lend her aid and counsel.

Marshall Democrat, November 14, 1860.

MISSOURI! BRIGHT LAND OF THE WEST!

English-born Harry Macarthy came to the United States in 1849, settled in Arkansas, and developed strong Southern sympathies. He became famous throughout the South as a traveling comedian; his best-known song was the rousing "Bonnie Blue Flag," chronicling the secession of the Southern states in 1861. Shortly after the outbreak of the Civil War, Macarthy wrote a hymn to Missouri, encouraging the state to join the new Confederacy.

MISSOURI! BRIGHT LAND OF THE WEST!

Missouri! Missouri! Bright land of the West!
Where the way worn emigrant always found rest,
Who gave to the farmer reward for the toil,
Expended in breaking and turning the soil;
Awake to the notes of the bugle and drum!
Awake from your peace the tyrant hath come.

Chorus:

> *And swear by your honor your chains shall be riven,*
> *And add your bright star to our flag of Eleven.*

They forced you to join in their unholy fight,
With fire and with sword, with power and with might.
'Gainst father and brother, and loved ones so near,
'Gainst women, and children, and all you hold dear;
They've o'er run your soil, insulted your press,
They've murdered your citizens—shown no redress—

> *So swear by your honor your chains shall be riven,*
> *And add your bright star to our flag of eleven.*

Missouri! Missouri! Where is thy proud fame?
Free land of the West, thy once cherished name?
Trod in the dust by a tyrant's command
Proclaiming there's martial law in the land;
Men of Missouri, strike without fear!
McCulloch, and Jackson, brave men are near.

> *Then swear by your honor your chains shall be riven,*
> *And add your bright star to our flag of eleven.*

T. Michael Parrish and Robert M. Willingham Jr., *Confederate Imprints, 1861–1865* (New Haven, Conn.: Research Publications, 1974), microform, reel 110, no. 3657.

MISSOURI DEMOCRATS PROCLAIM THEIR LOYALTY

The following pamphlet, published by ardent pro-Union Democrats, reveals the intense political rivalries among loyal factions in St. Louis. On February 9, 1861, a crowd of St. Louisans met at Verandah Hall to declare their staunch support for the Union.

RATIFICATION MEETINGS IN ST. LOUIS.

FULL ENDORSEMENT OF THE CONSTITUTIONAL TICKET.— REPORTS OF FRIDAY AND SATURDAY'S MEETINGS,

WITH LETTERS FROM

JUDGE GAMBLE, URIEL WRIGHT, ESQ., MAJ. TURNER, CAPT. WILLS AND COL. CLARKSON.

MONSTER MEETING

HELD ON

SATURDAY, FEBRUARY 9, 1861,

AT "VERANDAH HALL."

ADDRESS AND RESOLUTIONS.

We, citizens of St. Louis, opposed to the Black Republican party, in mass meeting assembled, declare, in the language used by the Father of his Country in his Farewell Address, *"that the unity of the government which constitutes us one people is dear to us."* In the language of WASHINGTON, in that same address, we say further, that "toward the preservation of our happy State, it is requisite not only that we discountenance irregular opposition to its acknowledged authority, but also that we resist with care the spirit of innovation upon its principles, however *specious the pretext.* One method of assault may be to *effect* in the FORMS OF THE CONSTITUTION alterations which will impair the energy of the system and thus *undermine* what cannot directly be overthrown."

We charge that the Republican party is, in the language of WASHINGTON, truly "characterized by *geographical discrimination"* as a sectional party, whose bond of union is hostility to an institution common to fifteen States of this Union—we charge that it is seeking *under the forms of the Constitution,"* to subvert its spirit by denying, as that party has done in its platform of principles adopted at Chicago, to the slaveholding States, their equality in the Union—by denying to the citizens of Missouri and her sister slaveholding States, their rights in the common Territories of the States. We, therefore, feel it to be our duty to *"resist any such innovation"* upon the principles of the Constitution which created this American Union, *"however specious the pretext."* . . .

RESOLVED, THAT WE ARE WARMLY ATTACHED TO THE GOVERNMENT UNDER WHICH WE LIVE; THAT WE RECOGNIZE THE FEDERAL UNION AS THE GREAT CONSERVATOR OF OUR LIBERTIES; THAT UNDER IT WE HAVE, BY GOD'S PROVIDENCE, PROSPERED BEYOND ALL OTHER PEOPLE, AND EVEN BEYOND THE EXPECTATIONS OF OUR PATRIOT SIRES, WHO

ESTABLISHED IT AS THE BEST MEANS OF PERPETUATING THE BLESSINGS WHICH THEY SO GALLANTLY FOUGHT FOR AND OBTAINED. . . .

THAT UNDER THIS GOVERNMENT WE ARE RESPECTED ABROAD, PROSPEROUS AT HOME, AND FAST TAKING OUR TRUE POSITION AS THE LEADING NATION OF THE EARTH. . . .

THAT ALTHOUGH CAUSES OF COMPLAINT EXIST AGAINST SOME OF HER SISTER STATES, WE DO NOT RECOGNIZE IN THEM SUFFICIENT CAUSES FOR THE WITHDRAWAL OF MISSOURI FROM THE UNION. . . .

THAT APPREHENSIONS OF WHAT MAY HAPPEN, DO NOT CONSTI-TUTE SUFFICIENT GROUNDS FOR SUCH WITHDRAWAL. . . .

THAT THE WELFARE OF ALL THE STATES WILL BE MUCH GREATER *IN* THE UNION THAN *OUT* OF IT; BUT THAT THE UNION CAN ONLY BE MAINTAINED BY JUSTICE AND EQUITY—NOT BY FORCE. . . .

THAT THE POSSESSION OF SLAVE PROPERTY IS A CONSTITUTIONAL RIGHT, AND AS SUCH OUGHT TO BE EVER RECOGNIZED BY THE FED-ERAL GOVERNMENT; THAT IF THE FEDERAL GOVERNMENT SHALL FAIL AND REFUSE TO SECURE THIS RIGHT, THE SOUTHERN STATES SHOULD BE FOUND UNITED IN ITS DEFENSE. . . .

THAT THE PEACE AND WELFARE OF THE UNION DEMAND SUCH AN ADJUSTMENT OF THE SLAVERY QUESTION AS SHALL BE PERMANENT, AND WE INVITE THE OTHER STATES TO MEET US IN THAT ADJUST-MENT IN A SPIRIT OF MUTUAL CONCESSION AND FORBEARANCE . . .

THAT WITH AN HONORABLE AND PERMANENT ADJUSTMENT OF THE EXISTING DIFFICULTIES, WE ENTERTAIN THE HOPE OF A RETURN OF THE SECEDING STATES INTO THE UNION, AND WE ARE OPPOSED AND WILL NOT SUBMIT, TO ANY ATTEMPT BY THE GENERAL GOVERNMENT, TO CO-ERCE THEM BY FORCE, FOR WE BELIEVE ANY SUCH ATTEMPT AT COER-CION WOULD BE CALCULATED NOT ONLY TO PREVENT A REUNION, BUT WOULD AGGRAVATE EXISTING EVILS PAST REMEDY. . . .

THAT, SO LONG AS A HOPE REMAINS OF AN HONORABLE SETTLE-MENT OF OUR DIFFERENCES, WE WILL OPPOSE, BY EVERY MEANS IN OUR POWER, THE SECESSION OF MISSOURI; AND WILL INSIST THAT ANY ORDINANCE OF THE CONVENTION CHANGING THE RELATIONS OF OUR STATE WITH THE FEDERAL GOVERNMENT SHALL BE SUBMIT-TED TO THE PEOPLE FOR THEIR APPROVAL OR REJECTION. . . .

Ratification Meetings in St. Louis. Full Endorsement of the Constitutional ticket.—Reports of Friday and Saturday's Meetings, With Letters from Judge Gamble, Uriel Wright, Esq., Maj. Turner, Capt. Wills and Col. Clarkson. MONSTER MEETING held on Saturday, February 9, 1861, at "Verandah Hall." St. Louis, Mo.: [1861?]. Copy in the collections of the Harry Elkins Widener Memorial Library, Harvard University, Cambridge, Mass.

Minerva Blow with daughter
Susie and baby Ella, ca. 1849. *Courtesy of Missouri Historical Society*

MINERVA BLOW'S FLAG IS STILL WAVING FOR THE UNION

*During the Civil War, prominent St. Louisan Minerva Blow wrote letters to her
daughter Susie, who was then living in Gramercy Park, New York City. The
Blow family, which lived in Carondelet (then a southern suburb of St. Louis),
had distinguished itself through abolitionist activities, including the liberating of
Dred Scott in 1858. Educator Susan Blow later founded the country's first public
kindergarten in 1873. The expression "viz" means "that is" or "namely."*

Carondelet Feb 4th [1861]

Dear Susie,

I am all alone this morning & as I am indebted to both Ella & yourself I will
make good use of the opportunity by answering your letters. It is very lonely
here during the day as we all miss you & Ella so much, & we all feel so sad about
the State of the Country. Even your dear Father who is naturally so bouyant

is at times depressed. The little ones are all very well. We have had beautiful
weather & indeed in every aspect as a family feel that we have good reason to
be thankful—Under other circumstances, we would have been more joyful &
happy this winter than we have been for several years. It is truly deplorable to
see how embittered & angry the people have become. Here in Missouri where a
number are identified with the slave interest, we who differ with them politically
are made to feel sensibly the alienation of feeling caused by it and it is not always
as pleasant as it ought to be to visit our old friends—we confidently look forward
to the time when the excitement of the present moment wears off, and that
every thing will return again to old ways and we [will] again be a united & happy
people—May our Heavenly Father preserve us from civil war & deliver us from
all our *sins*—for these have brought us to our present unhappy condition . . . .

Yrs devotedly & lovingly—Mother.

~

Carondelet, March 8th [1861]

Dear Susie,
    Your Father returned from the city this morning, feeling very unwell & tired,
& not having answered yours of the 1st he desires I will do so. I very cheerfully
comply as I feel very much like holding a little confab with my precious Daughter
to-night. This day has been a long one to me & as I have been alone . . . . I felt
so troubled about the State of the Country, & realized my ignorance of political
matters so much, that I devoted myself quite industriously to informing myself
in these respects & trying to understand the issues that are causing so much
distress to our beloved country. I have rejoiced over my little knowledge of its
history . . . —it has served me in many an argument & has filled my heart with a
patriotic sentiment that otherwise I should never have possessed. You remember
no doubt how often I have urged you to study our history well. If you feel
now that you have not done so do try & remedy this more in your education,
& learn the useful lesson it has taught me & which I hope to transmit to my
children—Never will I consent to abandon the Stars & Stripes, but hold firm
to it while life lasts—Our flag is still waving on the top [of] our sweet home—
consecrated as it has ever been to love & affection it has another charm added
viz the symbol of our country pride & glory—A few days since I was in the
city [St. Louis] & I saw accidentally a secession flag which was raised opposite
Pezolt's [a confectionary store]. You cannot imagine how the sight affected me!
I could have mourned aloud in sorrow. That in *my* native city where I grew up
& spent my whole life there should be those who would do such a . . . deed &
disgrace themselves forever. The Union sentiment is strong here, but we have

some very ultra politicians, who talk & threaten very hard all the time. Many despise the Republicans. This party you know does not embrace many of our circle of acquaintance. Consequently we are compelled to listen to many absurd & provoking things said by them—I have tried to feel kind & act the part of a Christian *lady* though at times I have had my feelings very much hurt. . . .

We confidently hope that the "clouds we so much dread

> *Are big with mercy & shall break.*
> *In blessings over our heads—*

That good does & can come out of evil we all know & we can safely & surely trust "Our Father." who is able & willing to bless & preserve all who love & trust "Him." . . . With heartfelt prayers for your health & happiness I am as ever with love & kisses from your Father joined to mine—your

Loving Mother

Minerva Blow to Susan Blow, February 4, 1861, and March 8, 1861, Blow Family Papers, Missouri Historical Society, St. Louis.

"PEACE . . . SHOULD BE MAINTAINED IN OUR STATE"

Christian Kribben, a St. Louis Democrat of German background, served as Speaker of the house of representatives in the Missouri General Assembly in 1860. Motivated by a desire for unity, Kribben wrote a public letter to Nathaniel Paschall, the editor of the Missouri Republican, *a pro-Union Democratic newspaper. Paschall had been involved in the newspaper business since the age of twelve, and by 1844 he had assumed control of the* Republican. *He endorsed Stephen A. Douglas's candidacy for president in 1860, by which time the* Republican *had become the most powerful Democratic newspaper in Missouri.*

LETTER TO THE EDITOR, MAY 16, 1861

Nathaniel Paschall, Esq.
Editor of the Missouri Republican:

Dear Sir:

You may well believe me that it is with a feeling of reluctance almost insurmountable that I appear before the public to offer an opinion on existing affairs. But the dangers surrounding us are so imminent and terrible, the circumstances so commanding, and the calls on me so many and moreover so earnest, that I would be untrue to myself were I longer to hesitate . . . .

I have for several years been more or less engaged in public life, and being withal of German birth, and associating much with citizens of German origin,

I may possibly have it in my power of somewhat allaying unnecessary and wicked excitement, by suggesting a few statements which are based upon a close and most intimate acquaintance with the German element in our midst, and prompted by the most devout wishes for the peace and prosperity of our city.

In the first place, then, Peace, in my opinion, should be maintained in our State; and I fully believe will be maintained. Every consideration or inducement which can impel or influence a citizen of our State must lead him towards peace. Unaccustomed, thank God, as American freemen are to military rule, the temporary submission to dire necessity with us in Missouri will not, in my opinion, humble either our State or our citizens, but will tend only to enable us the better to appreciate our wants and our interests hereafter. These days of terror and of folly will pass by—and shortly, too—and tranquility and wisdom will again mark our social and political condition. . . .

My political sentiments respecting the powers and workings of our government remain unchanged, and my opinion of President LINCOLN, and the wisdom of his councils, has not in any wise been heightened since his inauguration . . . ; therefore no blind admiration of the course of the present Administration impels my course. On the contrary, I regard the principles of the Republican party as political heresy, and I have looked in vain thus far for any sign of broad and comprehensive patriotism and policy in any act of our present Government. But such is my intuitive and irrepressible faith in the excellence of our system of government, and the good sober sense of the American people, that I fully believe that America will even survive the calamities and perils of 1861, and the unwise measures of misguided men, dressed, alas, in more power than may be good for the country.

Such are my political sentiments. My hopes, on the other hand, are altogether concentrated in the perpetuation of our Union, and the occupation of Missouri in that Union of as prominent and commanding a position as her greatness, her wealth and her geographical importance entitle her to.

The existing Government, I fear, may have employed very indifferent means to accomplish that great end; but should, after all, Mr. LINCOLN's failings be a cause of utter despair? Because the counsels of the Administration may be unwise, improvident and unfortunate, should we visit the indiscretion of a few men in power, but for a day, on the system, on the nation, on the perpetuity of liberal government? God forbid! By submitting to a power legally placed over us for the time being—however abused it may be on the minds of many—do we lose character, position or honor? By so doing have we not everything to gain, while by pursuing a different course, have we not all to lose? Is there a man in our midst who believes that the state of things at present existing, can be perpetuated? And as there can be none to so believe, will not the public mind, North and South, East and West, find its own balance again in a proper appreciation of, and respect for, the rights of all alike? I entertain not the slightest doubt of this. . . .

Chr. Kribben.

Missouri Republican, May 18, 1861.

"THE ATTEMPT TO OVERTHROW AN ESTABLISHED GOVERNMENT IS THE PLAINEST TREASON"

Massachusetts native William Greenleaf Eliot was a prominent Unitarian minister in St. Louis. He was a founder of Washington University in St. Louis in 1853, and after the war he served as its president and chancellor. He was also the father of Henry Ware Eliot and the grandfather of poet T. S. Eliot.

During the war, he participated in the Western Sanitary Commission, supported the recruitment of black soldiers, and provided aid to freed slaves in Missouri. In the first summer of the conflict, he delivered to his congregation at the Church of the Messiah this sermon, in which he rejected the validity of secession.

A DISCOURSE FOR THE TIMES,

DELIVERED IN

THE CHURCH OF THE MESSIAH, ST. LOUIS,

AUGUST 18ᵀᴴ, 1861,

BY REV. W. G. ELIOT, D. D.

ST. LOUIS:

PRINTED BY GEORGE KNAPP & CO., CHESNUT STREET.

1861.

. . . Revolution, even when successful, is a terrible means of redress. Nothing can justify it, except the sternest and most urgent necessity. It involves, in its progress, all manner of evil, whatever its final result. Temporarily at least, and probably for months and years, it stops all good influences upon which the welfare of society depends, and sets in active operation all the elements of evil, to do the work of devastation, of social ruin, of anarchy and crime. Therefore, whoever leads or abets in revolution, under whatever circumstances, assumes a fearful responsibility, and ought to be very sure of his ground. If he expects to do his work, peacefully, without bloodshed, without civil war and all its horrors, he must be equally ignorant of the principles of civil government and of the whole teaching of history. The beginning of revolution is nothing but rebellion, and is sure to be so treated. The attempt to overthrow an established government is the plainest treason, and nothing but complete success can save, or ever has saved, its promoters from the punishment and brand of traitors. SAMUEL ADAMS AND JOHN HANCOCK, if they had failed would have died upon the scaffold, and they knew that this was the alternative. The work of revolution cannot be done peaceably and amicably, under whatever ingenious name introduced, and they who unfurl its banner are *openly declaring war.* . . .

I know that some of you differ from me as to the propriety of introducing the subject, in this place. It is urged that offense will be given, that it is impolitic and unwise. But it is not a matter of policy, nor choice, with me; not of mere conventional propriety and taste; not of praise or blame. It is a matter of positive obligation. I may do no good, but I must try. No man can answer to his country, to his conscience, to his God, who does not do his best, however little that may be. . . . From the abundance of the heart the mouth will speak, and is very like to speak plainly. . . .

The radical defect in the existing state of the public mind, is slowness to perceive the magnitude and importance of the present controversy. The subject is often treated in conversation and in the public prints as if it were one of local, party, or temporary concern, like a municipal or Presidential election—as if it were merely to determine whether we are for or against the present Administration, in favor of Mr. LINCOLN or opposed to him. . . . The battle and defeat at Manassas Gap developed wonderful zeal for Secession, and the love of many waxed cold. At this moment there are hundreds anxiously waiting for the next news from Southern Missouri and Virginia, to decide them whether they will be for or against their country, friends of the Union or its foes. What wretched logic is this! What miserable and craven fidelity which depends upon sunshine and prosperity! . . .

And what is our cause? It is the existence of non-existence of our country. The permanence or dismemberment of a great nation. "Republican institutions are on their trial, and according to the result, will the verdict of the world be given." The plain question is, shall we be one, strong, united people, or scattered into, no one can tell how many, communities, republics or monarchies, at strife among ourselves, the scorn and contempt of the nations. . . .

W. G. Eliot, *Loyalty and Religion: A Discourse for the Times, Delivered in the Church of the Messiah, St. Louis, August 18th, 1861, by W. G. Eliot.* St. Louis: G. Knapp, 1861. A copy of this pamphlet is in the collections of the University of Missouri, St. Louis.

THREE

~

Missourians Confront War

*A*s states from the deep south seceded from the Union during the winter of 1860–61, Governor Claiborne F. Jackson urged the General Assembly to call a convention to consider the state's relationship with the federal government. He believed that in doing so, he was guiding Missouri along the path followed by the Southern states. In Missouri, however, the results were rather different: the state did not secede. The democratically elected Missouri State Convention, which met in February 1861, selected as its president the future Confederate general Sterling Price and seated mostly Southern-born delegates (eighty-six out of ninety-nine). Nevertheless, this body was made up primarily of men who remained loyal to the Union.[1] Indeed, the convention eventually accused Jackson of treason and removed him from his office. Missouri's long tradition of political moderation won out over the proslavery sympathies of individual political actors.

Missouri's battles were far from over, however. Unlike other midwestern states, Missouri had to struggle for control of the state militia as well as the diverse paramilitary organizations that sprang up on both sides. Missouri's long-standing internal conflicts profoundly influenced the state's response to war. Union loyalists and Confederate sympathizers had begun training and arming men in secret, as many young Missourians followed a less formal route into their respective fighting forces in 1861. In most other states, the usual practice was for new recruits to join state regiments that were raised and organized by politicians or other prominent men. Generally, the governors also deployed the state militia. In Missouri, the situation was more complicated. Although the governor was pro-Confederate, the state had not joined the Confederacy, so initially Missouri did not officially supply men to either army.[2] Political and military leaders were left to battle each other for control of the military apparatus of the state. At stake were Missouri's federal installations, such as barracks, arsenals, quartermaster depots, and river dockyards. Although most Missourians, even those who lived in the proslavery northwestern counties, still believed that the state's place was in the Union, the loyalty of many was conditional. A federal invasion or interference with their slave property might persuade some to heed the call for secession. Those who lived in cities or near the eastern boundary along the Mississippi River were more firmly committed to the United States, especially the Republicans in St. Louis. Still, as early as January 1861, secessionist sympathizers calling themselves the Minute Men had organized a paramilitary group whose principal purpose was to gain control of the St. Louis Arsenal. In the southeastern bootheel area, in the Ozarks near the Arkansas border, and along the border with Kansas, many Missourians could be counted on to support the Confederacy. In the same area, jayhawkers, or pro-Unionist bands, harassed residents regardless of their loyalties and proved trying to military commanders of both armies.

Republican congressman Frank P. Blair, leader of the pro-Union element, had been hard at work since February organizing men, protecting the arsenal, and finding ways of furnishing the United States government with the men denied by Governor Jackson. Part of his activities built upon the network of the Wide Awakes in St. Louis. The initial purpose of the Wide Awakes had been to escort and to protect Republican candidates in the 1856 and 1860 elections, and to this end, these young radicals had organized uniformed private regiments in St. Louis. Blair also called upon members of various Union Clubs to unite into a fighting corps. He began drilling them secretly in a warehouse whose floor was covered with sawdust to muffle the sound of marching.[3]

Blair called upon U.S. Army lieutenant John M. Schofield, a lecturer at Washington University, to muster the new regiments into service. To supplement the Missouri recruits guarding the arsenal, the federal War Department sent regiments from other states, including Kansas, to St. Louis. Finally, the Missouri Home Guard (not to be confused with the pro-Southern Missouri State Guard), a newly formed pro-Union organization from St. Louis, became the U.S. Reserve Corps under the command of the federal army. When their ninety-day term of service expired, many men joined other U.S. Army regiments. Pro-Union St. Louis officials also focused on local security. In March 1861, St. Louisans set up a Union Committee of Public Safety, whose responsibilities included overseeing the training and organization of men and matériel as well as maintaining peace on the city's streets.

Missouri's pro-Confederate leaders organized military support as well. On April 15, 1861, three days after the fall of Fort Sumter, President Lincoln had issued a national proclamation requisitioning 75,000 militiamen, who were to be raised within individual states throughout the North for three months' service. When Secretary of War Simon Cameron requested four regiments (4,000 troops) from Missouri, Governor Jackson refused, denouncing Lincoln's requisition of state militia as "illegal, unconstitutional, and revolutionary; in its objects inhuman and diabolical."[4] On the same day, Jackson met with the secessionist commander of the state militia, General Daniel M. Frost, and called up the state forces, ordering militia members in each district to report for training. As governor of the state, that was his prerogative.[5] The Missouri State Militia included such famous companies as the St. Louis Greys (who had fought in the war with Mexico and later joined the First Confederate Regiment), the Washington Blues, who later formed Company F of the Fifth Missouri Infantry Regiment (C.S.A.), and the Carondelet Guards.

In the midst of competing mobilization efforts in a state divided over its place in the war, it was hardly surprising when violence broke out in early May 1861, in what Unionists called the "Battle of Camp Jackson" and most Southern sympathizers called the "Camp Jackson Massacre." St. Louis had experienced riots between Irish and German immigrants as far back as the 1850s, but imminent warfare lent an additional sense of crisis to these underlying ethnic antagonisms. Both Unionists and Confederates recognized the vital importance of the federal arsenal in St. Louis. Confederate president Jefferson Davis had already told the governor that he hoped to take the arsenal's arms for the use of Southern soldiers—indeed, the arsenal could have provided one of the largest storehouses of weapons in their fledgling Confederacy. When Captain Nathaniel Lyon, a veteran of the Mexican war who had been assigned to protect the arsenal, learned that Jackson had called up the state militia and ordered them to drill on the western suburbs of the city, he quickly dismissed General Frost's request for negotiation. Lyon moved against the militia encampment and captured it with ease. Unfortunately, as Lyon's untrained soldiers were bringing their prisoners away from the camp, they encountered harassment on the streets. A riot ensued near Olive Street, and about thirty civilians lost their lives. Following the Camp Jackson tragedy, secessionist sentiment flared up, and residents demonstrated their support for the Confederacy by raising flags on public buildings and fighting in the streets.[6] On May 11, the day after the Camp Jackson incident, an anti-German riot broke out near the corner of Fifth and Walnut streets that resulted in severe injuries and two rumored deaths.

The incident at Camp Jackson had left the local population anxious, angry, and of dubious loyalty, and public support for the Union outside the city wavered. In early June, Lyon—who had by now been promoted to brigadier general for his role in saving the arsenal—tried to ameliorate the situation. The stern New Englander was probably not the best person to calm troubled waters. When he called a meeting with Frank Blair, Sterling Price, and Claiborne Jackson at the elegant Planters House Hotel, he hoped to convince Jackson and Price to cease their efforts to take Missouri out of the Union. Jackson, however, was already corresponding with Jefferson Davis, and the men argued for more than four hours. In the end, Lyon told Price and Jackson that nothing would induce him to meet their demands and declared, "This means war." Price and Jackson immediately returned to Jefferson City, the state capital, determined to save their government from a federal attack.

In the weeks that followed, Jackson publicly declared his loyalty to the Confederacy. The convention, which he had called into existence to ratify the decision to

United States volunteers attacked by the mob, corner of Fifth and Walnut streets, St. Louis, Missouri. *Mat Hastings, wood engraving, 1861. Courtesy of Missouri Historical Society*

leave the Union, instead promptly unseated him as governor and found him guilty of treason. The convention proclaimed the governor's seat "empty," and installed the moderately proslavery and well-respected Supreme Court justice Hamilton R. Gamble as Provisional Governor. They asked Gamble to serve until a regular gubernatorial election could be held in 1864. The convention was called into service from time to time whenever the state needed help deciding crucial questions. While the state legislature dealt with questions of finance, army mobilization, and legislation, the convention coped with such issues as the secession crisis and emancipation. A well-balanced and conscientious body composed of hardworking, moderate men from diverse backgrounds, the convention met five times during the conflict and kept Missouri solidly on a pro-Union course throughout the war.

A rival pro-Southern legislature, composed of the rebel senators and representatives who had left Jefferson City, followed Jackson to Neosho, a small town in the extreme southwest corner of Missouri. No one knows just how many men met in the exiled legislature; some historians have estimated that, at times, there were only two people in the room during sessions.[7] On October 28, 1861, both houses of the rebel legislature passed an ordinance of secession, which declared Missouri a free and independent state. Exactly one month later, Missouri was formally admitted to the Confederacy without ever having held a referendum on the issue. Elsewhere in the state, citizens mocked this rival government, which continued to make laws and regulate army affairs until the end of the war. When Jackson died of pneumonia in 1862, he left Lieutenant Governor Thomas Caute Reynolds to lead the pro-Southern Missouri government in his stead.[8]

Military and political blunders in 1861 had sharply polarized public opinion in a state already torn by internal divisions. Nearly every community experienced internal dissension and even fighting, and families were often bitterly divided. These problems were greatly inflamed by the hasty actions of Union military commanders, including Nathaniel Lyon and John C. Frémont, who angered Missouri residents and often exacerbated the problems of disloyalty and internal fighting. Missourians blamed the hotheads and fanatics of both sides for the ongoing violence that plagued them. After Hamilton Gamble was appointed Provisional Governor, however, he became a popular and trusted leader. His moderate politics, unswerving Unionism, and reputation for integrity did a great deal to keep pro-Union sentiment alive in Missouri.[9]

Although the administration in Washington certainly recognized the crucial importance Missouri, the western border state had to rely largely on its independent-minded populace for funding and assistance. In this, pro-Union residents fared better than their pro-Confederate neighbors. Union women, especially those who lived near the larger towns and cities, found more ready outlets for their patriotic efforts than did those women whose husbands and brothers fought for the rebels. The Union cause was always better organized, better funded, and more openly supported in most areas in Missouri, enabling wives and mothers of soldiers of Union soldiers to raise money and supplies through organizations like the Ladies Union Aid Society or through fund-raising fairs and bazaars. On the other hand, women who supported the Confederate cause faced ostracism or even threats to their safety, prompting many to keep their opinions to themselves or go into exile. Still, some women who lived near the Kansas border, in the Ozarks, or in the southern Missouri bootheel counties provided food and shelter to bushwhackers, activities that could become dangerous. By November 1861, a reporter for the *New York Herald* was already writing about ruined houses and destitute families who had the misfortune of living directly in the path of opposing armies.[10]

MISSOURI'S MINUTE MEN JOIN THE SOUTHERN CAUSE

This undated petition was probably drafted and signed during the secession crisis. The signatures indicate a predominance of young men of Irish descent, although there is at least one German name on the list. Little else is known about the men who joined this company.

MINUTE MEN PETITION

We, the undersigned, agree to form ourselves into Companies of "Minute Men," upon the following basis of principles:

1. That if any State or States of this Union, aggrieved by the hostile and unconstitutional acts of the Black Republican Party, shall exercise the right to secede from the present Confederacy, and the Federal Government shall, thereupon, attempt to coerce such State or states back into the Union, Missouri ought to resist such attempt, by arms, if need be.

2. That, on the event of a disruption of this Union, the honor and safety of Missouri impel her to espouse the cause of the Southern States, and, in such case, we should endeavor to unite all slave-holding States in one Confederacy.

[The following names are written in ink, all in the same hand; many are checked off, some with two checks. There are also penciled addresses, but most are too faint and smudged to read.]

Wm. A. Foster
Peter H. Tiernan
J. H. Foster
S. G. Pilkington
Francis Beilstein
Wm. Cochran
John Maker
Henry Grow
I. B. Smith
Syl. Watts
Wm. E. Sloan
Wm. McDowell
Francis Fitzgerald
John Slevin
J. L. Purdy
J. Meagher
Frank Smith
A. C. Howard
Chas. D. Paul
J. M. Douglas
D. R. Grace
B. M. Everest
J. J. Horan
Jno. M. Langdon
J. W. Sanford

Agreement to form companies of Minute Men, Civil War Collection, Missouri Historical Society, St. Louis.

LIEUTENANT COLONEL JOHN S. BOWEN REPORTS ON
JAYHAWKERS TO GOVERNOR CLAIBORNE F. JACKSON

*Georgia-born John S. Bowen graduated from West Point in 1853 and served in the
U.S. Army and Georgia militia until 1857. He enjoyed a successful career as an
architect in St. Louis until the outbreak of the war, when he reentered military
service. Because of his Southern loyalties, Bowen joined the Missouri State Guard
during the secession crisis and was one of the men captured at Camp Jackson. He
later became a general in the Confederate army, commanding in the western theater.
In March 1861, Bowen was drilling his troops and confronting jayhawkers in western
Missouri near the Little Osage River. He refers to James Montgomery and Charles R.
"Doc" Jennison, two notorious jayhawkers who intimidated, robbed, and harassed
pro-Southern families along the Missouri-Kansas border.*

LT COL JOHN S. BOWEN, LITTLE OSAGE, MO [COMMDG, SW EXPED], TO CLAIBORNE FOX JACKSON, GOV OF MO AND COMM IN CHIEF, MVM, JEFFC, 10 MAR 1861

I have the honor to report that during the past month my command have
improved wonderfully in drill, discipline and everything tending to render them
serviceable & efficient Soldiers, proving that it is possible to attain a good organization, by simply demonstrating to our citizens, the propriety of submitting while
on duty to military rule.

The systematic organization of this Battalion I am fully convinced has effected
much good upon the frontier. Passing over the confidence and security which our
own citizens have felt, as well as, the military instruction we have been enabled to
discriminate among them I am not satisfied that the "Jayhawkers" of Kansas are
now completely intimidated and temporarily broken up.

I have employed *every means* of procuring information of their movements and
designs, have kept myself posted in regard to every attempt made to resuscitate
[*sic*] their bands and am pleased to report that they have *utterly failed* for the present
and I believe will never have courage to make another attempt unless reinforced
by Eastern Abolitionists

They endeavored to organize under the guise of State Militia and after enrolling to adopt a species of Constitution & By Laws, in the companies, the main
features of which were "Death to Border Ruffians" ["]Freedom for Slaves" & "il-
licit acquisition of horses." But the majority were of the opinion that there was no
use in attempting such things at present; So the Companies have all disbanded.

Montgomery & Jennison are exceedingly chagrined at their failure and are fully
convinced that for the present they must abandon their calling. I am satisfied that
this failure to organize is due to no change of sentiment or to any kind of friendly
feelings for Missourians, but result from fear.

How long they will thus be restrained remains to be seen, their leaders have arms & munitions and whenever they can induce followers to join them who have courage, we may expect an outbreak

I have ascertained that there is a disposition among many of the Citizens of Kansas to have the parties guilty of murders last fall brought up for trial and if your Excellency would make an application to have the persons guilty of hanging the young man Hines (a citizen of Missouri) arrested and tried for the offence it would make an issue exceed[ing]ly annoying to Kansas and serviceable to us.

I have had the leaders in the affair hunted out and know where they can be found in fact, if authorized I could bring them into the state in twenty four hours.

The above is all the information I have been enabled to procure which would influence the retaining or disbanding the South West Battalion. I cannot predict what would transpire if we should leave, but there is certainly no danger while we are here. I have kept my men in ignorance of this fact to increase their zeal and interest in the service

My information as regards affairs in Kansas has been obtained from spies who have acted with a great deal of discretion and the parties there finding they could keep nothing private, have driven out several men on suspicion but fortunately have made blunders in every instance

Upon one occasion only have I Employed anyone connected with my command and that was simply to assure myself that I was not imposed upon or duped by others.

I trust that your excellency will approve of the course adopted for I found that only in that way could anything like truth be brought over the Boundary line and being fully aware that you were anxious to save useless service on our part involving an unnecessary Expense to the state I was anxious to glean some facts which might serve to settle the question definitely

I now believe unless the ringleaders: viz Montgomery Jennison Forbes Rice Snyder and one or two others are killed imprisoned or driven from the country they will again inaugurate their system of wholesale murder and plunder unless the people on this frontier (on their own account) establish a patrol.

These men are undoubtedly supported by Eastern Abolitionists and they are necessitated to continue this agitation or their pay will be stopped. Numbers of these "Free State Men" live out in the prairie in a cabin with not a vestige of an inclosure or any improvement which gives a semblance of farming, stock raising or obtaining an honest living in any way

Yet they do live, support large families and have always plenty to eat & clothes to wear.

I enclose herewith a Slip from the "Mound City Report" illustrative of the sentiment in that neighborhood also a note from the present commanding officer of the 3d Company Lieut Baughn which has just come to hand, showing that even such men as General Lane, admit, that our citizens have cause for complaint.

In regard to other matters in the Command I have the honor to report that one Company, Capt McDonald's have had a number of members sick with the measles but the general health of the Battalion is excellent

The hardest & severest duties are now over. the weather is comparatively mil[d], the men are becoming accustomed to the neccessary restraints and I now believe are rather pleased with service, they seem perfectly contented and evince an elacrity for duty which is very encouraging

Missouri Volunteer Militia Papers, 1860–65, Special Collections, Duke University Library, Durham, N.C.

GENERAL DANIEL M. FROST AND CAPTAIN NATHANIEL LYON
ARGUE OVER THE FATE OF CAMP JACKSON

The following correspondence highlights the situation at Camp Jackson, a military encampment in the western suburbs of St. Louis. The letters between Frost and Lyon hide as much as they reveal. Frost was already in communication with Jefferson Davis, and Lyon had by now removed most of the weapons in the St. Louis Arsenal to Illinois. It is likely that at least a third of the men present at Camp Jackson were loyal to the United States.

Gen. Daniel M. Frost sent the following message to Captain Lyon:

Hdqrs. Camp Jackson, Missouri Militia,
May 10, 1861.

SIR: I am constantly in receipt of information that you contemplate an attack upon my camp, whilst I understand that you are impressed with the idea that an attack upon the arsenal and United States troops is intended on the part of the militia of Missouri; . . .

I would be glad to know from you personally whether there is any truth in the statements that are constantly poured into my ears. So far as regards any hostility being intended toward the United States or its property or representatives, by any portion of my command, or, as far as I can learn (and I think I am fully informed), of any other part of the State forces, I can say positively that the idea has never been entertained. . . .

I trust that, after this explicit statement, we may be able, by fully understanding each other, to keep far from our borders the misfortunes which so unhappily afflict our common country.

I am, sir, very respectfully, your obedient servant,
D. M. Frost,
Brig. Gen., Comdg. Camp Jackson, M.V.M.

General Nathaniel Lyon. *Johnson, Fry and Company, steel engraving after Alonzo Chappel, 1862. Courtesy of Missouri Historical Society*

Captain Lyon dispatched B. G. Farrar with the following message to General Frost:

Headquarters United States Troops,
St. Louis, Mo., May 10, 1861.

SIR: Your command is regarded as evidently hostile towards the Government of the United States. It is, for the most part, made up of those secessionists who have openly avowed their hostility to the General Government, and have been plotting at the seizure of its property and the overthrow of its authority.

You are openly in communication with the so-called Southern Confederacy, which is now at war with the United States; and you are receiving at your camp from the said Confederacy, and under its flag, large supplies of the material of war, most of which is known to be the property of the United States.

These extraordinary preparations plainly indicate none other than the well-known purpose of the governor of this State, under whose orders your are acting, and whose purposes, recently communicated to the legislature, have just been responded to by that body in the most unparalleled legislation, having in direct view hostilities to the General Government and co-operation with its enemies.

In view of these considerations, and of your failure to disperse in obedience to the proclamation of the President, and of the eminent necessities of State policy and welfare, and the obligations imposed upon me by instructions from Washington, it is my duty to demand, and I do hereby demand, of you an

immediate surrender of your command, with no other conditions than that all
persons surrendering under this demand shall be humanely and kindly treated.
Believing myself prepared to enforce this demand, one-half hour's time, before
doing so, will be allowed for your compliance therewith.

Very respectfully, your obedient servant,

N. LYON,

Captain Second Infantry, Comdg. Troops.

The War of the Rebellion: A Compilation of the Official Records of the Union and Confederate Armies, ser. 1, vol. 3
(Washington, D.C.: Government Printing Office, 1881), 7.

ALICE CAYTON BELIEVES ST. LOUIS WILL BE CLEARED OF GERMANS

*When Lyon moved on Camp Jackson and captured Frost's men, the ensuing riot resulted
in the deaths of more than thirty civilians. Alice E. Cayton described the riot in a letter
to her brother, Alexander Badger. Alice and Alexander had moved to St. Louis from
Paducah, Kentucky, in 1850. Alexander worked as a clerk in the Quartermaster and
Subsistence Departments while stationed at Fort Vancouver, Washington.*

St. Louis, May 12th, 1861

My dear Brother,

I can scarcely realize as I sit down this calm Sunday morning that our city has
been the scene of so much *intense* excitement, as it certainly has been for the past
two days. I mention the last *two* as *intense,* because previous to this, it has been
in a state of nervousness, but not so great. You will probaly learn some of the
particulars of the cause of so much trouble, before receiving this, but I will try
and give you a correct statement of affairs as far as I know concerning the
city of "St. Louis".

. . . The "Governor of this state,"—"Governor Jackson"—last month called
out all the "Malitia" of the several districts to camp on the 6th of this month for
the purpose of drilling. The companies of this district—as you are aware of are
composed of American men, Germans, and Irishmen, all State troops of course.
They are however divided into two parties as regards politics, the Germans
belonging to the Federal army, and the American[s] and Irish to the "Confederate
Army" and are called "Minute Men," accordingly, the "Minute Men" went into
camp out at "Lindell Grove" that is between Garrison Ave, and Grand Ave, and
Olive and Market Street. The Germans went to the Arsenal where they have
been reinforced to the amount of seven or eight thousand.

On Friday the 10th, in the afternoon about three o'clock, they marched out
to Lindell Grove, surrounded the Camp, which then contained eight hundred

men, under the command [of] "General D. M. Frost." . . . They could do nothing
under the circumstances but surrender. . . . They were then made prisoners, and
were formed into a line ready to march to the "Arsenal," when a disturbance
took place between the citizens and the German soldiers, the soldiers fired
into a crowd of citizens killing about eighteen or twenty and wounding many
others. I cannot describe the scene to you fully. Imagine to yourself all of those
hills surrounding the "Grove" filled with people, for as soon as it was known
the "Minute Men" had surrendered their arms, it was natural to suppose there
would be no fighting, and just as soon as this Company commenced firing, the
multitude commenced running, men, women and children were there, some in
carriages, buggies, on horseback and on foot. Every body from Aunt Nancys and
our house, with the exception of Mother was out there; . . . Dora was there and
was knocked down by a man, and then run over by a horse and buggy, she was
severly bruised, but was lucky to have no bones broken. I never was so frightened
in all my life before. It was all done so unexpectedly, and so uncalled for. . . .

Harry Somers an engineer you recollect who used to be with Father, lost his
daughter a girl fourteen years old, she was shot in the breast, her funeral took place
this morning. The excitement continued Friday night and all day yesterday. . . . [goes
on to describe another riot on Walnut Street] on the part of the Germans, and four
of their soldiers were killed, and two citizens making six more to the list. . . . . [This
is] enough to mak every true American heart swell with indignation against the
Germans. I believe in time this place will be entirely cleared of them.

. . .

Take good care of yourself, so that you can bundle up and come home one
of these days, to see us. I must say Goodbye. Love to all again, the *biggest half* for
your *dear self.*

From
Alice

Alice E. Cayton to Alexander Badger, May 12, 1861, f. 1 of 2 (1832–61), Badger Collection, Missouri Historical
Society, St. Louis.

GOVERNOR JACKSON CONDEMNS THE "BLOODY AND REVOLUTIONARY SCHEMES" OF THE U.S. GOVERNMENT

*By early 1861, Governor Claiborne F. Jackson had already been in contact with
Jefferson Davis for some months and soon declared himself for the Confederacy. He
issued this proclamation to the people of Missouri about a month after the civilian
massacre at Camp Jackson in St. Louis in early May of that year.*

Jackson's fiery proclamation was carried in the pro-Southern Boonville
Observer *on June 12, 1861. Many Missourians considered Boonville to be the capital*

*of Little Dixie, and within five days of the governor's proclamation, the town
became the site of a skirmish—the first on Missouri's soil.*

BOONVILLE OBSERVER EXTRA.
GOVERNOR'S PROCLAMATION.
TO THE PEOPLE OF MISSOURI.

A series of unprovoked and unparalleled outrages have been inflicted upon the peace and dignity of this Commonwealth, and upon the rights and liberties of its people, by wicked and unprincipled men professing to act under the authority of the United States Government; the solemn enactments of your Legislature have been nullified; your volunteer soldiers have been taken prisoners; our commerce with your sister states has been suspended; your trade with your fellow-citizens has been, and is, subjected to the harassing control of an armed soldiery; peaceful citizens have been imprisoned without warrant of law; unoffending and defenseless men, women and children have been ruthlessly shot down and murdered; and other unbearable indignities have been heaped upon your State and yourselves.

To all these outrages and indignities you have submitted with a patriotic forbearance, which has only encouraged the perpetrators of these grievous wrongs to attempt still bolder and more daring usurpations.

It has been my earnest endeavor under all these embarrassing circumstances to maintain the peace of the State, and to avert, if possible, from our borders the desolating effect of a civil war. With that object in view, I authorized Major-General Price several weeks ago to arrange with Gen. Harney, commanding the Federal forces in this State, the terms of an agreement by which the peace of the State might be preserved. They came, on the 21st May, to an understanding, which was made public. The State authorities have faithfully labored to carry out the terms of that agreement. The Federal Government on the other hand not only manifested its strong disapprobation of it, by the instant dismissal of the distinguished officer, who, on its part, entered into it but it at once began, and has unintermittingly carried out, a system of hostile operations, in utter contempt of that agreement, and in reckless disregard of its own plighted faith. . . . [He goes on to describe various "humiliating conditions" he had to agree to, only to be forced to make even more concessions.]

Fellow citizens: All our efforts towards conciliation have failed. We can hope nothing from the justice or moderation of the agents of the Federal Government in this State. They are energetically hastening the execution of their bloody and revolutionary schemes for the inauguration of civil war in your midst; for the military occupation of your States by armed bands of lawless invaders; for the overthrow of your State Government; and for the subversion of those liberties which that Government has always sought to protect; and they intend to exert their whole power to subjugate you, if possible, to the military despotism which has usurped the powers of the Federal Government.

Now, THEREFORE, I, C. F. JACKSON, Governor of the State of Missouri, do, in view of the foregoing facts, and by virtue of the powers vested in me, by the Constitution and laws of this Commonwealth, issue this my PROCLAMATION, calling the Militia of the State, to the number of FIFTY THOUSAND, into active service of the State, for the purpose of repelling said invasion, and for the protection of the lives, liberty, and property of the citizens of this State. And I earnestly exhort all good citizens of Missouri to rally under the flag of their State for the protection of their endangered homes and firesides, and for the defense of their most sacred rights and dearest liberties.

In issuing this Proclamation, I hold it to be my solemn duty to remind you that Missouri is still one of the United States; that the Executive Department of the State Government does not arrogate to itself the power to disturb that relation; that power has been wisely vested in a Convention which will, at the proper time, express your sovereign will; and that meanwhile it is your duty to obey all the *constitutional* requirements of the Federal Government. But it is equally my duty to advise you that your first allegiance is due to your own State; and that you are under no obligation, whatever, to obey the *unconstitutional* edicts of the military despotism which has enthroned itself at Washington, nor to submit to the infamous and degrading sway of its wicked minions in this State. No brave and true-hearted Missourian will obey the one, or submit to the other. Rise, then, and drive out ignominiously the invaders who have dared to desecrate the soil which your labors have made fruitful, and which is consecrated by your homes!

Given under my hand as Governor, and under the great seal of the State of Missouri, at Jefferson City, this twelfth day of June, 1861.

By the Governor:

CLAIBORNE F. JACKSON

B. F. Massey, Secretary of State.

Boonville Observer Extra, June 12, 1861, Civil War Collection, Missouri Historical Society, St. Louis.

"I GOES TO FIGHT MIT SIGEL"

About one-third of the soldiers who fought in the Union army were foreign-born; nearly 180,000 were of German descent. Several St. Louis regiments, such as the Seventeenth Missouri Volunteer Infantry Regiment, were composed entirely of Germans. The pseudonym "O. N. E. Schnapps" in the 1863 sheet music publication translates colloquially as "one stiff drink." The real author, John F. Poole, was a popular Irish songwriter who also penned the lyrics to the famous labor protest song "No Irish Need Apply" (1863). Proud of his Irish descent, Poole was poking good-natured fun at the German immigrant soldiers and their eating and drinking customs. General Franz Sigel had left his native Germany during the revolution and had suffered a defeat at the battle of Wilson's Creek in Missouri in August 1861. He later achieved a victory at Pea Ridge, Arkansas, that saved Missouri for the Union. The word "schlauch" may be corruption of the German word "Schlacht," which means "battle" or "slaughter," and the word "tuyvel" may be "Teufel," or "devil." The allusion to "Fighting Joe" refers to General Joseph Hooker.

"I GOES TO FIGHT MIT SIGEL"

John F. Poole
Tune: The Girl I Left behind Me (traditional).

I've come shust now to tells you how, I goes mit regimentals,
To schlauch dem voes of Liberty, like dem old Continentals
Vot fights mit England long ago to save the Yankee Eagle;
Un now I gets my sojer clothes; I'm going to fight mit Sigel.

CHORUS
    Yah, daus is true, I shpeaks mit you. I'm going to fight mit Sigel.

Ven I comes from der Deutsche Countree, I vorks somedimes at baking;
Den I keeps a lager beer-saloon, und den I goes shoe-making;
But now I was a sojer been to save der Yankee Eagle,
To schlauch dem tam secession volks, I goes to fight mit Sigel.

CHORUS
    Yah, daus is true, I shpeaks mit you. I'm going to fight mit Sigel.

I gets ein tam big rifle guns und puts him to mine shoulder,
Den march so bold like a big jackhorse, und maybe someding bolder;
I goes off mit de volunteers to save der Yankee Eagle;
To give dem Rebel vellers fits, I goes to fight mit Sigel.

CHORUS
    Yah, daus is true, I shpeaks mit you. I'm going to fight mit Sigel.

For rations dey gives salty pork. I dinks dat vas a great sell;
I petter likes de sauerkraut, der Schvitzer-kase und bretzel.
If Fighting Joe will give us dem, ve'll save der Yankee Eagle,
Und I'll put mine vrou in breech-a-loons to go and fight mit Sigel.

CHORUS
Yah, daus is true, I shpeaks mit you. I'm going to fight mit Sigel.

Dem Deutschen mens mit Sigel's band at fighting have no rival;
Und ven Cheff Davis mens ve meet, ve schlauch em like de tuyvil.
Dere's only von ting vot I fear, ven pattling for der Eagle,
I vont get not no lager beer, ven I goes to fight mit Sigel.

O. N. E. Schnapps, A. C. Peters and Bro., Cincinnati, 1863

GERMAN LADIES PRESENT A UNION FLAG

The Daily Missouri Democrat, *a fervently pro-Union paper with Republican sympathies, published a poem written for the occasion of a flag presentation by ladies of German descent in April 1861. Women often sewed and presented flags to the soldiers in their communities. The author of the poem, Dr. Ferdinand Hoenssler (the name is misspelled in the article), was a German physician who had emigrated from the Kingdom of Saxony.*

SENTIMENTS OF THE GERMAN LADIES OF ST. LOUIS.

In presenting a flag of our Union to Company A, Union Guards, Missouri Volunteers: Dedicated to the Regiments of Missouri Volunteers who bravely responded to the call of "Our President."

By Dr. Ferdinand Hanussler.

Receive this flag and let it wave,
The emblem of the free and brave;
Support it with your valiant hand,
True to your God and Fatherland.

It is that flag which we once bore,
In days gone by, in days of yore—
Whose name is hailed in every zone,
As Freedom's bravest, noblest son.

It is that flag which proudly shone
At Sumter, o'er brave Anderson,
When he there with his little band
For Freedom took his manly stand.

Bear then that flag and hold it high
Let treason never it defy!
Protect it on the battlefield
And God on high will be your shield!

Daily Missouri Democrat, April 30, 1861.

"YOU MAY BE ASSURED THAT SHE TALKS SOUTHERN"

Although unsigned, this letter was probably written by a young woman named Euphrasie Pettus who lived in St. Louis during the Civil War. The Pettus family was passionately sympathetic to the Confederate cause and numbered among its friends several officers in the Confederate army. "Dutchmen" was a popular (and somewhat unflattering) nickname for German Americans. The St. Louis Fair Grounds were a gently rising area just north of the city, home to Benton Barracks, where new regiments were mustered in. Benton Barracks later housed refugee encampments, a military prison, hospitals, and cavalry stables.

Dear Sister,

The town is filled & surrounded by troops. Harney's regulars occupy Russell & Kennet's houses on 4th St & there are Dutch regiments out by the fair grounds, at the Water Works, all around & in the Arsenal, on the Gravois road, at the RailRoad depots, & everywhere. This of course ensures our quiet. Until we have a force equal to engage with them, there can be no resistance. Frank Blair is Dictator. He has assembled troops from all parts of Illinois & stationed them at Belleville, Caseyville, Alton, St. Charles, all within an hour's ride & if the slightest show of resistance is made, we will be crushed out. My blood boils in my veins when I think of the position of Missouri—held in the Union at the point of Dutchmen's bayonets. I feel outraged—you may imagine how hard it is for men to endure it. Frank Blair has stolen every weapon in town to arm his blood hounds against us & we must submit. But the sullen submission of down-trodden men will be avenged the more terribly in the day of their uprising. May I live to see that day!

Mrs. Henry Kayser came for me one day last week to take dinner with her. I had a very pleasant day. We were entirely alone & we almost talked ourselves to death. You may be assured that she talks Southern or I wouldn't have talked with her. Her home is surrounded by armed men. The adjoining buildings filled with them & two sentinels stand at her gate & challenge people that go in or out after dark. We talked almost in a whisper, lest we should be over-heard. It is like the French Revolution. . . .

Euphrasia [Euphrasie] Pettus [?] to sister [Mrs. Charles Parsons?], May 20, 1860, Pettus Family Papers, 1861–68, Missouri Historical Society, St. Louis.

THE LADIES UNION AID SOCIETY VISITS BENTON BARRACKS

Prominent pro-Union ladies living in St. Louis during the Civil War regularly visited the sick and wounded soldiers hospitalized at Benton Barracks. Although most of them lacked nursing skills, they were able to provide soldiers with shirts and socks as well as Bibles and other reading matter. A few of their regular reports have survived, detailing their activities from 1862 through 1863. The following report was probably from early 1863.

REPORT FROM WARDS 1 & 2. BENTON BARRACKS.

Since our last report we have made three visits at Wards 1 & 2 Benton Barracks— all interesting but with little variety of incident. The physicians in these wards have been changed more than once in this time, & we have not met either of them in our late visits. We have had pleasure in watching the improvement of some of the patients, who have now the prospect of restored health and vigor—some whose faces had become familiar in our repeated visits, and whom we looked upon as old acquaintances, have just received their discharge and are on their way home.

One young man whose gradual wasting we had watched with painful interest, died the day before our last visit. We had feared that he must die, but did not think that we should so soon miss his cordial greeting, and the pleading look with which he accompanied the inquiry "Don't you think I look better than when you saw me first?" He had seemed to be feeling after the Savior—we must *hope* that his anxious heart accepted the gracious invitation "Come unto me," & that so coming it found "rest."

In the first ward there are now only two or three who are quite sick. The most interesting of our friends in that room is Reuben Bolinger, a young man who was for some time a prisoner in Jackson and who can tell many interesting facts respecting the experiences of our soldiers in Dixie. His right limb is paralyzed, so that he can only walk with crutches. He is intelligent and thoughtful, and loves to study his Bible, & anything which may help him to understand it. At our last visit but one he asked us if we could bring him our Almanac, and when at our last visit we gave him one of the beautiful copies published by the New York branch of the Am. Tract Society, which are so full of useful information, he immediately began to read it from the commencement. We hope that his persevering efforts to obtain a discharge may . . . soon be successful. He has already sent five letters to his Captain, for the necessary papers, without receiving any response.

Among other requests—we receive the usual variety—one man lately asked for a dictionary—he found so many Latin words in his books that he could not understand them. When we carried the dictionary two other men begged for it, before we found the first applicant.

One rather intelligent appearing youth, whom we found reading Tom Paine's Age of Reason is now interested in Nelson's Cause and Cure of Infidelity, though he does not seem yet decided who has the best of the argument.

We have been asked for a Norwegian Testament by a man who can read only in that language. One of his comrades told us that this man had only one book a Norwegian hymn book which he had read through both ways, and he seemed quite in earnest for something else that was good to read. We promised to do our best for him.

There has been a very marked increase in the demand for Testaments & Bibles. We no longer find them barely accepted when offered with "I don't care if I take one"—they are now eagerly sought for, and gladly welcomed. Two weeks ago we promised several Bibles & Testaments—at our next trip we carried a larger number than we had promised, thinking to meet all demands. When we had disposed of the last one, a lad whose face we recollected immediately came up & asked "Have you brought my Testament?" We were obliged to tell him that though we had brought his Testament it had been given to another. His disappointed face haunted us until our last visit we had the satisfaction of placing the promised book in his hand—the pleasure expressed in his face & in his voice seemed a pledge that the Testament would be valued.

We have distributed 17 pr socks 4 towels & 6 handkerchiefs, besides paper, envelopes & stamps taken from these rooms.

Our visits were made Jan 17th, 21st, & 27th [1863].

Mrs. Nelson

Ladies Union Aid Society Reports, 1862–63, Western Historical Manuscripts Collection, University of Missouri, Columbia.

STEPHAN WERLY REFUSES TO SERVE UNDER A COLONEL WHO "DOES NOT SEEM TO KNOW ANY RELIGION"

Stephan K. Werly, a deeply religious young Methodist of German descent, served as a drummer in Company K of the Twenty-first Missouri Volunteer Infantry Regiment. He was about eighteen when he enlisted. The Twenty-first was made up primarily of men from Missouri and nearby counties in Iowa and Illinois. Although

> Werly and his compatriots at first refused to serve under Colonel David Moore, he
> eventually made his peace with the Twenty-first Regiment and later fought with
> them at the battles of Shiloh and Corinth. Moore was the son of Irish immigrants,
> which may account for Werly's reluctance to serve under him.[11]

TWENTY FIRST REGIMENT OF MISSOURI VOLUNTEERS, COMPANY "K".

La Grange, February 1, 1862

It was on Friday, February 1, when we were ordered to leave La Grange
for Canton, to be paid for our 6 months time of service, as we were told, but
when we arrived at Canton, there was first something else to be attended to
than to be paid, and that was to be enrolled for the United States' service in
the 21st Missouri Regiment under Colonel Moore, and we had believed until
now that we belonged to the 2nd Northeast Missouri Regiment under Colonel
Woodyard. That was a hard task for our company, as we knew Colonel Moore
to be a man who did not seem to know any religion and who would swear
and curse and mistreat his troops. We, as a company then named "B," [asked]
not to let us enroll under such a man. When they started with the enrolling,
they called off our names, and we put ourselves in two ranks. Then they proceeded to take our oath and to enroll us, but there was not a single one who
raised his hand, and therefore they being unable to do anything else with us,
but to take us under guard, and pretty soon we were really taken under guard
in a big two-story high hall, with a sentinel at the door. We were in the belief
that we had a right and sufficient reasons and ground, not to serve under such
a man, with a different oath than we previously took; but the "men up higher"
and our general stuck together and soon they ordered our officers to come to
the officers' room. They soon found out that there was no other way, without
perhaps being taken under guard for a long time and to be dragged around as
prisoners.

Oh, how miserable I felt, to find myself to be a prisoner, but firmly believing
to have a clear conscience, as I had promised to stick to our community; and I
thought, would it be an honor to my children, that it would be said, their father
is a prisoner? And I had my family at heart. Should I be dragged around all over
the United States? However, as a soldier, God knows how far away from my dear
little five children, among whom the second youngest one is very ill at present . . .
and my dear companion through life, and my dear, old, invalid mother, as well as
all my other blood relations, and to be separated for three years? That was a hard
task for me. But thank the Lord, I had confidence in my God while I only believed
to have done my duty in having joined my company to help maintain and save

the rights and the liberty of our country, as well as to subdue the rebels; and also believing that the Almighty who manages everything as he thinks best, and who has promised us to be father and helper to the widows and orphans, and that he would carry out and guide everything beautifully, could unite us again in happiness, as he in His wisdom would think best.

Soon the decision came, when the major returned with our officers and asked the company, if we were willing to be enrolled with our officers as a company of the 21st Regiment of Missouri under Colonel Moore? If not, then we would be separated and distributed among other companies—. And as all our officers were willing and ready to join, we nearly all were also willing and treaty to stick to our officers and with them together to join than to be dragged around for a long time as a prisoner; and besides, the humble one has to submit to the man higher up.

Oh, how good it is that we can look forward in faith to a land where there is justice! May God strengthen my faith and revive my hope that I may always trust in child-like confidence in my dear Saviour and Redeemer, Jesus Christ. May He help me to be persistent in prayer and that I may hereafter enter the holy land with all my dear loved ones, and never to be separated again, for the mercy of the bitter sufferings and death of Jesus Christ's sake. This is my supplication. Amen!

Stephan Werly Diary, Western Historical Manuscripts Collection, University of Missouri, Columbia.

THE LADIES UNION AID SOCIETY RAISES FUNDS FOR THE CAUSE

As a response to the Camp Jackson incident, a group of patriotic St. Louis ladies gathered to form the Ladies Union Aid Society (LUAS). By September 1861, the LUAS was working with the Western Sanitary Commission (WSC) established by General John C. Frémont at the suggestion of the Reverend William Greenleaf Eliot. (The WSC was not connected with the U.S. Sanitary Commission, a national organization that distributed medicines, food, and other necessary supplies to soldiers.) Together, these two women's organizations established hospitals for nursing sick and wounded soldiers, both in St. Louis and on board hospital ships such as the City of Louisiana and the Red Rover. In addition, the WSC organized the Mississippi Valley Sanitary Fair, which raised over $620,000.

MISSISSIPPI VALLEY SANITARY FAIR.
CIRCULAR.

St. Louis, Mo., February 5, 1864.

Although its sphere of action is geographically limited to the States west of the mountains, in spirit it recognizes no State lines nor sectional divisions or prejudices, but treats all soldiers alike, whether from the East or West, and, so far as in its power, permits none to suffer or be neglected. It also co-operates with the Untied States Commission and its branches, with the Christian Commissions, and with all local organizations, seeking in all cases, without rivalry, to increase the amount of good accomplished, as there is more than enough for all to do. . . . In view of the new call for soldiers, adding three hundred thousand new recruits to the armies in the field, and the enlistment of colored troops, the sanitary demands are not likely to decrease, and for a year's supply a fund of at least FIVE HUNDRED THOUSAND DOLLARS should be provided.

The undersigned . . . propose to themselves and to their fellow-citizens to RAISE THAT AMOUNT by one great effort of patriotism and humanity. A Herculean labor, but by united and general effort it can be accomplished. They believe that there is a heart to do it, and "where there is a will there is a way." So long as our self-sacrificing soldiers, our sons and brothers, are freely offering health and life in our country's cause, we, who stay at home, defended and guarded by them, will give them the gratitude of our hearts, the labor of our hands, the fruits of our industry, however long and at whatever cost, until the national triumph is perfectly secured, with all the blessings of undivided nationality and universal freedom. . . .

We ask [the loyal men and women] to remember how magnificently the armies of the West have fought, often under circumstances of the utmost difficulty and discouragement. How victory has almost uniformly attended upon them, and they have never lost an inch of ground once gained. How Missouri, beset and beleaguered and almost betrayed, held to her first allegiance, and although devastated by fire and sword has steadfastly refused to be forced into the madness of rebellion. How St. Louis, with paralyzed trade and with commercial ruin staring her in the face, with a divided community and the whole Southern sympathy pleading with her for fellowship, did not hesitate for a moment, but with conjoined American and German strength anticipated attack and destroyed treason at its birth. . . . What would have been the effect upon our national cause if St. Luis and Missouri had been recreant, or if, in the Mississippi Valley, defeat, instead of victory had been found! . . .

The undersigned, therefore, respectfully but earnestly solicit the prompt and active assistance of all persons to whom this circular comes or this enterprise is made known. Contributions of every sort and kind will be received and all can be advantageously used. Large buildings for the Fair will be erected and the bulkiest articles will find abundant room. All the fruits of the garden and farm, the produce of the mine, iron or gold or whatever else, every variety of manufactures from the needle to the steam-engine, works of art and fancy, home made and imported goods, hardware and silverware and queensware, groceries and dry goods, India rubber goods, boots and shoes, curiosities and relics, books and pictures, live stock of whatever kind from the farm, yard or prairies, and in short whatever is bought and sold by rich or poor, wise or simple, young or old, will find a welcome place in the Mississippi Valley Fair and contribute to its success. Every dollar, or dollar's worth, will relieve the suffering of some sick and wounded soldier and perhaps save him from death—it may be a stranger to you, of whom you will never hear— it maybe your kinsman or your dearest friend.

It will be . . . A UNION LOVE FEAST, which will bring back the kindly relations of former times. A new era will soon dawn upon our State and Nation, the era of Union, of Freedom, and enduring Peace. Let it be inaugurated here by a hundred thousand welcome guests, and there will be room enough for all that come.

Major-General W. S. Rosecrans, President.
Gov. Willard P. Hall, First Vice-President.
Mayor Chauncy I. Filley, Second Vice-President.
Brig. Gen. Clinton B. Fisk, Third Vice-President.

St. Louis Sanitation Papers, Missouri Historical Society, St. Louis.

CONFEDERATE SOLDIERS EXHORT PRO-SOUTHERN WOMEN TO STAND FIRM

The Missouri Army Argus *was published by soldiers in the pro-Southern Missouri State Guard. Here they call upon their sisters and mothers to emulate the women of ancient Rome in their struggle against the intrusions of the federal government. "Oseolo" was probably a misspelling of Osceola, a town in the western part of the state, halfway between Springfield and Kansas City.*

THE MISSOURI ARMY ARGUS

CAMP NEAR OSEOLO, MISSOURI, SATURDAY, 30 NOVEMBER 1861

VOL. I, NO. 4

THE WOMEN OF MISSOURI.

Daughters of Missouri! Have you less of that moral heroism, characteristic of your sex, than the ladies of other times and other States? Do you not behold a country bleeding under the inflictions of a cruel and barbarous foe? We write these words from a scene of desolation and blackened ruin, caused by the torch of the oppressor. Osceola is in ruins. Women and tender children have been driven out to hunt shelter or starve in the cold by the ruffians who bear commissions from the Federal Government. Warsaw is in ruins; and then these lyiug cut-throats publish in the Tory sheet of St. Louis that the secessionists have burnt their own property!

Women are insulted. Old men are murdered. Defenceless communities are scattered in terror. Millions of our substance destroyed. The self-sacrificing men of Gen. Price's army have done and suffered for home and country all that sublime devotion could require. They cry to their brethren and fellow-citizens for force enough to drive out the brutal hirelings from the land. Daughters of Missouri! send your husbands, sons and brothers out to battle. Shame the laggards who ingloriously loiter at home. Say, as the Roman matron said to her sons—"Go, and see my face no more until our country is free!" Exert your great moral influence to save your bleeding country. If you are conscious of the promptings of woman's great nature, help, help, help! Let MEN know they will merit and receive your scorn and contempt by an exhibition of poltroonery.

Condemn the cravens to wear a bonnet, and surrender all claims to the dignity of glorious manhood! "Only the brave deserve the fair!" You can do more than regiments. You can wield an influence mightier than the sword. It is woman's mission to exalt and ennoble, to comfort and to bliss; it is man's mission to protect and defend, to preserve liberty and country and hedge the domestic sanctuary with security and peace. What are the men doing to make you free, and to protect your hearth-stones from violence? Have they shouldered their guns? Have they drawn the sword? Or do they cling to your apron strings and cry for protection? Are they men? Can you respect a coward? Are these lords of creation to creep, and hide, and dodge, and beg, and tremble; and crouch like servile menials? Daughters of the land! tell these white-lipped, lilly-livered gentlemen that you will yourselves meet the foe, if there be no MEN to defend you. Drive them out to battle.

Civil War Collection, Missouri Historical Society, St. Louis.

THIS WAR AMONGST NEIGHBORS AND BROTHERS

The following editorial from the Missouri Republican *of November 10, 1861, was published under the pseudonym NORTHEAST. Despite its name, the* Republican *was actually a Democratic paper with proslavery sentiments. It was, however, loyal to the Union. Hannibal, Missouri, the birthplace of Samuel Clemens (Mark Twain)—who briefly joined a Confederate regiment—was a prosperous town on the west bank of the Mississippi River in the northern county of Marion. As the starting point for the Hannibal–St. Joseph Railroad, the town was strategically important for both sides. Like most northern areas in the state, Marion County was mostly pro-Southern, but when Union forces occupied the town in the autumn of 1861, they were able to subdue the worst of the partisan warfare in the neighborhood.*

THE WAR IN MISSOURI.

BURNT PRAIRIES AND THE WAR PLAGUE—HORSE THIEVES—PEACE IN NORTH MISSOURI.

HANNIBAL, MO., November 9, 1861.

Out again upon the road, gliding over the wide prairies between Hannibal and St. Joseph—not those pictured plains which a few months ago so charmed the eye with their beauty of flowers and wreath of verdure, dotted over here and there with herds of cattle and sheep, but for miles and miles along the road scorched into blackness by the desolating fire that has swept over their surface. No green or living thing is left; no grass, no flowers, no animals, wild or domestic, but everywhere a scene of silent, black desolation. The land is left, but that is all.

How truthfully do these burnt prairies typify that other fire that has swept back and forth across our distracted and devoted State. In the present scenes of wretchedness and gloom, in many portions of Missouri, the resemblance is perfect, for the miseries that have come with this war amongst neighbors and brothers are far greater than any physical evils which follow the ravages of the uncontrolled elements. This storm of human passion—this civil and social war—now sweeping with hurricane-violence through the land, has not only blasted the flowers of hope, truth and trust, but has stained its whole course with the blood of friends and kindred. Many a father mourns his first born who has gone down in the storm of battle, or in some bloody fray; and many a widowed mother, with a grief too deep for tears, sets about the care and support of children, left without their natural protector. . . .

The only remains of the war in Northeast Missouri consist in straggling banks of horse thieves. These gentry have grown out of the war as maggots grow out of a carcass under the influence of an August sun. It will take some time, under the most vigilant police system, aided by military detachments, to effectually rid the country of these miscreants. As an example of how they operate, I will mention an incident connected with their transactions: A few days since, a man arrived at Macon City with four horses, which he shipped for St. Louis, stating that he had purchased them in Linn County. Next day he was followed by the real owner of the animals, from whom they had been stolen. But he was too late, for in the twenty-four hours intervening Mr. Thief had taken the horses to market, pocketed the money, and was seen on his way back, with *two confederates*, (true in both senses of the word,) to renew their acts of plunder.

These scoundrels generally profess to be good secessionists, engaged in the laudable, patriotic work of confiscating the property of "d___d Abolitionists." . . . I do not assert or believe that all the horse thieves in Missouri are secessionists, but it being convenient to do so, they use the doctrine as a cloak for the crime.

Without some unexpected disaster to the Union cause in Southern Missouri, there need be no fear entertained with regard to the peace of this part of the State. Travelers need not indulge in apprehension for safety on the railroads, for, in addition to being well guarded at all important points, the disposition to burn bridges has either died out, or the authors of this kind of mischief have gone South. The trains upon the North Missouri and Hannibal and St. Joe roads make their trips upon time, and meet with no obstructions. The business on these lines is increasing and promises to be much better than could have been anticipated one month ago.

NORTHEAST.

Missouri Republican, November 10, 1861.

FOUR

Missouri's Battles

$\mathcal{V}$IOLENCE AND BLOODSHED had plagued the boundary areas of Missouri for years before the Civil War began, especially in the western and northern counties of the state. During the war, battles over the future of slavery continued or renewed old conflicts originating in the state's territorial period, and political allegiances intensified as open warfare gripped the state. For the first two years of the war, pro-Southern political and military leaders desperately fought to take the state out of the Union but received little aid from the Confederate government. Missouri's northern counties, those most sympathetic to the Southern cause, were far removed from Confederate supply lines. The most important city in the state—St. Louis—was too solidly in the Union camp to be a viable target. Nevertheless, General Sterling Price and former governor Claiborne Jackson continued to believe (or to hope) that if they could achieve military victories in Missouri they would precipitate the state's secession; surely then young Missouri rebels would flock to the Confederate standard. But those who joined the Confederate forces soon experienced what became chronic shortages of money, clothes, food, and weapons. Confederate military leaders in the state found their troops inexperienced, poorly trained, and lacking in discipline. Moreover, many of these soldiers were fiercely devoted to the cause of states rights and had no intention of leaving Missouri to fight for Confederate independence. They intended to defend their homes from the "foreigners."

Federal commanders, for their part, struggled to drive Confederate forces from the state and to neutralize guerrilla violence. Beginning in May 1861 with the Camp Jackson incident and continuing through March 1862 with the battle of Pea Ridge, federal commanders sought to keep a precarious peace with only raw, untrained troops at their disposal. Most of the St. Louis men who joined the U.S. Army were Germans and young Republicans. In other parts of the state, recruiting efforts had not gone well, at least in part because former governor Jackson had flatly refused the call to raise volunteer regiments in April. Because Missouri was so far from the center of operations in the eastern theater, money, troops, and supplies were always slow in coming. The Lincoln administration certainly recognized the vital role of the state, situated as it was on two of the most important rivers in the nation and possessing an abundance of many crucial resources, but found it difficult to support the war effort there adequately. Even before the outbreak of war, St. Louis residents had already begun forming private armed organizations, especially among Germans. Some of these recruits lacked discipline, and some harbored bitter enmity toward slaveholders. Others suspected foreigners—not only Germans but any men from outside the state, a hostility that led to clashes between soldiers and civilians. Still, despite of the state's long-standing moderation on slavery and political and military blunders that antagonized even pro-Union citizens, at least two-thirds of Missourians remained committed to the Union.[1]

Missouri's soldiers, both those in blue and those in gray, represented the diverse nature of the state's population. Their ethnic and racial divisions reflected long-standing animosities and differences that had lingered in the state for the first half of the nineteenth century. Black Missourians had already joined the fight some time before President Lincoln authorized their recruitment, when the jayhawking senator James H. Lane impressed or encouraged them into service. On November 14, 1863, General John M. Schofield issued General Order No. 135, which provided for compensation for Missouri slave owners who permitted their slaves to join the U.S. Army. Although there is no definitive information on how many black men from Missouri fought in the Civil War, some historians suggest that more than eighty-three hundred African Americans from Missouri (both slave and free) entered Union regiments, though most served in regiments from states other than Missouri.[2]

Like the residents of other Southern states, Missouri families suffered as opposing military forces marched through their towns and homesteads. Residents in all parts of the state endured maltreatment at the hands of soldiers of both sides. Missouri's wartime history, then, reveals several recurring themes: military blunders that alienated and polarized civilian populations; rough treatment of citizens that triggered ever-more-brutal reprisals; and heroic efforts by both sides to build up, fund, and train volunteer armies.

Missouri, as one historian has observed, was hard on its generals. Federal commanders faced nearly insurmountable difficulties as they attempted to cope with internal divisions along with the military effort. Generals Ulysses S. Grant and William T. Sherman needed Missouri men in other theaters of the war, including the Vicksburg, Atlanta, and Carolinas campaigns, and they removed experienced commanders from the state. General John C. Frémont had assumed command over the Department of the West and established his headquarters in St. Louis, where he faced a divided city—though firmly in the Union camp, the city had suffered outbreaks of riots and even a civilian massacre in 1861—as well as guerrilla activity on the western border and a chronic shortage of manpower. Both Union and Confederate commanders found that many Missourians refused to leave their home state to fight.

General Sterling "Pap" Price, who had served as governor of Missouri from 1853 to 1857, took command of the Missouri State Guard. Although the State Guard never officially merged with the Confederate army, it did cooperate with the Confederate States Army of the West during the Wilson's Creek campaign in 1861. Individual state guardsmen eventually joined newly established CSA units, and the guard continued to exist in limited numbers until late in the war. Price, along with most of his guardsmen, waited to join the Confederate army until early 1862. Price's men clashed briefly with units under the command of General Nathaniel Lyon at Boonville, Missouri, on June 17, 1861, where Lyon's two thousand troops easily defeated Price's untrained and poorly armed Missouri State Guard. While the battle of Boonville was later considered to be a small skirmish, it did keep Confederate forces away from the state capital and the Missouri River. Price took his troops southward, where he remained for the next few weeks in order to drill his raw recruits and join with Confederate general Benjamin McCulloch and his Arkansas troops. When Price fell ill, Claiborne Jackson took command of the forces.

Lyon commanded Union forces that included four Missouri regiments as well as Iowa and Kansas troops and regular infantry and artillery at Springfield in the southwestern part of the state. His aim was to prevent Price's forces from entering the state and gaining control of the Missouri and Mississippi rivers. Lyon pleaded with Frémont to send him additional troops and supplies, but Frémont, already worried that his own troop strength was inadequate, refused. It was a poor decision. On July 5, 1861, the pro-Southern forces under Jackson achieved a victory over the outnumbered Colonel Franz Sigel and his troops at the battle of Carthage in the southwestern corner of Missouri, not far from Arkansas. This first battle of the Civil War cheered pro-Southern forces in the state, and encouraged Jackson to believe that Missouri could still be drawn into the Confederacy. A month later, on August 5, 1861, Jackson declared the state of Missouri an independent republic, and he gained Missouri's admission to the Confederacy at the end of October. The government established by Jackson moved out of the state, first to Arkansas and later to Texas, where it operated as a conduit for information and Confederate recruiting until the end of the war.[3]

On August 10, 1861, ten miles southwest of Springfield, Price and Lyon clashed at the battle of Wilson's Creek, a terrible defeat for Union forces. Lyon was wounded in the leg and head, and did not survive the battle, becoming the first Union general killed in the Civil War. In that battle, 1,317 Union soldiers were killed or wounded, and Confederate and State Guard casualties numbered 1,222. Although the rebels won the battle, they did not pursue the federal armies.[4] After Wilson's Creek, Price wanted to move north, but McCulloch refused to advance any farther into Missouri with Price's undisciplined, untrained troops. Price then set out on his own with just the Missouri State Guard in an attempt to reach the

Missouri River and to recruit more soldiers to the cause. He was sure that men with Southern sympathies would flock to his marching lines as soon as he reached the north-central part of the state. Price left Springfield on August 25, 1861. On September 2, his Missouri State Guard attacked and routed a Union force under a notorious jayhawker, the former Kansas senator James H. Lane, at Dry Woods Creek near the Kansas border. Price reached Lexington, Missouri, not far from Kansas City, on September 12. On September 18, the State Guard initiated a siege of the Lexington garrison, which had also pleaded in vain for reinforcements from Frémont. After three days of fighting, Union commander Colonel James A. Mulligan surrendered on September 20, 1861. Confederate casualties included 33 killed and 150 wounded against 40 Union soldiers killed and 120 wounded.[5]

The Union defeat at Wilson Creek exacerbated Frémont's difficulties in St. Louis. The secessionist element among the populace had become more strident than ever, contributing to civil strife in the city. Moreover, Unionists criticized Frémont for his refusal to send more troops to the martyred hero, General Lyon. In response, Frémont arrested a loyalist newspaper editor for publishing editorials critical of his actions. Lacking men and money and with some three-month Union recruits refusing to reenlist, Frémont struck a blow against Confederate sympathizers. On August 31, 1861, Frémont declared—without first obtaining presidential approval—that henceforward any rebels found in arms were to be summarily court-martialed and, if found guilty, executed. Moreover, all slaves belonging to rebels were freed and the property of persons in rebellion against the government was to be confiscated. Radicals throughout the nation applauded Frémont's bold move, but Lincoln revoked the proclamation because he felt that it would cause further unrest in Missouri and other important border states. Furthermore, Frémont's proclamation, which confiscated the property of all who sympathized with the rebel cause, violated the recently enacted federal Confiscation Act, which authorized seizure only of the property of persons in arms against the United States. When Frémont refused rescind the proclamation, Lincoln overruled him and later removed the general from command.

In October 1861, Lincoln replaced Frémont with Major General David Hunter, who stayed in Missouri about a month before being sent to Kansas, and then with Major General Henry W. Halleck. Halleck was a more professional, even-tempered officer. Although he faced the same problems of a divided population, and instituted some stringent policies against civilians, Halleck worked well with the moderate Provisional Governor Hamilton Gamble. By spring 1862, Union forces had pushed the Confederate troops out of Missouri, though Price would continue in his desperate struggle with a greatly reduced force for nearly two more years. Brigadier General Samuel R. Curtis, who commanded the Army of the Southwest, decided to chase the Confederates all the way into northwestern corner of Arkansas with his 10,250 men and fifty artillery pieces. On March 6, 1862, Major General Earl Van Dorn, who now commanded the C. S. Army of the West, divided his army into two columns, one led by Price and the other by McCulloch, and sent them toward Pea Ridge, Arkansas. There he hoped to catch the federals, who were dispersed across northwest Arkansas. When Curtis learned of the Confederate advance, he retreated northward while attempting to unite his scattered forces. After two days of desperate fighting around Elk Horn Tavern, during which the Union army was driven nearly to defeat, Price's column was finally forced to retreat, resulting in a Union victory. There are no complete figures for Confederate casualties, although some historians place them as high as 4,600. Union casualties at Pea Ridge included 203 killed, 980 wounded, and 201 missing or captured.

Missouri witnessed more than a thousand battles and skirmishes over the course of the war, several of them of national significance. After the victories at Carthage and Pea Ridge, there was very little hope left for a Confederate Missouri. Over the next two years, Price tried several more times to lead his men into the northern and central part of the state and toward St. Louis, in an effort to capture the principal cities and rivers. Each time he failed; each time he had fewer men and less support. When he was at last driven out of the state after the decisive battle of Westport in October 1864, Price achieved one of his goals, although not the way he had hoped: he finally had influenced the political situation in his home state. His defeat caused a major pro-Union upswing in the state, resulting in the election of Governor Thomas C. Fletcher. Fletcher had been one of the heroes at the siege of Fort Davidson at Pilot Knob in September 1863. Although he had to abandon the fort, he had prevented Price from taking the gunpowder stored nearby. As a result, his name became a household word. An ardent antislavery man, Fletcher would play an important role in emancipating Missouri's slaves.

REMEMBERING BOONVILLE: THE FIRST BATTLE ON THE SOIL OF MISSOURI

At the beginning of the Civil War, New Hampshire–born Thomas Wallace Knox volunteered for the California National Guard, with whom he fought in Missouri. The following excerpt was taken from his recollections of the battle of Boonville, in which he was wounded. After his discharge sometime in 1863, he worked as a war reporter and encountered serious problems when he published troop movements in northern newspapers. General U. S. Grant accused Knox of espionage and had him court-martialed. Knox appealed to President Lincoln for clemency and was exonerated.

Daybreak on the 17th found us slowly moving up the river toward Booneville. General Lyon sat forward of the steamer's cabin, closely scanning both banks of

Fortifications and entrenchments of Pilot Knob, Missouri. *W. A. Hinchey, wood engraving, 1862–65. Courtesy of Missouri Historical Society*

the stream. Four miles below the town his glass sought out two pieces of artillery, partially concealed in a clump of trees, and trained upon the channel by which we were to pass. At once our engines were reversed, and the boats moved back to a landing about eight miles below Booneville. A little before seven o'clock we were on shore, and our column of fifteen hundred men began its advance upon the Rebel camp.

It was the story that has found its repetition in many a battle since that time. The enemy's pickets were driven in. The enemy, in line of battle, was discovered on a long ridge, and our own line was formed on a ridge parallel to it. Then we opened fire with our artillery (one battery was all we possessed), and received no response, save by a desultory discharge of small-arms. Next our infantry added its tenor notes to the bass of the field-guns; the Rebel forces melted steadily away, and the field was in our possession, twenty minutes after the opening shot had been fired.

Once in retreat, the Rebels did not halt until out of harm's reach. Their camp lay in the line of retreat, but they made no stop in passing it. Following in the rear of our column, I entered the camp, and found many signs of hasty departure. I found the fires burning, and dozens of coffee-pots and frying-pans filled with the materials for breakfast. Here was a pan full of meat fried to a crisp, from the neglect of the cook to remove it before his sudden exodus. A few feet distant lay a ham, with a knife sticking in a half-severed slice. A rude camp-table was spread with plates and their accessories, and a portion of the articles of food were carefully arranged. The seats for the breakfast party were in position, two of them being overturned. I could not help fancying the haste with which that table had been abandoned, only a few moments before. The tents were standing, and in some the blankets were lying on the ground, as if they had been very suddenly vacated. In one tent was a side-saddle, a neat pair of gaiters, and a hoop-skirt. The proper connection of those articles with the battle-field I was unable to ascertain.

In that camp was a fine lot of provisions, arms, equipments, and ammunition. Saddles were numerous, but there were no horses. It was evident that the hasty evacuation left no time for the simple process of saddling. . . .

The flags captured in this affair were excellent illustrations of the policy of the leading Secessionists. There was one rebel flag with the arms of the State of Missouri filling the field. There was a State flag, with only fifteen stars surrounding the coat of arms. There was a Rebel flag, with the State arms in the center, and there was one Rebel flag of the regular pattern. The rallying-cry at that time was in behalf of the State, and the people were told they must act for Missouri, without regard to any thing else. In no part of the country was the "State Rights" theory more freely used. . . . The flags under which Missouri soldiers were gathered clearly blended the interests of the State with secession.

Our troops entered Booneville amid demonstrations of delight from one portion of the inhabitants, and the frowns and muttered indignation of the other. The Rebels had fled, a part of them by land, and the balance on a steamboat, toward Lexington. . . . We had lost twelve men, the enemy probably twice as many. The action, three years later, would have been considered only a road-side skirmish, but it was then an affair of importance. Every man with General Lyon felt far more elation over the result than has since been felt over battles of much greater moment. We had won a signal victory; the enemy had suffered an equally signal defeat. . . .

From Thomas W. Knox, *Camp-Fire and Cotton-Field: Southern Adventure in Time of War. Life with the Union Armies, and Residence on a Louisiana Plantation.* New York: Blelock, 1865.

UNION SOLDIERS ARE SPOILING FOR A FIGHT

Irish and German Missourians made up two companies of the U.S. Reserve Corps that were organized at Turner Hall, St. Louis, a German patriotic stronghold. The Reserve Corps, mustered into service in May 1861, was soon attached to Lyon's Army of the West, and three companies of the Third Regiment left for southwest Missouri on July 1. The Third Regiment fought at Fulton on July 17 and was mustered out just a month later, on August 18, 1861. Companies K and D published the Camp Sweeny Spy *while encamped near Rolla in central Missouri. General*

"Fightin' Thomas" Sweeny, for whom the camp was named, was born in Ireland and later fought at Forsyth and Wilson's Creek in Missouri, as well as at Shiloh, Iuka, and Corinth. Adolphus Busch, founder of the Anheuser-Busch Brewery, was a corporal in Company E. Eberhard Anheuser, his father-in-law, served as a private in Company C.

CAMP SWEENY SPY.

ISSUED BY CO.'S K. AND D. THIRD REG. U. S. RESERVE CORPS OF MISSOURI.

CAMP SWEENY, ROLLA, MO., JULY 4, 1861.

DAILY REVIEW OF THE ROLLA MARKET.

[CORRECTED BY HAM.]

Ashes—No sales. Market flooded from camp fires.

Butter—"Prime" sales 4 lbs. 2 oz., at 15 cts.

Corn Bread—Going down fast. Sales 116 loaves at 15 cts.

Eggs—Fresh 15 cts. per doz.; do. with chickens 25 cts.

Fish—Only a few caught for private use.

Pork—Under "marching orders."

Gun Shot—All in the hands of Jeff. Davis.

Hens—Dull, having received a command to "rear open order," causing them to "halt" for three weeks, when they are expected on with "fresh recruits."

Muskets—Speak for themselves.

Negroes—None in town, all being kept *dark* by the former inhabitants.

Potatoes—*Going down* with the officers.

Quarters—None given to seceshers.

To the Editor of the Camp Sweeny Spy:

I am in a bad fix. As you may be aware, I belong to Company K, 3d Regiment U. S. R. C., under command of Capt. Geo. A. Rowley, and with said company volunteered on the 22nd ult. for an expedition of thirty days in Southwest Missouri. The urgency of the demand for our services was said to be extreme. We were led to believe that upon us would mainly rest the duty of repelling a host of invaders from the Arkansas border, and also the administration of cathartics to rebels within our own State. Our campaign was to be short, but very bloody. We were to return home covered with glory, and be toasted and feted *ad infinitum*, or die game before the bristling steel of Price, Jackson & Co. We were to tear down the dirty rag of secession, and rear the glorious standard of our fathers all along our track.

But, Mr. Editor, we have been bamboozled from the start. The major part of our command, under Gen. Sweeny, left us on the 24th ult., and we waited, first for ammunition, then for arms, which we were to transport to Springfield, then for wagons, until we have concluded that all the officials of the circumlocution office are in league to keep us just where we are, in this most attractive young city, Rolla, among the lizards, ticks, and blackjacks, with which the country abounds. Our thirty days are passing away; our captain has left us in search of wagons; our navy bread is very hard; our pork very fat, and beginning to manifest signs of insubordination; our rice is always badly cooked, (we get it twice a week;) our clothes are becoming dingy, and the boys generally, look decidedly hard.

Yet we haven't seen a *secesher,* nor a rattlesnake, since we left home. No wreath of laurel has been twined for our brows, though we have done all the dirty work of camp life for near two weeks. To crown all, our wife hasn't written a line to us since our departure, though we have sent letters to her after each meal of pork and hard bread, and watched every train with the most intense anxiety.

In view of all these grievances, we have *spiled* for a fight, until we are *spilt;* and we want your advice as to the best means of drawing the coils of the *boa constrictor* around our enemy—the pork barrel—and closing the campaign. We think secesh is dead in our State, and want Gov. Jackson's permission to go home and see our babies, and wait till game is more plenty, or hunters more *few.* I trust you will allow no one to see this, but send an early reply to

"Any Other Man."

TO THE VOLUNTEERS.

AN OLD SOLDIER'S ADVICE.

1. Remember that in a campaign, more men die from sickness than by the bullet.

2. Line your blanket with one thickness of brown drilling. This adds but four ounces in weight and doubles the warmth.

3. Buy a small India rubber blanket (only $1,50) to lay on the ground, or to throw over your shoulders when on guard duty during a rain storm. Most of the eastern troops are provided with these. Straw to lie upon is not always to be had.

4. The best military hat in use is the light colored soft felt; the crown being sufficiently high to allow space for air over the brain. You can fasten it up as a continental in fair weather, or turn it down when it is wet or very sunny.

5. When it is very hot, to avoid melting, or sun stroke, wet your pocket handkerchief and put it in the top of your hat, on the crown of the head.

6. To cure and prevent sore feet, rub bar soap on the inside of your stockins.

7. Avoid the use of ardent spirits, which are more injurious in a hot than cold climate.

8. Let your beard grow, so as to protect your throat and lungs.

9. Keep your entire person clean; this prevents fevers and bowel complaints in warm climates. Wash your body each day if possible. Avoid strong coffee and oily meat. General Scott said that the too free use of these (together with neglect in keeping the body clean) cost many a soldier his life in Mexico.

10. A sudden check of perspiration, by chilly or night air often causes fever and death. When thus exposed, do not forget your blanket.

11. Put this in your pocket and read it daily.

Civil War Collection, Missouri Historical Society, St. Louis.

"I FEEL ANY THING BUT LONESOME WHEN I GET AMONG THE ST. LOUIS BOYS"

Joseph Boyce was born in Donegal, Ireland, and joined the First Missouri Infantry Regiment (CSA) after serving in the dashing St. Louis Greys. The twenty-year-old was one of the pro-Southern men captured at Camp Jackson. By the time he mustered out of service, he had risen to the rank of second lieutenant. He later became an insurance agent in St. Louis.

Memphis, Tenn., C. S. A.

July 20th, 1861

Messrs. Keogh & Dowell

S. W. Cor. 11th & Franklin Ave.,

St. Louis, Mo.

Dear Sirs:

I hope this letter will be more interesting than any I have sent yet. I have just returned from a visit to the navy yards and Batteries along the River. . . . We arrived at the navy yard and there met with Pete Keogh a distant relation of Mr. Keogh of your firm. He is *foreman* of the moulding shop they mould canon under his direction. He also intends to make revolvers here after Colt's Pat. They are to furnish him with tools to carry on his good & holy work. They turn out compleet three (brass 6 pounders) Cannons per week mounted and ready for use, also swords three Dozen a day done up in the most improved style, to see the shot they have around the works would astonish you, why they turn out about two ton of shot a day ready for the cartridages. They make from grape up to sixty four pounders all nicely polished for to go into the affections of the Hessians. We then paid a visit to the Batteries on the River Bank, first you come

to the main one commanding the bend in the River it is composed of two 64
Pnds. & two 32 Pnds. that is in the upper part of town, in the lower part they
have five 64 Pndrs. commanding the Arkansas shore in case of attack from land,
in the middle of the Levee they have three Canonades which can throw shot or
shell any way that is necessary so now you can see how well fortified Memphis
is. I must state that those guns are manned by big double-fisted Irishmen sixteen
to each piece. They will shortly be supplied by Flying Artillery to come with us
to Missouri. There will be other men then detailed to work those pieces that
commands the river. . . .

Jim is going to be foremen of the Blacksmith shop, on Monday, he has to
oversee the Iron work on the Gun Carriages he will get about twenty five dollars
per week if you know of any more good hands in St. Louis that is true blue and
if they want work send them down and encourage them to come as they have
not mechanics enough to do the work here. They also want Shoemakers, it
would pay a good Irish Shoemaker to come here for I can tell you the Dutch in
Memphis is very scarce. . . .

[I]n the Memphis Light Dragoons, it has cost every man in the troop $600
to equip himself. They are going to Missouri with us. . . . We have not had
our election yet, the boys say that I must be first Lieut. or they will leave the
Corps. they will not serve under any country Jake in war times as they do not
understand the drill, I suppose I will have to accept as you all know I am a
conservative boy in some respects . . . I got some St. Louis men yesterday to
join and when they heard I was in town and in a company they joined right away
and among [them] was a man named Stevenson he is the Husband of Laura
Honey the actress. . . .

We had a good time last night Capt. Burke, Jim Harrington myself went up to
Jim's room and you should have seen Martin dance. He is an awful *heavy dancer.*
Jim played the Fiddle till 11 o'clock I feel any thing but lonesome when I get
among the St. Louis Boys. I send you enclosed in this letter the particulars of the
fight at "Bulls Run." I know how we'll get the news by the "Lincoln Dynasty."
The southerners welted them right & left. I hope you will soon hear of our Regt.
on Battle and when you do you will know the dutch are whipped. Give my kind
regards to Mrs. Capt. Burke and tell her Martin often speaks of her and he is all
O. K. Also remember me to Mr. Jim Sweeney, Mr. William Taylor & Mr. Tiernan
and all my friends—I remain

Yours Truly

(Signed) Jos. Boyce

Joseph Boyce Collection, Missouri Historical Society, St. Louis.

The Battle of Wilson's Creek and the death of General Lyon. *Johnson, Fry and Company, steel engraving after Alonzo Chappel, 1867. Courtesy of Missouri Historical Society*

"THEY WERE EVER SEEN IN THE THICKEST OF THE FIGHT, CHEERING ON THEIR MEN": THE BATTLE OF WILSON'S CREEK

Colonel Thomas J. Churchill, a veteran of the Mexican War, raised the First Arkansas Mounted Riflemen (Confederate) in Arkansas in early June 1861. The following reports were taken from official military correspondence from both the Union and Confederate sides of the battle. Churchill's report, which may have been written for General Benjamin McCulloch, stressed the bravery of his men in the face of overwhelming odds, though his information was incomplete at the time he wrote. Price and McCullough commanded about twelve thousand men in all. Lyon had about six thousand at nearby Springfield. Colonel Franz Sigel's letter to General John C. Frémont emphasizes his need for reinforcements and explains his retreat to Rolla, a city that was strategically accessible from Springfield, Jefferson City, and St. Louis. The final letter in this series was written by McCullough, who by this time was disheartened by the lack of training and discipline of the Missouri State Guard. He did not mention his misgivings in his report, however.

Camp on Wilson's Creek
Aug. 10th 1861

Gen.

I have the honor to report that about breakfast the enemy opened one of
their batteries upon my camp. Being in an open field and exposed to a raking fire
of grape and shell and not supported by any of our own batteries, I fell back to
the woods and then formed my regiment—I then moved down the road in the
direction of Springfield.

Having reached the hollow, I was met by an Aide of Gen Price asking for a
reinforcement to come to the support of General Slack—I immediately moved
up my regiment to his aid amid a shower of grape and musketry, and took my
position on his left, and ordered my men to commence firing—we disputed the
ground there with the enemy inch by inch for about three or four hours amidst
a most terrific fire from their battery posted on the hill, supposed to be Totten's
and continued volleys of musketry—I there encountered the forces commanded
by General Lyons in person, mostly all regulars with a Regiment of Iowa
troops—The battle raged fiercely, and the firing scarcely ceased for a moment.
The contest seemed doubtful. At times we would drive them up the hill and in
turn they would rally and cause us to fall back. At length we shouted, made a
gallant charge and drove them over the hill.

At this moment the Louisiana regiment with Col. Dockery's flanked them upon
my left made a charge and drove them completely from the field. This was the last
position they abandoned and the last stand they made. In the engagement I had
two horses shot under me. The Adjutant James Hasper was shot down mortally
wounded at his post, with his sword in hand, leading and cheering on the men. The
Sargeant Maj. N. T. Roberts was wound[ed] in the shoulder while leading on the
left. My volunteer Aide A. H. Sevier was wounded in the breast while encouraging
our men to stand by their colors and had to be taken from the field. Capt.
McAlexander was killed advancing on the enemy at the head of his company. At
the same time fell Lieutenants Dawson Chambers and Johnson; Captains Ramsaur
and Porter and Lieutenants Thomas King, Adams, Hardesty, and McIvor severely
wounded. Captains Pearsons and Gibbs and Lieutenants Sadler, Nair and Head
slightly wounded. Major Harper at one time was taken prisoner by the enemy, but
made his escape. Captain Reynolds was thrown from his horse early in the action
and was cut off from his company. The Lieutenant Col. and Major evinced great
bravery in leading their different wings to the charge; and I must say that no men
displayed greater coolness than they did on the field.

Too much praise cannot be bestowed upon the officers of my command
for they were ever seen in the thickest of the fight, cheering on their men, who

always gallantly responded to the call. I lost in the engagement 42 killed and 155 wounded. I have the honor to be, General, very Respectfully, your Obedient Servant

T. J. Churchill
Command First Arkansas
Mounted Riflemen
The Regiment fought on foot

Civil War Collection, Missouri Historical Society, St. Louis.

~

Niangua Crossing, 28 Miles East Of Springfield,
August 12, 1861.

SIR: I respectfully report to you that after a battle fought 10 miles south of Springfield, on Saturday, the 10th, between our forces and the rebel army, and in which General Lyon was killed, I have taken temporarily the command of the Union troops.

Arrived after the battle at Springfield, on the evening of the 10th, it was found necessary to retreat towards Rolla. We are now here with 3,000 men of infantry, 300 cavalry, and thirteen pieces of artillery. The Irish Brigade, about 900 strong, will meet us at Lebanon. The Home Guards amount to about 200 infantry and 500 mounted men, who are more or less valuable. The enemy's forces cannot be less than 20,000 men, of which about one-fourth are infantry, the others cavalry, besides fifteen pieces of artillery.

Once in possession of Springfield, the enemy will be able to raise the southwest of the State against us, add a great number of men to his army, make Springfield a great depot, and continue his operations towards Rolla, and probably also towards the Missouri (Jefferson City). I do not see the probability of making an effective resistance without reinforcement of not less than 5,000 men, infantry, one or two regiments of cavalry, and at least two batteries. To meet the momentous danger we want re-enforcements, and to be prepared against the last reverses which may befall us in this State, I would respectfully propose to you to make, in the shortest time possible, the necessary preparations for two intrenched camps, one at Saint Louis, the key to the Southwest, and another at Jefferson City, or, perhaps better, between the Osage River and Moreau Creek, on the heights of Taos Post Office. At the same time it would be necessary to be master of the river between Jefferson City and Saint Louis, and to arm the two intrenched positions by heavy ordnance.

The Missouri will now become our natural line of defense, with the Osage River in advance, and the two places, Tuscumbia and Linn Creek, as the most important points where *têtes-de-pont* could be constructed. I make these remarks because I am aware of our strength and weakness. Our 4,000 men will be crippled by the discharge of the three-months' men, who cannot be kept longer in our midst because they are anxious to go home, and would be of more damage than use if forced to serve longer.

I therefore respectfully request you to give your kind attention to our little army, and enable us to take up anew the struggle with our enemy.

With the greatest respect, your obedient servant,

F. SIGEL,

Colonel, Commanding.

Major-General FRÉMONT,

Commanding Department of the West.

The War of the Rebellion: A Compilation of the Official Records of the Union and Confederate Armies, ser. 1, vol. 3 (Washington, D.C.: Government Printing Office, 1881), 85.

~

Headquarters Mcculloch's Brigade,

Camp Weightman, near Springfield, Mo., August 12, 1861.

SIR: I have the honor to make the following official report of the battle of the Oak Hills on the 10th instant:

Having taken position about 10 miles from Springfield, I endeavored to gain the necessary information of the strength and position of the enemy stationed in and about the town. The information was very conflicting and unsatisfactory. I, however, made up my mind to attack the enemy in their position, and issued orders on the 9th instant to my force to start at 9 o'clock at night to attack at four different points at daylight. A few days before General Price, in command of the Missouri force, turned over his command to me, and I assumed command of the entire force, comprising my own brigade, the brigade of Arkansas State forces under General Pearce, and General Price's command of Missourians.

My effective force was 5,300 infantry, 15 pieces of artillery, and 6,000 horsemen, armed with flint-lock muskets, rifles, and shot-guns. There were other horsemen with the army who were entirely unarmed, and instead of being a help, were continually in the way. When the time arrived for the night march, it commenced to rain slightly, and fearing, from the want of cartridge boxes, that my ammunition would be ruined, I ordered the movement to be stopped, hoping to move the next morning. Many of my men had but twenty rounds of ammunition, and there was no more to be had.

While still hesitating in the morning the enemy were reported advancing, and I made arrangements to meet him. The attack was made simultaneously at 5.30 a.m. on our right and left flanks, and the enemy had gained the positions they desired. General Lyon attacked us on our left, and General Sigel on our right and rear. From these points batteries opened upon us. My command was soon ready. . . .

A terrible conflict of small-arms took place here. The opposing force was a body of regular United States infantry, commanded by Captains Plummer and Gilbert. Notwithstanding the galling fire poured upon these two regiments, they leaped over the fence, and, gallantly led by their colonels, drove the enemy before them back upon the main body. During this time the Missourians, under General Price, were nobly attempting to sustain themselves in the center, and were hotly engaged on the sides of the height upon which the enemy were posted. Far on the right Sigel had opened his battery upon Churchill's and Greer's regiments, and had gradually made his way to the Springfield road, upon each side of which the army was encamped, and in a prominent position had established his battery. I at once took two companies of the Louisiana regiment which were nearest me, and marched them rapidly from the front and right to the rear, with orders to Colonel Mcintosh to bring up the rest. . . .

Having cleared our right and rear, it was necessary to turn all our attention to the center, under General Lyon, who was pressing upon the Missourians, having driven them back. To this point McIntosh's regiment, under Lieutenant Colonel Embry, and Churchill's regiment on foot, Gratiot's regiment, and McRae's battalion were sent to their aid. A terrible fire of musketry was now kept up along the whole side and top of the hill upon which the enemy were posted. Masses of infantry fell back and again rushed forward. The summit of the hill was covered with the dead and wounded. Both sides were fighting with desperation for the day. Carroll's and Greer's regiments, led gallantly by Captain Bradfute, charged the battery (Totten's), but the whole strength of the enemy were immediately in rear, and a deadly fire was opened upon them.

At this critical moment, when the fortunes of the day seemed to be at the turning point, two regiments of General Pearce's brigade were ordered to march from their position (as reserves) to support the center.

The order was obeyed with alacrity, and General Pearce gallantly marched with his brigade to the rescue. Reid's battery was also ordered to move forward and the Louisiana regiment was again called into action on the left of it. The battle then became general, and probably no two opposing forces ever fought with greater desperation. Inch by inch the enemy gave way, and were driven from their position. Totten's battery fell back. Missourians, Arkansans, Louisianians, and Texans pushed forward. The incessant roll of musketry was deafening, and the balls fell thick as hailstones, but still our gallant Southerners pushed onward, and with one wild yell broke upon the enemy, pushing them back and strewing the ground with their dead. Nothing could withstand the impetuosity of our final charge. The enemy fled, and could not again be rallied, and they were seen at 12 m. fast retreating among the hills in the distance. Thus ended the battle. It lasted six hours and a half. The force of the enemy, between nine and ten thousand, was composed of well-disciplined troops, well armed, and a large part of them belonging to the old Army of the United States. With every advantage on their side they have met with a signal repulse. The loss of the enemy is 800 killed, 1,000 wounded, and 300 prisoners. We captured six pieces of artillery, several hundred stand of small arms, and several of their standards.

Major-General Lyon, chief in command, was killed, and many of their officers high in rank wounded.

Our loss was also severe, and we mourn the death of many a gallant officer and soldier. Our killed amounts to 265, 800 wounded, and 30 missing.

Colonel Weightman fell at the head of his brigade of Missourians while gallantly charging upon the enemy. His place will not easily be filled. Generals Slack and Clark, of Missouri, were severely wounded; General Price slightly. Captain Hinson, of the Louisiana regiment; Captain McAlexander, of Churchill's regiment; Captains Bell and Brown, of Pearce's brigade; Lieutenants Walton and Weaver, all fell while nobly and gallantly doing their duty. . . .

Where all were doing their duty so gallantly, it is almost unfair to discriminate. I must, however, bring to your notice the gallant conduct of the Missouri generals—McBride, Parsons, Clark, and Slack, and their officers. To General Price I am under many obligations for assistance on the battle-field. He was at the head of his force, leading them on, and sustaining them by his gallant bearing. . . . To Colonel Mcintosh, at one time at the head of his regiment and at other times in his capacity of adjutant-general, I cannot bestow too much praise. Wherever the balls flew thickest he was gallantly leading different regiments into action, and his presence gave confidence everywhere.

I have the honor to be, sir, your obedient servant,
BEN. McCULLOCH,
Brigadier-General, Commanding.
Brig. Gen. S. COOPER,
Adjutant-General C. S. Army.

The War of the Rebellion: A Compilation of the Official Records of the Union and Confederate Armies, ser. 1, vol. 3 (Washington, D.C.: Government Printing Office, 1881), 85.

THE RAY CHILDREN WITNESS THE BATTLE OF WILSON'S CREEK

Prosperous farmer John Ray served as postmaster and ran a stagecoach stop from his home in Wilson Township, where he lived with his wife Roxanna and three children as well as a slave woman named Rhoda. His house stood on the Wire (or Telegraph)

Road, a main thoroughfare that led from Jefferson City through Springfield to
Arkansas. The three Ray children had been sent out before dawn on the morning
of August 10, 1861, to take the family's horses to pasture. While they were on this
errand, a stranger rode toward them and shouted, "Children get out of here! They'll
be fighting like hell in less than ten minutes." The children immediately returned
home. Lavinia Ray Bruton, who was six years old in 1861, later recalled the battle
of Wilson's Creek in an interview recorded in 1934.

Mother was greatly alarmed when we came running to tell her what the stranger
had told us, for she knew the Confederate troops were encamped in a valley a
short distance from our farm. . . . She knew of course that there would be a battle
royal if General Lyon moved his troops from Springfield, ten miles away, to meet
the Southerners.

Mother found Father on the front porch. There he was holding the baby, calm
as you please, with Mother trying to convince him that all of us would be killed
if we didn't run to cover. All she could get out of him was, "Roxanna, don't be
alarmed. Some fellow told the children this story to frighten them," and there
he sat throughout the battle that ensued, with bullets striking all about him and
bombs bursting in the yard.

Just as Father was telling Mother not to be alarmed all of us saw what appeared
to be a black line moving in the distance, and as we watched it we recognized it as
an Army of marching men. Mother got all of the children lined up, both white and
black and hustled them together with grown-ups into the cellar, colored Mammy
Rhoda bringing up the rear. The cellar was under the house with an entrance at
back, the outside steps being sheltered within [an] enclosed cellarway. The door
opened out instead of having to be raised. On the hill which was visible from both
the back and front of the house the battle was in progress.

The older boys, anxious to see what was taking place kept trying to steal a
glance by opening the cellar door. Finally one of the men Julius Short, the mail
carrier, became so bold as to open the door, only to have it slammed in his face
from the concussion of a bomb that crashed through our chicken house a short
distance away. Firing had now become so constant and so heavy that none of us
had any desire to peep. We younger children munched biscuits that mother had
snatched from the oven in passing, for this battle had driven us to cover before
breakfast. The battle began at sunrise and continued until early noon.

Father never left his dangerous position on our front porch until the firing
ceased and the family emerged from their retreat. Then he was pressed into service
to guard Confederate prisoners. After a while General Lyon's body was brought
to our home and laid upon a bed in the front room. Doctor Melcher, an army
surgeon and General James S. Rains, of the Confederate army, were present. Mother

was nervous and weakened. I recall General Rains said, "She weeps because the roaring Lyon is dead!"

Wounded Confederate soldiers were brought in and the women were kept busy carrying basins of water and towels. After a while the wounded were taken away in ambulances drawn by horses. The body of General Lyon was wrapped in a counterpane and delivered to the home of Governor Phelps in Springfield, where General Lyon had made his headquarters.

Battle of Wilson's Creek, Western Historical Manuscripts Collection, University of Missouri, Columbia.

GENERAL JOHN C. FRÉMONT DECLARES MARTIAL LAW AND FREES SLAVES

When Major General John C. Frémont issued his proclamation of martial law and emancipation, the situation throughout Missouri had deteriorated to such an extent that neither the military nor civil authorities could control the violence. Frémont had long espoused abolitionist views and, like most Republicans living in Missouri at the time, blamed slaveholders for the violence and unrest in the state.

PROCLAMATION.

Headquarters Western Department,

Saint Louis, August 30, 1861.

Circumstances, in my judgment, of sufficient urgency render it necessary that the commanding general of this department should assume the administrative powers of the State. Its disorganized condition, the helplessness of the civil authority, the total insecurity of life, and the devastation of property by bands of murderers and marauders who infest nearly every county in the State and avail themselves of the public misfortunes and the vicinity of a hostile force to gratify private and neighborhood vengeance, and who find an enemy wherever they find plunder, finally demand the severest measures to repress the daily increasing crimes and outrages which are driving off the inhabitants and ruining the State.

In this condition the public safety and the success of our arms require unity of purpose, without let or hindrance, to the prompt administration of affairs. In order, therefore, to suppress disorder, to maintain as far as now practicable the public peace, and to give security and protection to the persons and property of loyal citizens, I do hereby extend and declare established martial law throughout the State of Missouri.

The lines of the army of occupation in this State are for the present declared to extend from Leavenworth, by way of the posts of Jefferson City, Rolla, and Ironton, to Cape Girardeau, on the Mississippi River.

All persons who shall be taken with arms in their hands within these lines shall be tried by court-martial, and, if found guilty, will be shot.

The property, real and personal, of all persons in the State of Missouri who shall take up arms against the United States, or who shall be directly proven to have taken active part with their enemies in the field, is declared to be confiscated to the public use; and their slaves, if any they have, are hereby declared freemen.

All persons who shall be proven to have destroyed, after the publication of this order, railroad tracks, bridges, or telegraphs, shall suffer the extreme penalty of the law.

All persons engaged in treasonable correspondence, in giving or procuring aid to the enemies of the United States, . . . in disturbing the public tranquillity by creating and circulating false reports or incendiary documents, are in their own interest warned that they are exposing themselves to sudden and severe punishment.

All persons who have been led away from their allegiance are required to return to their homes forthwith. Any such absence, without sufficient cause. will be held to be presumptive evidence against them.

The object of this declaration is to place in the hands of the military authorities the power to give instantaneous effect to existing laws, and to supply such deficiencies as the conditions of war demand. But this is not intended to suspend the ordinary tribunals of the country, where the law will be administered by the civil officers in the usual manner, and with their customary authority, while the same can be peaceably exercised.

The commanding general will labor vigilantly for the public welfare, and in his efforts for their safety hopes to obtain not only the acquiescence, but the active support of the people of the country.

J. C. FRÉMONT,
Major-General Commanding.

The War of the Rebellion: A Compilation of the Official Records of the Union and Confederate Armies, ser. 1, vol. 3 (Washington, D.C.: Government Printing Office, 1881), 466–67.

"WE ARE ENGAGED IN WAR WITH AN ARMY OF DESPERATE ADVENTURERS"

The Zouave Register was published by the American Zouaves, members of the Eighth Missouri Volunteer Infantry Regiment, a primarily Irish unit. Most of these men were deckhands, boatmen, and dockworkers at Cape Girardeau under Colonel Morgan L. Smith, who later rose to the rank of general. The Eighth Missouri soon earned a reputation as one of the toughest fighting units in the trans-Mississippi theater. The regiment fought in the battles of Forts Henry and Donelson as well as at Shiloh, Corinth, and Vicksburg.

THE ZOUAVE REGISTER.
CAPE GIRARDEAU, MO., SEPT. 4, 1861.
VOL. 1, NO. 1.
THE WAR.

We are engaged in war with an army of desperate adventurers, who have, without excuse, save the desire to pillage and destroy, ruthlessly invaded our territory. It is a source of the deepest regret to see so many Missourians sympathizing with, and aiding and abetting the enemy. These Missourians are like men taking the torch from ruffians and applying it to their own dwellings—like men wresting the knife from the assassin to use against the throats of their own kindred. Never since the beginning of human history has there been an invasion so thoroughly barren of justification. In all America there is not that man who can, with the least truth, assert that the Government of the Union ever oppressed him. In Missouri there is not that man in the rebel ranks but who owes more than he could have possibly repaid to that Government, for its protecting care and its blessed encouragements. It is a sad thing to see so many apparently enlightened and christianized men, throwing themselves so energetically into the vortex of civil strife, for the purpose of overthrowing a Government . . . [illegible] . . . This . . . Claib Jackson shamelessly . . . and with an impudence, which would be sublime if it did not stamp him as a monomaniac, or a scoundrel, declares the millions of Missouri to be the subject of a "slave oligarchy," and not of their own chosen Government. The "secret session" last spring would have passed a *secession ordinance* had it been thought safe to trust the people upon it at the ballot box. The CABAL knew the people were unalterably opposed to secession. What was to be done? A military law was passed, and a stupendous terror was organized to coerce the people into the policy and treachery of that basest of all perjurers, Claiborne F. Jackson.

While Union loving people were being driven out by scores and outraged in person and property by secession coercionists, it was all well enough, but if an occasional incident turned the weapons of the oppressor against himself, then all secessiondom cried out in holy horror, and shouted "constitutional rights." Were it not for the Federal Government a system would have been inaugurated here which would have transformed this beautiful State into an Indian dependence whose jungles would have been crowded with fugitive loyalists, whose valleys would have been laid waste by the destroyer, and whose streams would have been crimsoned with patriot blood . . . [the rest is missing].

PRIVATE HENRY VOELKNER COMPLAINS
ABOUT THE ARMY'S LACK OF INFORMATION

Henry Voelkner enlisted in Pfanninghausen's Battery of Flying Artillery in August 1861. He later served as an orderly sergeant in Landgraeber's First Flying Battery, Missouri Artillery, where he rose to the rank of second lieutenant. He participated in operations in southern Missouri and northwestern Arkansas. He resigned his commission in 1862. This letter, written just six months after the onset of warfare in Missouri, describes the devastation that had already overtaken the southern and central part of the state. Warsaw is a town north of Springfield, in central Missouri, close to the Wilson's Creek battlefield.

Springfield, Missouri,
October 31, 1861.

Dear Mother:

It is now 12 midnight and I am taking advantage of a period of watchful waiting to write this letter. We, i.e., the whole army, are fully prepared for a march and every one is waiting with keen ear for two successive cannon shots, which are to be the signal that the enemy is advancing and at the same time the signal for breaking camp. The devil knows whether I will be able to finish this letter or not. About the enemy's number and position we are absolutely in the dark. If our generals are equally ill-informed, it will be a sad story, which I indeed hope is not the case. Wild rumors are being circulated about these conditions, and I will tell you of those in which I place most reliance. I would rather begin where I left off in my last letter.

As I was writing the last letter from Warsaw, I was interrupted by marching orders. We were glad to be able to remain in camp at Warsaw for a while; we had made ourselves quite comfortable in an old chicken house, when after a half a day we received those orders. We crossed the Osage over a bridge, the like of which will scarcely be found anywhere. In Germany they would not have dared let a dog valued at 3 pennies across. Then we made a forced march to Springfield, where we arrived on the afternoon of the 29th. Springfield was occupied by 2,100 secessionists, the rear guard of the army. While we were still 2 days from our destination, 150 men of General Fremont's body guard were wiped out.

Springfield must have been a pretty place, but now presents a sorry sight, as all towns and villages which we passed, through the steady movements of both armies and the alternative occupation of the cities, the houses are largely destroyed or totally forsaken. The stores are plundered and other houses are burned down, etc.

The entire army, the size of which I had no certainty, is now here in Springfield. Two divisions are still en route here. Gen. Siegel is with his division,

forming the advance guard, and has as spies 50 Delaware Indians who most likely
will offer most valuable service. These, or others, will be used for reconnoitering
purposes, in all probability. At any rate, the news reached us that the secessionists
under Gen. Price have stopped rationing about 40 miles from here, and that Price
merged with McCulloch and turned back with the entire merged army, between
forty to sixty thousand men, as it is said, toward Springfield, and that the advance
guard of 6,000 cavalry is already approaching us at about 10 miles.

In consequence thereof, everything is in readiness. According to the orders, 2
o'clock is given as the probable time, at which the two cannon shots will be fired,
as signal that the enemy is really approaching. It is a queer sight, when one looks
over the imposing camp, like a large dead city, where thousands of living are very
much alive, with hearts beating, waiting for the sound of cannons. While I write,
the call of a sentry occasionally diverts my thoughts. No other sounds are heard;
my only thought is that it may start at any moment. Still, I have an idea that
the night will pass quietly and that at daybreak we will either advance or draw
rations, all depending upon the information available. Let things go to the devil,
as they please.

We are still well. We are still eating, with the exception of bread, of which I
had no bite for ten days. We have an abundance of meat and fowl of every kind,
but due to lack of bread and vegetables, my teeth have loosened that I can hardly
chew. I would never have believed that one misses bread so much and that it is so
essential for the subsistence of man. Today, however, we obtained confiscated corn
meal and everyone is anxiously waiting for his bread. I think I could devour nothing
but bread for two days. What kind of bread it will be, only the devil knows,
because we must bake it ourselves without the proper utensils. Really, we can
only prepare pancakes, and if we get them finished, only the gods know. My only
consolation is that I swiped some whiskey yesterday, which we sorely missed. I will
take a sip now before I proceed with writing, for it is darned cold, and we have no
ovens. But something comes to mind, I brought 15 cents along from St. Louis, that
is all I had in my pocket, and I will send you an imprint (10) (5). But I think if we are
still here in the morning I will buy tobacco with it, for I cannot exist without it.

I must quickly come to the end, because the Adjutants are running back and
forth in a most peculiar manner, and besides I am out of paper.

Now farewell, Father, Mother, Brothers and Sisters, and think often of

Your son and brother,

Henry,

As well as Louis, who was kept from writing by the call of duty; he is well and
happy and will write later.

Henry Voelkner Letters, Western Historical Manuscripts Collection, University of Missouri, Columbia.

EDWARD BATES DISCUSSES GUNBOATS AND POLITICS WITH HIS SON

Edward Bates served as attorney general for the United States from 1861 to 1864. His eldest son Barton, whom Governor Hamilton Gamble later appointed a judge of the Missouri Supreme Court, worked with James Eads to construct armor-plated gunboats for the U.S. Navy. James Eads was a self-educated engineer and brilliant inventor who constructed the famous City Class ironclads in about three months. These ironclads were a group of seven gunboats that provided vital support to Union land forces and enabled them to gain control over the Mississippi River. Eads built ironclads, monitors, and warships at Carondelet (at that time a village south of St. Louis) and at Mound City, Illinois. After the war, he designed the famous Eads Bridge that still spans the Mississippi River from St. Louis, Missouri, to East St. Louis, Illinois.

Cheneaux October 10, 1861
Edwd. Bates
Washington City.

My Dear Father,

Certainly I think I can pay Mr. Vaughn & the other bill you mentioned also. I have no money at home it is true, but I am sure that I can get it [from] St. Louis. In fact all the available means are now in Gunboats, but Eads would always be able to pay few hundred for me. . . . Mr. V. goes to "Barnum's" & Eads is boarding at the same house.

I saw Mr. Vaughn in St. Louis directly after the Lexington surrender & offered to him & his brother Isaac a home at my house for their families. I did not think of it that he might be in want of ready money for present expenses or I would have offered to lend him some though I should have had to squeeze it out of as hard pressed a man as Eads. . . .

This is day on which they [gun boats] were by contract, to have been delivered to Cairo. He will be a few days behind time, but every single day counts largely as he is to forfeit $250 per day for each of the seven boats. The Govt has delayed him somewhat by ordering additional work on the boats & by interfering somewhat with his operations. They took a steamboat which he had towing lumber and kept it a while to transfer troops from Cape Girardeau to Cairo . . . & they took a part of the ways at Mound City . . . where he is building 3 hulls, to haul out & repair the bottom of one of the Gun Boats in use about Cairo. The Govt also delayed very unreasonably the stipulated payments. This I don't think delayed the work any, for Eads managed to push it [the construction work] as fast as possible all the time, but it made the cost greater to him & ought to be considered in exacting forfeitures from him.

* * *

Every man, in these times, in debt as I am stands on ticklish ground. . . . If we
could only get the Rebels subdued in Mo, I might have better hopes of devising
better measures of relief. . . .

You may depend upon it that there will be trouble in Mo until the Secesh
are *subjugated* . . . . If Fremont be retained in command here, even *he* must
see the propriety now of sustaining the loyal men of the State, if he ever gets
able, which seems doubtful now, while he allows Sterling Price (& the drink)
to out-general him, but I yet hope that he will be recalled & (as Frank Blair
phrases it) an *able* man put in his place, & any such a man would necessarily cooperate with the State authorities in putting down rebellion. Did you ever hear
of such a superb jackass as "John C. & Jessie Benton Fremont Major-General
commanding". And poor Missouri has to suffer for their folly & crime. Numbers
of fugitives from South of the Missouri have passed through this county. The
men generally express a determination to go back & get *revenge* & some of
them express a desire to get their first shot at Fremont & others denounce the
President bitterly for leaving them unprotected, when they were willing to do
their full share of the fighting if it could only be done with some hope that they
were not thereby bringing destruction on their families.

If a reasoning & reasonable man had been in command here since the first
of last July with half the means Fremont has had, there would not have been a
rebel company in the State and Gov Gamble would have had 30 or 40 000 men
in the field ready & able to keep the rebels in order. As it is, not only is Missouri
scourged to the bones, but ulterior operations are postponed indefinitely. . . .

Your Son
Barton Bates

Bates Family Papers, Missouri Historical Society, St. Louis.

A SENATE IN EXILE

*Claiborne Jackson's pro-Southern rival government removed to Neosho, Missouri,
in October 1861 and, as the following excerpt from their senate journal indicates,
passed military and defensive legislation. Miles Vernon, the illiterate president of
the senate, had fought with Andrew Jackson at the Battle of New Orleans.*

JOURNAL OF THE SENATE OF THE STATE OF MISSOURI

Begun and Held at the Town of Neosho, Newton County, Missouri on the
twenty-first day of October, Eighteen hundred and sixty-one in pursuance of the
Proclamation of the Governor issued on the twenty-sixth day of September last, it
being the third and special session of the twenty-first General Assembly . . . .

Tuesday Morning, November 5th, 1861

The Senate was pursuant to adjournment. Message from the House of Representatives by Mr. Murray, Chief Clerk:

. . .

"Mr. President:

The Speaker of the House has signed Senate enrolled bill entitled 'An Act to provide for the defense of the State of Missouri.' Senate joint resolution of thanks to officers and troops engaged in the several battles in Missouri, has been amended in the House and passed. Senate joint resolution in reference to signing the rolls of the Act of Separation and Annexation has been indefinitely postponed in the House.

. . .

Message from the House of Representatives by Mr. Murray, Chief Clerk.

"Mr. President:

The following bill has passed the House of Representatives: 'An Act to amend an Act entitled An Act to provide for the organization, government, and support of the military forces of the State of Missouri, approved May 14th, 1861.'" The further consideration of the bill under consideration was passed over.

On motion of Mr. Lyday two thousand copies of the act of the Confederate Congress entitled "An Act to perpetuate testimony in case of slaves abducted or harbored by the enemy and of other property, seized, waisted [sic] or destroyed by them" was ordered to be printed for the use of The Senate, the same to be paid for out of the contingent fund of The Senate.

The further consideration of the military bill was resumed. Mr. Goodlett moved to amend Section 2 of the bill by striking out the first clause of said section down to the word "army," in second line, and inserting in lieu thereof, "Any commissioned officer who shall be found drunk on the battlefield, in the hospital, or camp or within three miles of said camp or hospital shall be cashiered." Which was read a first time and second time and withdrawn.

Mr. Goodlett moved to amend by way of new section as follows: "Section ???—The Governor, Major General, and the several Brigadier Generals of the Missouri State Guard shall have the power to remove any aid or other officer now in office or, hereafter, to be appointed by them respectively." Which was read a first and second time and agreed to. Mr. Peyton moved to amend by additional sections as follows:

" . . . The Governor shall have the power and is hereby authorized to appoint one chief of ordinance with the rank of colonel and two assistants; the first with the rank of major and the other with the rank of captain; one inspector general with the rank of colonel; One judge advocate general with the rank of colonel, and one assistant with the rank of lieutenant colonel; one commissary general with the rank of colonel, and five assistants the first named with the rank of Colonel, one assistant Surgeon General with the rank of major and the others each with the rank of captains; one chaplain with the rank of major, one surgeon general with the rank of colonel, one assistant surgeon general with the rank of major, one paymaster general with the rank of colonel, one military storekeeper with the rank of captain (who shall take charge under the direction of the Quartermaster General) of the clothing beausener[?], and the Governor shall further have the power, and it is hereby made his duty, to displace whenever in his opinion it becomes necessary any one of the officers who shall be appointed under this section, which was read a first and second time and agreed to.

Mr. Peyton moved to amend by way of additional section—

Section ???—The Brigadier Generals of each division shall have the power, and they are each hereby authorized to appoint for their respective divisions one chief of ordinance with the rank of lieutenant colonel and one assistant with the rank of captain. Which was read a first and second time and agreed to.

Mr. Peyton moved to amend by striking out of Section 2, all after the word captain in the 14th line, which was read a first and second time and agreed to.

The President laid before the Senate the following communication from the Governor.

Cassville, Nov. 5, 1861
To the President of the Senate

"Sir:

I have this day approved and signed Senate bill entitled "An Act to provide for the defense of the State of Missouri."

Respectfully
CF Jackson"

On motion of Mr. Thompson, the Senate adjourned until 2 o'clock p.m.

Evening Session [Tuesday, November 5, 1861]

The Senate met pursuant to adjournment.

. . .

Mr. Hardin moved to amend by way of a new section as follows: "Sec——The Board of Commissioners authorized by law to issue defense bonds are hereby authorized to allow to the owner or, if he be dead, to his representatives, of any horse lost in battle in the service of the state by any incident thereof the value of such horse, and shall pay such value in defense bonds. They shall keep a record of their proceedings, noting the name of the owner, the date and amount of the allowance and a minute abstract of the Bond's delivered in payment. No allowance shall be made except upon satisfactory evidence of the correctness of the claim and all applications for allowance shall be supported by the affidavit of the owner if living and if dead of his representatives, and all evidence shall be by affidavit and authenticated by some judicial officer or Justice of the Peace to the effect that the officiant is personally known to him to be entitled credit. The application and all affidavits shall be preserved by the Commissioners. No oral testimony shall be received by the Commissioners, nor shall the application of the Owner or his representation be taken to be evidence"

Which was read a first and second time and agreed to.

Mr. Hardin moved to amend the Bill by adding a new section:

Section———The Major General shall appoint a 'Medical Board' of the persons of habitual sobriety and learned in the profession of surgery and medicine. Whose duty it shall be to grant a certificate of qualification to any person deserving an appointment in the army as surgeon or assistant surgeon. But, no person shall be granted a certificate who shall not have successfully stood a rigid examination before said board and have the same requisite qualifications in all respects as a member of said board is required by this section. No person shall be appointed a surgeon or assistant surgeon in the army who has not obtained such a certificate from said medical board. The Major General shall have power to remove at discretion any member of said board. Each member of said Board shall have the rank and enrollment of a Colonel in the army and when not engaged in his duties as a member of the Board, he shall discharge as any other duty pertaining to his profession that may be assigned him by the Major General. One surgeon and one assistant shall be appointed to a regiment of three hundred men and upward, but he shall have no assistant when the regiment contains a less number of men than three hundred. Should any regiment be reduced to a less number of men than three hundred then the office of assistant Surgeon for that regiment shall be vacated nor shall it again be filled till the regiment shall be renewed to the number of three hundred men.

Which was read a first and a second time and agreed to.

The Bill was then read a third time and passed as amended.

On motion of Mr. Hardin it was resolved that the Major General be requested to furnish The Senate a copy of the Joint Resolution to the people of the State of Missouri and the Major General of the Missouri army.

. . .

On motion of Mr. Lyday the Senate went into second session. After sometime spent therein, the second session was dissolved and on motion of Mr. Thompson, the senate adjourned until tomorrow morning at 9 o'clock. . . .

November 7, 1861

On motion of Mr. Goodlett the Senate adjourned.

John T. Crisp

Secy

Miles Vernon
president protem

Senate Journal, Wilson's Creek National Park Service Battle Field Archives.

REBEL SOLDIERS DECLARE,
"OUR CAUSE IS AS SURE TO TRIUMPH AS GOD REIGNS IN HEAVEN"

The Missouri Army Argus *was edited by Joseph W. Tucker and published by William F. Wisely, two Missouri rebels who fought with the State Guard under General Sterling Price before joining the Confederate army in 1862. Publication of the* Argus *probably ceased with the fourth issue.*

THE MISSOURI ARMY ARGUS.

CAMP NEAR OSEOLO, MISSOURI, SATURDAY, NOVEMBER 30, 1861

VOL. I, NO. 4

OUR HOPES.

We know but one principle of action—but one rule of moral conduct, of universal application, and that is, to speak the truth and pursue the right, if the heavens be rent asunder. We, therefore, declare the truth as we understand it, when we affirm our conviction, that our cause is as sure to triumph as God reigns in Heaven, if we are true to ourselves and plumb the track of duty. If we should prove unworthy Agents, others will be raised up to do our work—theirs the glory—ours the shame.

What has the Federal Government accomplished after a year of effort to crush the rebels? Their hireling bands have been met at every point and defeated with slaughter. The Confederate Government has maintained itself with dignity and honor; and has shown its great ability to take rank among the nations of the earth. The hand of Providence can be discerned in many events affecting our safety and our interest. The destiny of Missouri is now and forever the destiny of the Confederate States, and our future, contemplated in the light of history and by the aids of just induction, is a bright and glorious future. Let no man despond—let no man leave his post—let no man cast away the wreath of imperishable renown that will reward the brave and true—let no man shrink from duty, labor, hardship, or sacrifice—let men think less of PROMOTION and POSITION, and more of country and patriotic devotion. Let our best men go into the ranks if necessary; and set the example of order and obedience to authority. Let us be MEN—high-minded men, who are capable of the noblest devotion to principle, and the sublimest self-sacrifice. Let no man be afraid his merits will not be known. You can no more obscure merit than you can extinguish the rays of the sun. Our hopes were never brighter, stronger or more inspiring.

Missouri Army Argus, November 30, 1861, Civil War Collection, Missouri Historical Society, St. Louis.

DAVID MONLUX TELLS HIS FATHER,
"WE HAVE A FIRST RATE TIME IN OUR TENT"

David Monlux, of Farmington, Illinois, served in Company G of the Eighth Missouri Volunteer Infantry Regiment (USA). The Eighth Missouri Infantry was organized at the St. Louis Arsenal, then served at Cape Girardeau, Missouri; Paducah, Kentucky; Forts Henry and Donelson in Tennessee; and Pittsburgh Landing, Corinth, and the siege of Vicksburg in Mississippi.

Paducah ky Dec the 23 1861

Well pop i got your letter about ten minutes ago and i was glad to hear that you was all well i am well and harty i weigh one hundred and fifty pounds and i Can do as much duty as any other man in the Company. we are at paducah ky yet. the weather is kinder somewhat Cold here now we have got good Clothes our overcoats are first rate they are as good as a blanket at night we Can take and button them together and spread them.

Frank dog-on-it sit over i haint got room to write well i will go on with it story pap I will tell you the different kinds of medicine he gives for diseases well for headaches he gives blue pill for the shite blue pill for the sore eyes blue pill for the measles blue pill to kill body lice we get the pills and feed it to them in the little bite he gives blue pill to every kind of Disease you Could think of

Well dad it rained all day yesterday and last night it froze about a half an inch that is as hard as its been froze this winter pap I have not got only one single blanket and I keep [w]arm as a fried flitter in a chicken roost well dad I was out on picket the other night and there was [an] old darkey lived there and he give me a Chicken and I went to puling the feathers off of it without skalding it well I got them pretty near all off but then around by its legs and I took and burnt them off and I took and gutted it and cooked it in a Coffee pot I made some broth with it too and so i did it was good

Too so it was well dad the nigger that gave it to me was in a too story building and he jumped out and run away and they had another one tied up in a room and he got leave and got away I dont mean the souldiers but Citizens I was glad to hear that they wanted me to take them in some morning as Contraband but I would not do it it was not my place to do it

Well pap I havent shaved but once since I left home my beard is getting quite long I would like to be at home at Christmas we have not got our money yet we

will get our months pay when we get payed off again then I am going to send
some of it home frank is making some tea for him and I I have been on fatigue
to day I got on the first relief I am excused from dress parade to night our first
lieutenant was married last night he treated the boys to day to penny grab well
pap there is about ten ton of powder in one magazine in fort anderson it is a nice
place I expect when I Come home I Can ride home on the Cars right in town
things are looking verry dull now dad there is some of the prettyest girls in this
place that I ever saw well pap you said you Could not think of any think of any
thing to write. you Could but you think that I know every thing that is going on
but it is not so. I cannot think of any ting more to write than you Can there is no
fighting on here we have a first rate time in our tent it is warm we are going to
Cook in it after pay day. I am going to make a Duch oven in it to bake bread in I
can make as good biscuit as an body can wait untill I get home and I will show
you some of my Cooking pap I can keep warmer here with one blanket here
than I could with six up there you would not believe the difference here. I have
not took a blanket on picket but once this winter and was not cold neather well
pap I guess I will have to quit for this time I am getting [t]ired of writing tell me
how they are getting along with the railroad I gues we are good for three years if
not longer I hope not though I dont like it any to well I tell you I would rather do
it than farm though well pap good bye write soon

David Monlux to Jonathan Monlux

Well mary I would like to see you and bub sis you must help mother all you
can bub if you are a good boy and help mother and pap and learn to read well I
will send you a dollar and if you dont I will give it to sis . . .

Company G 8th regiment
Missouri volunteers

David Monlux Letters, Civil War Collection, Missouri Historical Society, St. Louis.

A JESUIT CHAPLAIN SUFFERS ALONGSIDE HIS SOLDIERS

*Charles Joseph Truyens, S.J., a Jesuit priest who had established missions among
the Miami Indians in Kansas in the 1830s and 1840s, served as a chaplain for Union
troops in Missouri and Kentucky. He later observed that he had lost his health
during the time he marched alongside his spiritual charges. An anonymous note in
his file, written on the occasion of his death on December 19, 1867, indicates that
he had been particularly interested in the plight of free black people in Kentucky,
instructing them and saying Mass for them every week.*

January 11st, 1862

Revd. & Dear Father,

I believe this is the last letter which I will be able to write for some time. We have left Columbia and are pursuing our route towards Summerset. We are now 38 miles from that place. It will take us at least four days to reach it, as the roads are very bad and places us under the necessity of walking very slowly. The 10th Indiana is camped by the side of us. Thus far I have been obliged to do my journeys on foot in the rear of the regiment but to morrow I will have a horse as the Colonel just told me now. You can easily suppose that this life is very hard on me, I have suffered already very much from hunger and can hardly recollect myself for a few minutes. I try to make my meditations and examens, but I hope Alm. God will be satisfied with my endeavours. I feel also grieved not to be able to approach the Sacraments, there are no Catholics Chaplains here. When I will be able to say mass I do not know. I requested Mr. Merrimee to ask for the vestments etc. etc. to say mass, but if you have not as yet sent them do not send them, because I believe he will not be able to forward them to me. Please give my best respects to all

Your devoted B [brother] in Christ
C. Truyens, SJ

Please communicate the contents of this letter to Revd Fr Provincial.

Please tell F. Levisse to let Mrs. Moore know that George has received her letter. All the Bardstown boys are doing well.

Midwest Jesuit Archives, St. Louis, Missouri.

A CONFEDERATE SOLDIER AT THE SIEGE OF VICKSBURG

John T. Appler fought in the Vicksburg campaign with Company H of the First Missouri Infantry Regiment (CSA)—the same regiment as Albert O. Allen (see his letter dated December 3, 1863). Shortly after making the last entry in his diary, Appler fell seriously ill with typhoid fever. The widow of his commanding officer took him home to St. Louis, where he recovered. His jacket and trousers, of butternut-dyed handwoven woolen cloth, are still in the collection of the Missouri Historical Society. Appler wore this uniform at veterans' events over the next six decades. Both Appler and his friend Charles Mills had been wounded in a charge at Corinth, Mississippi, and each had believed the other dead; but they met again at a reunion in St. Louis in 1916 when Appler was 74 and Mills 77. Appler later recalled that the three hundred Confederate veterans present wept.

April 1863

Thursday 16th. Clear—Orders to march at 8 o'clock, to go back to camps on the other side of the river, came 2 miles down the river, got on Steamer Charm & came to Grand Gulf, good news in the papers, our mail carrier from Mo. Arrived to-day.

Clear Friday 17th. All is bustle & confusion to-day gunboat fight at V-g [Vicksburg], last night 5 passed the batteries there, all the troops withdrawn from the other side of the river, battle at [Charleston,] our forces victorious, 1 gun-boat sunk.

Clear Saturday 18th. All quiet to-day, nothing seen of the gunboat yet, no news.

Cloudy & rain Sunday 19th. Hard storm last night, heavy rains, firing up the river to-day, gunboats prowling around, no news to-day, on guard.

Clear Monday 20th. To-day pay day, orders to march to the breastworks, gunboats coming down.

Tuesday 21st. To-day hard rain storms, nothing from the gunboats.

Rain Wednesday 22nd. To-day gunboats came in sight, our batteries opened on them, drove them back, no news.

Clear Thursday 23rd. Last night 1 gunboat and five transports passed V-g, 3 sunk, no news.

Clear Friday & Saturday, 24th & 25th. No news of importance gunboats occasionally shell our batteries, on guard to-day 25th.

Cloudy Sunday 26th. No news of importance, the gunboats still in fight.

Rain 27th & 28th. No news to-day. Col. Cockerell takes command of the Brig. 27th, no news to-day, 28th.

Clear Wednesday 29th This morning at 8 O'clock feds attacked this place [Grand Gulf] with their gunboats, fought 7 hours, our loss 4 killed, 25 wounded, feds loss not known, 1 gunboat disabled.

Cloudy Thursday 30th. Last night gunboats attacked our batteries again, no damage done, gunboats and transports passed landing, troops below on the river, orders to cook 3 days rations at 2 o'clock & marked at 9 o'clock.

Clear Friday May 1st. Federals attacked our forces at or near Port Gibson, our forces fell back across bayou La-pier & burnt the bridges, our loss slight, Gen. Tracy killed.

Cloudy Saturday 2nd. Last night I throwed up breastworks, to-day had a skirmish with the ffeds, 2 horses killed, feds took possession of Port Gibson at 8 o'clock.

Clear Sunday 3rd. Last night evacuated our position, this morning had a skirmish with the feds, our Co. skirmishers fell back acros big Black river & destroyed the bridge, bivouacked for the night.

Clear Monday 4th. To-day marched at 7 o'clock, marched all day, bivouacked for the night, on clear Creek.

Cloudy Tuesday 5th. Stayed on clear Creek all day, ordered to cook rations at dark, & move in the morning at day-light, big battle in Virginia [Chancellorsville, April 30-May 4, 1863.]

Cloudy Wednesday 6th. Did not move to-day, sent away all extra baggage, victory in Virginia confirmed, 5000 prisoners taken, victory in Alabama, Forrest took 1600 prisoners. [Battle of Day's Gap, April 30, 1863.]

Clear Thursday 7th. To-day our Regt. was armed with Enfield Rifles, another victory in Via., federal army routed no move yet, 400 prisoners arrived from St. Louis Missouri, Winn one of them. Nat Kunkle arrived from Jackson.

Clear Friday 8th. To-day all is quiet, no move yet, no news of importance, papers confirm the victory in Via., went on guard this evening, regt. orderly.

Clear Saturday 9th. All quiet along the lines, working on breastworks to-day, papers still contain good news, to-day the news of Gen. Van Dorn's & Capt. King's assassination reached us, it happened in Tenn. by parties unknown.

Clear Sunday 10th. To-day Co. went on picket, skirmish with gunboats at Warrenton, Van Dorn's and Capt. King's death confirmed.

Clear Monday 11th. To-day all quiet, the sad news of Stonewall's death reached us, news of Kirby Smith defeating Banks in La.

Clear Tuesday 12th. To-day ordered to breastworks, made forts for artillery with cotton, all of the regt. throwed up breastworks, a fight expected, skirmish to-day.

Clear Wednesday 13th. Marched out of the ditches at 2 o'clock last night, came 7 miles & formed line of battle, our Co. as skirmishers made a reconnoiter & returned to-night & took our former position.

Rainy Thursday 14th. To-day returned to the regt., no fighting yet, all quiet in front, ordered to cook two days rations.

Cloudy Friday 15th. To-day orders to march at 2 o'clock marched till 9 and bivouacked for the night in line of battle, seen Gen. Pemberton & Reynolds today, feds captured Jackson Miss. On the 12th.

Clear Saturday 16th To-day hard fought battle, our forces retreated, myself, Albert & Lambert wounded, myself dangerously & all three prisoners, laid on battle-field all night.

Clear Sunday 17th. Moved to hospital at 12 o'clock today all of the wounded doing well, Lt. Dobyns killed, all the Co. F officers wounded.

Clear Sunday 24th. One week has passed and no news from our army at V-g yet, Thursday hard rain, all the wounded got wet, I was moved to Clinton Hospital that day Saturday moved to Jackson Hospital, lots of good news to-day.

Clear Sunday 31st. Another week passed and wound not any better, rain during the week, no news from V-g, Saturday moved to another Hospital, Sisters of Charity.

Clear Sunday [June] 7th. No news from V-g yet, good news from Port Hudson, feds badly whipped, my wound doing very well.

Clear Sunday 14th. Nothing of importance has transpired during the week, Bowman House burnt Monday night, set on fire, my wound is doing very well, all the wounded doing well.

Sunday 21st. All is quiet, no news from V-g. good news from Port Hudson, feds repulsed and left with great slaughter, I am improving fast with my wound, all doing well.

Clear Sunday July 5th. Last week was one of many important events. Gen. Taylor's victories in Louisiana are all confirmed, To-day sad news has reached us to the effect of the fall of the noble Vicksburg, the garrison all taken, and paroled, Gen. Johnston's forces fell back to this place (at Jackson) wounded doing well.

Clear Sunday July 12th. To-day is a day of dread to all, the feds are daily throwing shells in the city, doing but little damage, they commenced on Wednesday and have been at it ever since, to-day they shelled the city doing a little damage. The Hospitals were all moved, seven shells took effect in the one I was in, I was sent to Meridian & from there to Lauderdale Springs, wound is doing well.

Sunday 19th. This week has been one of great importance about Jackson, Johnson evacuated on Friday night, & fell back to Brandon 12 miles from Jackson, the V-g prisoners arrived at Brandon on Wednesday.

Cloudy & rain Sunday 26th. To-day is another blustery day rained and hard storms every day last week, lightening struck near Dr. Green's H. Q. No news of importance during the week, Vicksburg prisoners in the service again.

Clear Sunday Aug. 2nd '63. All is quiet and no news of fighting, no news from any quarter, it is rumored that Gen. Pemberton was shot by a soldier in Alabama, my wound doing well. . . .

Aug. 16th All is quiet, I left Lauderdale Springs Tuesday eve arrived at Mobile Wednesday morning, went to Soldier's Rest Hos. Seen several of the boys at this place.

Rain all week Sunday Aug. 23rd. This week has been one of great importance, all is anxious to hear definitely from Fort Sumpter, the south side of the fort in ruins.

John T. Appler diary, "Confederate Soldier, 1862–1863," Civil War Collection, Missouri Historical Society, St. Louis.

SERGEANT ALBERT ALLEN WANTS TO EMIGRATE TO MEXICO TO GET AWAY FROM GERMANS

Albert Otis Allen was an ordinance sergeant with the First Missouri Infantry, CSA, commanded by Colonel John S. Bowen. The First Missouri Infantry fought at Shiloh, Vicksburg, and Corinth. The quotation in this letter comes from William Shakespeare's Julius Caesar, *and the reference to the popular song "Joe Bowers" is an ironic comment on women's infidelity.*

Camp Near Meridian, Miss.
Dec. 3, 1863

Dear Jap [Pinnell]:

Your kind letter of the 28th was received today and I hasten to reply. I can give
no reason why my letters do not reach you promptly; I write you regularly twice
a week.

I agree with you that we will emmigrate to some of the cotton states when
the war is over and let the Northern men of Southern proclivities have Missouri.
There is no doubt that the Federal rule in that state has completely altered the
complexion of its politics. The United States government has been very active
in encouraging emigration from the loyal states to Missouri, and they now
offer inducement to foreigners to settle up the border states in place of those
misguided persons who have taken up arms and resisted the authority of the
United States government. I am the lucky owner of a bald-hill in Missouri and if
a Dutchman locates on it, if I live, he will wish himself at home on the Rhine, for
I shall certainly dispute his possession. Imagine a raw Dutchman who can't speak
our language teaching me the principles of Republican government!

It is my opinion that you are right in your conjecture that Mr. Lincoln will
"hold over" until the rebellion is crushed, before he vacates his place of military
dictator. He may allow an election to be held, he being a candidate himself, on
the Unconditional Union Ticket, and anyone that opposes him will be a traitor
and be punished accordingly by banishment or imprisonment.

I did not cry nor feel bad over the news that my old sweetheart was about to
be married and will claim what you were so kind as to guarantee. I am afraid
your friendship for me makes you overrate my personal beauty and you will
find it an easier undertaking to offer the guarantee than to make it good. Our
national song, "Joe Bowers," was written for the present time. Joe's experience
is that of many a bold soldier boy from our old state. You may put me down for
a young widow when the war is over. I will be 21 years old the 12th day of this
month; so you must select a very young widow.

The news from General [Braxton] Bragg at this time is very discouraging.
[Major-General Carter L.] Stephenson's division has made another inglorious
run, lost us a victory, and covered our arms with shame. It is reported in camp
that the Federals put to death all the Vicksburg soldiers captured in Tennessee at
the late battle [at Chattanooga] for violation of parole. I don't think it was done
by any order of any Federal general (if at all). It might have been done by the
men believing the tale circulated in the northern newspapers, that the Vicksburg
garrison took up arm without being exchanged.

A great deal depends on the result of the battles between Bragg and Grant. If Grant succeeds in cutting us off from the Department of Virginia, we will have to resort to a guerilla warfare in this department and when it comes to that, may God have mercy on the women and children for the Federals will not. I joined the rebellion cool and deliberate with the determination to see the South free from Yankee dominion, and I will not quit it until our independence is secured or seal my faith with blood.

"Live or die, sink or swim, survive or perish," I am with the Confederate States. I was with her in prosperity and will be with her at her death, if she dies. Our prospect is gloomy: but with an eye of faith I believe I am enabled to see the clouds begin to break. The darkest hour is just before daybreak.

> "There is a tide in the affairs of men
> Which, taken at the flood leads on to fortune;
> Omitted, all the usage of their life
> Is bound in shallows and in miseries.
> On such a full sea are we now afloat
> And we must take the current when it serves
> Or lose our ventures."

As much as I dislike fighting, if I was under General Bragg I think I could go into battle with a will. I have every confidence in General Bragg's whipping Grant in the decisive battle soon to be fought.

Our brigade is in fine spirits. Since we left Vicksburg we have been flattered so much that the boys think themselves invincible and are anxious to show their colors on the battlefield. We are very well clothed and fed, as well as any part of the Confederate army. I don't hear anyone express a desire to go to the trans-Mississippi department for the news form there is anything but encouraging.

William Phillips left here yesterday for Bellville (Ala). I don't know whether he will ever find you. I requested him to go by Selma [Alabama] and see Captain Kinney in your behalf.

Charlie Barxell is well again and will write you in a few days. You must write to Charlie.

I am glad to see that you are taking pains to write more plainly, It is true that but few great men write plainly, but you know there are many men who are not great who write badly. I think writing a good handwriting is a much more valuable accomplishment than dancing.

The company send their regards to you. Write me immediately on receipt of this.

Your friend truly,

[Albert O.] Allen

Missouri Collection, Western Historical Manuscripts, University of Missouri, Columbia.

FIVE

~

Civilians Cope with War

*T*HROUGHOUT 1861 AND 1862, Union army commanders struggled with two urgent problems: how to eliminate outrages committed by guerrilla bands and how to drive regular Confederate forces out of the state. Groups of guerrilla fighters, both pro-Southern bushwhackers and pro-Union jayhawkers, were targeting enemy soldiers and civilians alike. The laws of warfare at the time did not recognize or protect combatants who were not in uniform. Captured Confederate soldiers were treated as prisoners of war, but guerrilla fighters (armed men in civilian clothing) had no such standing and were considered spies or criminals. Complicating matters further, "partisan rangers," as Confederate guerrillas were euphemistically called, sometimes did attach themselves loosely to the Confederate army or to the Missouri State Guard. Bill Anderson, for example, assumed the rank of captain in the State Guard because General Sterling Price briefly used his services in 1863.

All over the state, farm families suffered harassment and robberies. Conditions were especially volatile along the Kansas border. Lingering bitterness over the Kansas troubles of the mid-1850s, marauding gangs of horse thieves, and attacks by Confederate and Union sympathizers wreaked havoc in the area. Kansas jayhawkers like Jim Lane and "Doc" Jennison ranged across the border and through the northwestern counties along the Missouri River, justifying their raids on settlers by characterizing their victims as Confederate sympathizers. Jennison, for example, plundered Osceola and Morristown in 1861, stealing horses and livestock, burning buildings, and terrorizing women and children.

These raids by jayhawkers and bushwhackers caused endless problems for Union commanders who were attempting to maintain order in the western part of the state. Missouri civilians were caught up in this process of pacification, in part because federal commanders believed that local residents were not doing enough to rein in the guerrillas. In late July 1861, Major General John Pope, who had been assigned to the northern counties of Missouri, found the "entire population in a state of excitement and apprehension." The area was rife with secessionist sentiment, as marauding bands destroyed bridges and railroad tracks and attacked pro-Union residents.[1] Like most Union commanders in the border states,

Pope blamed the local citizens for sustaining guerrilla warfare, and his efforts to reestablish order further alienated northern Missourians. He held the local committees of public safety responsible for maintaining the peace and called on men to serve in militia units and put down guerrilla violence. Refusal to do so would bring an occupying force of federal soldiers into their counties.[2]

Such incidents exacerbated the border violence, inspiring ever greater atrocities in retaliation. Major General Henry Halleck told General John C. Frémont in September 1861 that the only way to prevent Claiborne Jackson from taking St. Louis was to remove Jim Lane from the Kansas border. "A few more such raids," Halleck explained, would render Missouri as "unanimous against us as is Eastern Virginia."[3] He might have been exaggerating about the threat to St. Louis, but he was correct in claiming that jayhawkers alienated otherwise loyal citizens. By late 1862, Provisional Governor Hamilton Gamble had earned the respect and cooperation of military leaders through his moderation. He determined to use the Missouri militia to keep the peace internally, releasing men badly needed in other theaters of the war. Yet political opponents continued to blame Gamble for the violence along the Kansas border.[4]

Missouri families suffered depredations by both paramilitary forces and federal soldiers. Often, it simply did not matter where their allegiances lay.[5] Internal divisions, already troublesome before the war, erupted into bitter enmities by the end of the first year of the conflict. Old friendships and even family ties were destroyed by mutual accusations, personal assaults, or by neighbors' informing on one another. That situation was particularly difficult to resolve in southwestern Missouri, a wooded, mountainous region that concealed guerrillas and proved nearly impossible for the U.S. Army to patrol. Civilians in the area wanted to be left alone and had little love for federal soldiers. Union soldiers were frustrated in their attempts to bring the murderous raids to an end and received little cooperation from the people they were supposed to protect.[6]

Official military policy against guerrillas only exacerbated the suffering of many civilians. When Halleck decreed that disloyal Missourians would be forced to pay $5,000 for each Union soldier or pro-Union resident killed as a result of guerrilla violence, many innocent people lost their property to unscrupulous informants. Orders that targeted civilians usually caused more strife than they resolved. Moreover, proclamations of martial law had rendered personal security an issue, since private citizens (including women) could be arrested, detained, and even banished for seditious speech. Indeed, the situation was particularly frightening for women. Many who had been left at home without their husbands or fathers had to take up the burdens of running farms or businesses and protecting their homes. Those whose men were serving in the Confederate army often experienced difficulties communicating with their loved ones, since any letters intercepted by federal forces could be construed as colluding with the enemy. The penalties for such activities were detention or banishment.[7]

The only way to avoid imprisonment under these circumstances was to sign a loyalty oath, and some women refused even to consider such an act. By the close of 1861, test oaths (swearing loyalty to the Missouri and U.S. constitutions) were required of all attorneys, jurors, teachers, city officials, and railroad officers—indeed, all prominent citizens in the state. When the Missouri State Convention postponed elections until August 1862 and established a test oath for voters, protests broke out throughout the state.[8] Anyone unwilling to sign the oath could be removed from office, and the provisional government could fill the vacant offices with reliable men. Around the same time, Gamble began to implement a policy of amnesty for secessionists who agreed to lay down arms and swear loyalty to the United States. Because Gamble and Halleck always enjoyed a close working relationship, this policy eased at least some of the tensions in the state.

Once the initial anger over the Camp Jackson affair had died down, Unionism gradually came to the fore again in the city of St. Louis. In other parts of the state, including the western border, the northern counties, and the southeastern bootheel, the citizens remained divided. The line between military and civilian was not always clear; women tried to aid the war effort by smuggling medicines and information; some men turned their faces from violence, either refusing or simply fearing to speak out. Others (so-called mossbacks) fled to the woods to avoid conscription; and still others, disgusted by attacks on civilians, decided that the time had come to volunteer to protect their home state. In August 1862, one of the many Union clubs that had sprung up around St. Louis issued a call for volunteers to join the Missouri State militia, declaring that anyone who did not come forward had to be considered disloyal. Such bitter words created long-lasting enmities, as the battles raged across Missouri's soil and families were caught in an increasing spiral of violence.

Prominent women in St. Louis led fund-raising and charitable efforts. Like patriotic women in other northern cities, they joined sewing and knitting circles and held fund-raising fairs. By the end of the war, the Western Sanitary Commission had raised more than half a million dollars in one of its St. Louis fairs, the second-largest sum raised by any charitable organization in the Civil War. The St. Louis ladies were outdone only by the Philadelphia Great Central Fair, which raised just more than a million dollars. Poorer women supported the war effort by taking over their husbands' responsibilities or providing for their families by going out to work. Some sewed uniforms, others packed hardtack, and still others cooked or washed clothes for soldiers. For women who depended on their husbands' salaries, the wartime deprivations could be particularly trying. Because of problems with disbursing payrolls, some Confederate soldiers had to wait for months, while others never received any pay at all.[9]

Jessie Benton Frémont. *Carte de
visite photograph by E. Anthony,
New York, ca. 1861. Courtesy of
Missouri Historical Society*

Civilians who remained loyal to the Union, especially those who lived near
cities, were safer and therefore more able to express their support for the cause.
The more prosperous enjoyed greater opportunities to participate in the war effort than did those in more rural areas or in regions of divided loyalties. St. Louis
women from prominent families sewed flags and presented them in stirring cer-
emonies, made up patriotic tableaux, and founded soldiers' aid societies to help
provide food and clothing for the men in arms. Jessie Benton Frémont invited the
famed reformer Dorothea Dix to St. Louis to help found the Western Sanitary
Commission (similar to but not officially related to the U.S. Sanitary Commission)
in order to make food, medicines, and other supplies available to Union soldiers.
The hundreds of sick and wounded men who were flooding port towns such as
Cape Girardeau and St. Louis required immediate care. Because there were almost no medical facilities in place to care for them, women like Sarah Jane Hill
and Cordelia Chester volunteered their services, even though few of them had any

background or training as nurses. Before the Civil War, nursing had not been considered an appropriate profession for women, so they had to overcome opposition and criticism in order to work in hospitals. Within a year, however, some Missouri newspapers recognized the valuable service that these women were rendering to the sick and wounded and praised them as "angels."[10] The Catholic Sisters of Charity and Sisters of Mercy, the only groups of women with any medical training before the war, were especially active and useful on hospital boats like the *Red Rover* and the *Empress* that coursed along the Mississippi River, bringing the sick and wounded from battlefields as far away as Shiloh.[11]

By early 1863, however, pro-Union forces were able to keep the secessionist impulse in check, largely through the institution of martial law, test oaths, and arbitrary arrests. Historian Mark Neely has found that during the Civil War, arrest rates were higher in Missouri than anywhere else; he estimates that more than four thousand civilians were held without charge or indictment during the war years.[12]

In fall 1862, Missouri voters faced a series of political contests in which emancipation was a central issue. Pro-emancipation Republicans won five out of nine congressional seats, leaving no doubt that the test oath had a strong influence on the election outcomes. Gamble had reluctantly consented to continue in office as provisional governor until 1864. He was exhausted and faced increasing criticism from the growing radical element in the state, but he agreed that this was not the time to step down. Although still a moderate, he took the results of the 1862 elections as a sign that the state was ready for more serious action on the issue of emancipation. On December 29, 1862, Gamble sent a message to the Missouri legislature, asking them to consider a plan for gradual and compensated emancipation.[13]

"FASHIONABLE SECESH LADIES" WRITE THEIR FRIENDS IN THE ARMY

In September 1862, the Daily Missouri Democrat *(later known as the* St. Louis Globe-Democrat*), a pro-Union paper, published letters purportedly obtained from a captured "rebel mail bag." The letters of "Fashionable Secesh" ladies included references to the Picot family, wealthy Southern sympathizers who had fled St. Louis after being forced to take a loyalty oath. The writer of the first letter was mistaken in her estimation of Provisional Governor Hamilton Gamble. It was General Henry Halleck, who recently taken command of Union forces in Missouri, who had instituted assessments and outright confiscations of the property of rebel citizens. The comment on conscription refers to General John M. Schofield's July 1862 order, which mandated that every man between the ages of eighteen and forty-five join a militia on pain of imprisonment.*

RARE REVELATIONS.
INSIDE VIEW OF THE FASHIONABLE SECESH OF ST. LOUIS.

The richest expose of the season will be found in the following letters, which were captured a few days ago in the rebel mail bag:

ST. LOUIS, AUG. 28, 1862

Dear Sam: . . . They say they are going to commence drafting next week. The last two days they have been impressing men by going to different drinking shops and theaters, and even the jail, and taking men from them and obliging them to enlist. Gamble, in a speech made a few nights ago, advocated shooting the "guerrillas" the "non-combatant secesh" to be assessed and then sent South. Picot's property has all been confiscated; his family ordered to leave their house and everything in it. They lived in Carondelet.

I have heard a great many say they do not think L——e G——s deserving all the praise given her; at any rate she is full as kind to the Federals. She is walking, riding and flirting with them all the time. I can assure you there are not many southern women in St. Louis would speak to a Federal. Her mother has done a great deal, and so have a great many others in a quiet way.

Last winter L——e G——s and some other young ladies, visited families where there were prisoners every day. They would kiss some of the prisoners every morning and quarrel which should have such a one to walk with or for a beau. . .

.

LIZZIE.

. . .

ST. LOUIS, AUGUST 28, 1862

CAPT. PREDELL: You see your letter was appreciated, that I answer it so soon; and I hope this mail will get safely through. St. Louis is very stupid now. We have nothing in the way of amusement, and there is not the visiting there used to be, for we have no beaux to visit; indeed, our streets would be deserted if it were not for shoulder-straps. . . .

MISS L.

Newspaper clippings in the Chouteau Family Collection, Missouri Historical Society, St. Louis.

A ST. LOUIS "SHE-DEVIL" PROMISES REVENGE

The Robbins family moved from Kentucky to St. Louis sometime in the mid-1840s. Emily (Em) Robbins was about eighteen when she wrote the following letter to her brother, Lieutenant Edward (Ned) C. Robbins, who was a Confederate soldier serving under General Price. In the months that followed, Ned saw service at Corinth and Vicksburg. Emily and Edward's father, Samuel, was exiled in May 1863 *for his pro-Southern views. Near the time he wrote to his son, his wife gave birth to their seventh child, whom he named Sterling Price Robbins. (See "Martyrdom in Missouri," chap. 8.) When Samuel returned to St. Louis after traveling through the South during his exile, he swore the loyalty oath and gave a bond for $5,000. After the war, Emily married Nathaniel W. Davis, a sergeant from a New York regiment, and moved with him to Tioga. Peter Lindell was the wealthy farmer who owned Lindell's Grove, the site of Camp Jackson.*

Friday Afternoon
September 16 th, 1862

My darling brother:—

Major Cochran has just been over to tell me that he would send a letter for me by Gen. Ed. Price if I wished it so I sit down to write you a few lines.

As I have been told not to put anything contra band, in my letter I have very little news to tell you. Every one is so engrossed in the military affairs, that they talk or think about little else.

You said in your letter that you hoped the draft would drive out some of the St. Louis boys that are still here doing nothing, but they have all gotten their exemption papers, The smell of powder and the whistle of the minnie ball are not very pleasant to them. Cornelia Baker has spent the summer in Berlin and says she has had a delightful time. Mary Huntington is coming here on a visit and Cornelia and Ike are going to New York to meet her. Old Peter Lindell is dead and has left all of his relatives an immense fortune.

I have not written to Walter Howland yet but will do so very soon, I do not like to write to Yankees very well but I would do almost any thing that you asked me to do.

Thee has been several marriages in the Church and there will be two or three more before long. Edith Green and Mr. McLanahan. Annie Ranney and Mr. Wallace. Annie surprised us all when we heard that she was going to be married. She met him at a Festival and was married just two months after she met him. Anita Alexander and Lizzie Kingsland are both going to be married soon.

I wish all the nice St. Louis boys would come home we have the dullest times imaginable. Old Dr. Marshall is about the only beaux left to Pine Street Church Young ladies. Miss Isabel arrived in St. Louis a few days ago and gave us quite an encouraging account of you. I hear Ned that you have not forgotten how to cut up with the girls yet. I am glad you have something once in a while to enliven you for I think that camp life must [be] dreadful dull.

Tillie Stephenson came to see me the other day and told about your doings in Memphis. They tell a good many tales on the rebel girls of St. Louis or *she-devils* as the Democrat calls us about the fuss we made over the rebel prisoners. It was published in a Boston paper that the Young ladies of our Church kissed the buttons on a rebel prisoners coat as he was coming out and all such outrageous stories, to make us appear as rediculous as possible. Never mind, our day will come before long and then we will pay them with interest.

Our club will begin to meet very soon and I [hope] *you* will be at some of the meetings before winter is over. Ask Sam Kennard if he recollects what a nice talk I had with him at Mrs. Webbs and how much I eat standing by that old [side] board. I little thought when I was laughing and joking with him that night that he would see you before I did.

I hear that there has been an engagement between Price and Rosecrans and that Price has been defeated which I do not believe. Oh Ned I hope that you are safe. It would almost set me crazy to hear that you were wounded and not able to get to you. If anything ever does happen to you (which I pray God will not) if you can by any possible means let us know you must do it. Tell the gentlemen that I know that their friends are well. But I must close my letter as the Major has come for it.

Everybody sends you plenty of love and good wishes.

With much love your devoted
Sister Em.

P.S. You must excuse bad writing for I am in a great hurry

Em.

Put the enclosed letter in an envelope and send it to Gerard Foote it is from A. A.—

Okalono, Miss. May 22nd, 1863

Dear Son,

I Have been banished from St. Louis during the war with many other citizens we convened at this place Last Night, Mr. Daniel Donovan, will try and get this to you if you should not see him you will write to me at this place. I left them all well at home Em has gone to Kentucky with Miss Sue Willfolk to spend the summer all your friends are well at home. Terror Reigns Supreme in St. Louis and they are trying to subjugate all the Southern people. We heard of the disaster at Jackson and the investment of Vicksburgh. My hope and prayer to God is that you are well and safe. I shall come down to see you as soon as I can find out where you are. If it is possible to reach you. . . . Be Son Courageous & Brave but Not Rash. My Prayer is that your Life will be Preserve[d], but if God orders otherwise I Pray that he will give me Strength To Bear.

Your Father In Love
Saml. Robbins

ELVIRA SCOTT LAMENTS THAT HER HOME IS "NO LONGER A SAFE ASYLUM"

Elvira Ascenith Weir Scott was a pro-Southern lady who lived in Miami, a town in north-central Missouri, during the Civil War. Like so many other proslavery Missourians, Elvira's parents had originally come from Virginia, though she herself had been born in Indiana. She was educated at the Washington County Seminary in Salem, Indiana, married John P. Scott in 1844, and had two daughters, Eva and Hebe. From time to time during the war, federal soldiers came to the Scott home to ask Elvira and her seventeen-year-old daughter Eva ("Pet") to play the piano for them. "Jno." was a common mid-nineteenth-century abbreviation for the name "John."

Sunday, March 9th, 1862. The past summer & fall have been passed in such a state of excitement, in such feverish anxiety, that I have had no time to record the terrible events. Many of them will live in history. The past year of '61! What horrors it has witnessed! Sometimes we almost imagine it a frightful dream from which we will awake to the old peace & prosperity, but evidences of its fearful realities are everywhere the most painful of all. Thousands of bloody graves, disease & the sword have made the whole land to mourn. Where it will end, if God in his mercy does not interpose? We seem to be plunging deeper & deeper into the vortex. Men seem to be transformed into fiends. . . .

There is a class of men in every country—the low & shiftless, who live from hand to mouth by fishing, robbing, roaming from place to place, a tax on the communities in which they live; Dutch & Irish laborers, who have nothing at stake. Such men in Missouri are generally Union men, who by becoming "Home Guards" can prey upon their neighbors, or jayhawk. Generally they have a malicious, envious feeling toward their neighbors who by honest industry have surrounded themselves by the comforts of life. They openly boast that they will have possession of their fine farms, & they think that the time has arrived for them to take the time to better their fortunes. Such are nine-tenths of the Union refugees. We know some of them from the east in this county,. They owned nothing, were in debt, & had lived off the community as long as they could. They left of their own free will & became Union refugees. Now they are creating sympathy by their support of the free States. Or they are jayhawking in other counties of the State. . . .

If the maintenance of the Constitution is the object why don't they begin at home, where it was first violated? The cause lies in the North, the effect is in the South. Let them remove the cause. If they do not intend to interfere with slavery why have Federal soldiers stolen thousands of slaves from their masters? These are now wandering in Kansas as vagabonds, stealing everything they can lay their hands upon. . . .

April 26. . . . I suppose there is little if any hope of Missouri ever maintaining her independence of the Federal government, & of course every citizen will be obliged to give his allegiance. It seems a terrible state of affairs when all sub-stantial, worthy men must be fettered down from a free expression of opinion, deprived of arms, deprived of the privilege of voting & kept under subjection by the lowest most unprincipled Dutch, with a very few American hirelings. This is what the Federal government is doing now. . . .

[July] Wednesday 9th. . . . I was busy cleaning up my room, when one of the soldiers came in & handed me a document. I thought it was something for John, & was going to lay it on the table, when I discovered that it was directed to Mrs. Jno. P. Scott. I sat down to peruse it. To my amazement it was a military arrest, stating that the time had passed when treasonable conversation would be allowed. But I will hand down to posterity the Original Document, first stating that I had been careful to give no offence to the military authorities, although they had annoyed us by calling at all hours. We had never failed to treat them politely, playing when they asked us, for the soldier is merely the instrument in the hands of others. They were all an ignorant, degraded class of men, many of them never having seen a piano before. No doubt idle curiosity, as much as anything, brought them into people's houses unasked, & as none of them displayed any rudeness, more than going into people's houses unasked, [we] were in their power. It was also prudent to be care-ful, & I had been careful. The Document referred to is as follows:

Miami Saline Co. MO. July 9th 1862
NOTICE
to
Mrs. Jno P. Scott

The time has past when treasonable language goes unpunished. A Ladies place is to fulfill her household duties, and not to spread treason and excite men to rebellion. Since you cannot do the first, but be on the contrary all times at the last,
YOU ARE HEREBY ORDERED
to report yourself once a week every Fryday morning at 11 A M oclock to the Commanding Officer. at this place in person at the camp of the company in the fair ground at Miami and the same time once a week by letter to Cap W Love Provost Marshall, at Marshall Mo.

This order will remain in force until the commanding officer is fully convinced that you behave yourself as a Lady Ought. The non compliance with this order will be punished by transferring your resp. husband to the Military Prison at Marshall MO to be kept there in durance for the remainder of the War.
By Order of
Adam Bax

1st Lieut Co O, 7th MO.
Commanding at Miami, MO.
To Mrs. Jn P Scott
Miami MO.

To say that I was *indignant, outraged* would express nothing of the tempest raging within. My first impulse, of course, was to carry it to the store. It was wrong, I should have waited until I was composed, & not gone to excite John in business hours, with soldiers coming in & out of the house. I repented it after coming home.

I thought that there must be other ladies treated inn the same manner. I went to Mrs. Pendleton's; found that she had a like Document; also Mrs. Lewis & Mrs. T. P. Bell. They took it coolly; said they would report without their husbands, & before we separated we arranged how we should go, & I came home more composed, but had a bad headache.

After dinner the mail came & I was reading the paper when three soldiers came in. John had told me at dinner not to speak to another one, or to play for them. I had made up my mind that Pet should play no more for them. I asked them to sit down & they asked me if there was any news. I remarked that if there were perhaps I had better not tell them, as I had been arrested that morning & I did not know the offense, that it might be telling them some contraband news, as Mr. Parsons had been reprimanded for telling news the day before. They looked amazed & one said to the other, "Jim, don't that get you, arresting women? Lieut Bax must be a damned fool & will get himself in a scrape. But after that I suppose we can't ask you for any music." I told them that I played but little & was not well, but would play them a tune or two if they wished it, & did so. I thought of the *captives* in the *Scripture* who were commanded to sing to amuse their captors. My heart was full. This playing to amuse them had been a daily going on for weeks. I felt no animosity to the poor, ignorant soldiers, but could not but feel it a degradation to be intruded upon. Home was no longer a safe asylum, a sacred place. These were the last I had to play for. They thanked me kindly. The rudest & lowest can be touched by kindness.

Elvira Ascenith Weir Scott, diary, 1860–87, Western Historical Manuscripts Collection, University of Missouri, Columbia.

LUCY THURMAN ASKS HER COUSIN TO COME HOME IF HE CAN "GET OUT OF OLD ABE'S CLUTCHES"

Lucy Thurman, a young lady of somewhat doubtful political persuasion, was the daughter of a wealthy farmer. She was about twenty-four when she wrote this letter to her cousin Larkin Ramsay, who was then a private with the Fifth Missouri Infantry (CSA), to tell him that if he took a loyalty oath he could come home and prosper. Pin Oak was a village in Warren County, in the northwestern part of Missouri. The phrase "for it hurts im orfully" is undoubtedly a sarcastic reference to the Republican administration's sensitivity to criticism.

Larkin A. Ramsey, Esqr.

Pin Oak, Mo.

July 1ˢᵗ, 1862

Dear Cousin Lark,

I now for the first time seat myself to write to you: I am really ashamed that I have not written before but I hope you will not think that I [have] forgotten you for I think of you every day and wish you were here with your friends. We are all well as usual and the relations are generally well. I was out to Uncle Tommys that Sunday—they were all well then.

We have not heard from the boys since they went to Dixie but hope they are all right on the "goose," and will soon come home. Lark I do want you to come home if you can get the chance, by taking the oath and giving bond you could do very well if you were here for hands are so scarce they are offering two dollars a day for harvest hands and can hardly get them at that. Wheat is tolerable good but oats and grass are not worth cutting on account of the dry weather. We have had a very dry spring but we are having rain enough now. Corn is very small some people have not plowed their corn yet: but they *dont manage well* you know.

Times are hard here yet and no prospect of being better, but we have enough to eat which is a great blessing.

I will tell you of some weddings we have had since you have been gone I dont know whether you have heard of them or not . . .

Lark do come home if you can get out of old Abe's clutches, for I think you have served the old ape long enough unless you were getting better wages. O I tell you we are getting along first rate now since the negro stealers are all gone to Dixie to *whip* the southern boys. But I tell you they *cant do it* for they have not got the *pluck* to whip a swam of gnats.

But I guess I had better not say much, for it hurts im orfully. Your Mother and family are well she is talking about coming to see you if you dont come home soon.

Well Lark I will quit for this time for what I have done you will never be able to read my pen is so bad it lookss like the chickens had scratched it. Write to me as soon as you can accept my best wishes for your welfare

Yours truly

Lucy Thurman

Lucy Thurman letter, Alphabetical Files, Missouri Historical Society, St. Louis.

"LET US SEE IF WE CAN'T HAVE A 'RAID' OURSELVES"

Although the battle of Pea Ridge in March 1862 halted the Confederate advance into the state, pro-Union civilians still faced danger. Confederate forces remained on the state's borders and enjoyed some support among local sympathizers. The Weekly Central City and Brunswicker *(published in Chariton County, in northwestern Missouri) expressed impatience with officers of the U.S. Army who appeared to be dozing while guerrillas attacked civilians. The same edition in which the following editorial appeared also reported William Quantrill's assault on Olathe, Kansas, as well as Colonel Joseph C. Porter's attack on Union families in Palmyra on September 17. On the same day, Union forces under General George B. McClellan won a victory at the battle of Antietam in Maryland, but the news had not yet reached Missouri.*

THE SITUATION IN MISSOURI.

No large force of rebels tread the soil of Missouri in "solid column," but we are not to understand from this that our situation is one of perfect security. We hear of the amassing of rebel troops in Arkansas, and we know that rebel sympathizers in Missouri are confidently looking for an irruption of their friends and our enemies from that quarter.—Should their expectations be realized, and our State be invaded again by an army coming from the southwest, there is reason for fearing that it would be greatly augmented as it progressed, should it be able to make headway into the State at all. Possibly, our military authorities have their eyes open, and need not be reminded of the perils that environ us, but forewarned, we should be forearmed; hence no harm can result from a glance now and then at our real situation.

The Union status of Missouri is fixed. The combined powers of rebeldom cannot change her position as a member of the Federal Government; but this fact has no weight with the rebels who have undertaken the job of engineering her out. The more hopeless the undertaking, the more desperate and dashing their efforts, as seen in the late movements on the Potemac and in the invasion of Maryland.

Suppose, then, an army should again invade our State from the Southwest, and the small camps of rebels now nestled in the brush all over the State, should simultaneously emerge from their hiding places and dash to some converging point, or agreed upon center, for combining their forces, what incalculable damage could be done just as those bold raids in Virginia have done.

Our present situation in Missouri admits of just such a possibility—in view of the fact that camps of rebels are thick in almost every county in the State. Such being our situation, let us not be caught napping. Let us see if we can't have a "raid" ourselves—just one, to see how we could succeed with it. A Union raid would startle the country, and wake up our dozing officers.

Weekly Central City and Brunswicker, September 18, 1862.

WILLARD MENDENHALL IS HARASSED BY FEDERALS

Willard H. Mendenhall settled in Lexington, Missouri, where he owned a farm and ran a store. Although strongly proslavery, Mendenhall himself owned no slaves and remained loyal to the Union in spite of abuse he suffered at the hands of federal soldiers in late 1862.

Sept 24 [1862]

. . . hundreds yes Thousands of men of my political opinions wer joining the southern army. some from preference, others because they considered it unsafe fore them to remain at thare homes. I will stay at home. in order to do this I must in the first place gaurd my toung. many have suffered from talking too mutch. in this land of liberty at the present day a man is not alowed to speak his sentiments. in the second place, my doctrine is, abide by the laws of the country you live in, if it is Rome. 3rd make no private enemy! thare has bin many men ruined by enemy's that cared little abought thare country. all they wanted was to gratify a malicious feeling that existed in thare bosom. I thought if I done this I could not go far astray from any one's opinion of right. I had done so to the present time. Col Henry Neal's militia commenced marauding on my place taking potatoes etc. . . . went to John Ewings broke thare furniture took his and his wifes clothes then sett the house on fire. at Tho. Shields (They have nearly every thing taken from them) they looked at thare piano, said they had broken many of them since they left Independence. they must thank them if they did not brake thares. They forced Mrs Grigg to play fore them while they danced. as they left the house, one of the men remarked to Mrs Thos. Shields, (who is quite a fine looking young woman) that he liked her looks and would come back that night and stay with her. at Cal Belle's they took his hoarse, gold watch some money I do not know how mutch, and abused his wife shamefully felt of her person, and useing insulting language. The outrages are to numerous to write. I heard that Col Stevenson had them put under arrest. he appears to try and do what is right, as far as keeping his men in order is concerned, after the men took all they wanted from Cal Belle's they scattered them abought the room and set it on fire. Thos. Calaway told me that one of the men approached him pulled his watch out of his pocket, and left the place he has not heard of it since.

Mendenhall Diaries, Western Historical Manuscripts Collection, University of Missouri, Columbia.

STEAMERS AND SHIPS ON THE MISSISSIPPI RIVER

This editorial from the Daily Missouri Republican *(one of the more moderate Democratic newspapers published in St. Louis) reveals the vital role of the traffic on the Mississippi River. Steamers transported men and supplies, supported land forces, and occasionally emancipated slaves along the way. About a month after this editorial appeared, the* Empress *became a hospital steamer on which many prominent St. Louis women and Catholic sisters nursed the wounded and sick.*

FROM THE TENNESSE RIVER.
STEAMER EMPRESS OFF FOR THE WARS.

On Tuesday, the 4th instant, the steamer Empress left St. Louis, having on board some 700 tons Commissary stores for Cairo and Paducah, 150 head of cattle for Fort Henry and Col. Bissell's Engineer Regiment, destined for Gen. Pope's Division at Commerce, Mo.; Wednesday landed the troops at Commerce and Commissary stores at Cairo, coaled and arrived at Paducah on Thursday morning, received on board the Forty-eighth Ohio Infantry, Col. Sullivan commanding, coaled and arrived at Fort Henry Friday morning, being the first arrival for the new expedition; the water had almost completely inundated the Fort; no landing there; proceeded up the river about seven miles; landed in the brush, alongside the Gladiator, Gen. McClennand's headquarters, received a present from Lieut. Col. Parker, of the Forty-eighth, of a splendid American eagle, whose perch is now on the pilot house of the Empress. Here, on Saturday, the 8th, commenced a new phase in steamboating—the Empress is converted into a slaughter house to supply the much needed beef to the army, but "some things can be done as well as others," and there is room on the Empress to do almost anything, and Captain Jas. Gormley and his crew are the men to put things through.

The bully Forty-eighth, however, did not wait for the butcher, but went ashore, and finding a number of porkers that were evidently "secesh," (as they would not take the oath,) they "captivated" them, and soon were frying spare-ribs and tenderloins. . . . Left the bridge on Monday afternoon with the entire fleet. The departure of this fleet of ninety boats was a sight seen but once in a life time, and if ever the writer regretted the lack of artistic powers it was there; but to the Empress. She held her way in the midst of the fleet until about 4 p.m., when, espying a large pile of what turned out to be staves, she landed and took them on board. Not finding the owner, word was left with some neighbors that she had taken them and would pay for them. During the evening she passed every boat ahead but one, when a fog arose, compelling the whole fleet to lie by. . . .

Tuesday morning the fog having cleared away about 9 a.m., started for Savannah, meeting many demonstrations of loyalty along the shore, and without accident, except that just above Clifton a man rose up behind a cedar bush and fired at the boat, fortunately injuring nothing but the collar of a soldier's coat. . . . Landed on the west side of the river, opposite Savannah, at the plantation of Mr. Cherry, a loyal citizen, who has narrowly escaped hanging two or three times on that account. His residence is in Savannah. He is the owner of some forty slaves. Here some of the officers were presented with bouquets of hyacinths and other early spring flowers. Savannah is a pretty village, situated on the bluff on the east side of the river, the plantation above alluded to being opposite in the "sandy bottom," and bounded by a large cane brake, to which the soldiers betook themselves, returning with thousands of fishing rods, which of course were of no use to them. At night saw the light of a conflagration to the southwest of Savannah. Laid here until Friday noon, dispersing commissary stores, when General Sherman's division (to which the Empress is attached) started for Yellow Creek, on the west bank of the river just inside the line of Alabama, where we arrived about 8 p.m. Just before landing, a young soldier of the Forty-eighth died and was here buried on Saturday. . . .

Sunday morning, 16th, found us at Pittsburgh landing. Here occurred a curious fulfillment of a presentiment. Capt. Ireland, of the Forty-eighth, had on Sunday the 2d, requested the regimental band to practice a funeral march to play at his funeral two weeks from that day. He also asked a minister (one of the Seventeenth regiment) to preach his funeral sermon. He was then in good health, at twenty-five minutes past 12 o'clock he died of pneumonia, and was buried as he predicted. . . .

19th, 7 p.m., left for Savannah. 20th, discharged balance of commissary stores; river all over the bottoms opposite Savannah at least eighteen feet higher than when we went up 20th, left for "home, sweet home." Twenty miles above Duck river, the timber for some distance along the east bank had been recently torn down by the wind—not a tree left standing in the track of the hurricane. Found Fort Henry completely under water. It is, however, dismantled. The morning of the 22d found us on the Father of Waters. 23d, head wind and slight boat have kept us from our homes all day. Home again. Oliver.

Note.—The conflagration mentioned turned out to be the burning of forty bales of cotton by the rebels. The cotton belonged to Mr. Cherry, of Savannah. It was within three miles of that place. We learned at Savannah that on the day previous to our first arrival, there had been a squad of rebel cavalry there, pressing every able-bodied man into their service. Many fled to the woods and got aboard the gunboats, and some 160 enlisted for the war.

Daily Missouri Republican, March 25, 1862. I am indebted to Ms. Vicki Betts of the University of Texas at Tyler for this editorial.

HENRY CRAWFORD DESCRIBES THE EXECUTION OF A BUSHWHACKER

Henry C. Crawford and his brother, William H. Crawford, served with the Third Missouri Cavalry, Missouri State Militia, and later with the Seventh Missouri Cavalry, Missouri State Militia. The Third Missouri was recruited in spring 1862 and had a reputation for being "poorly clad and scantily fed." The Third Missouri served in southwestern Missouri and northwestern Arkansas; the Seventh Missouri, in southwestern and central Missouri.[14] In his letter, Crawford referred to Colonel John T. Coffee, who had served under General Price until April 1862. At that time, Coffee chose not to leave Missouri with Price, but instead joined Colonel Stand Watie's command in the southwest part of the state. Coffee's cavalry and Watie's Cherokee soldiers routed the federals near Neosho, the stronghold of the exiled Missouri legislature.

H. C. & W. H. Crawford
Aug. 8th 1862
Sedalia Pettis Co. Mo.

Dear friends

I hasten to Answer your Letter of July th 15th which just came to hand. we Was glad to hear from you as we had Not had a Letter for some time

We left the South West the 29 July And Arrived here to Day I think we will Leave here tomorrow or Next Day for . . . booneville or somewhere in that part of the country some . . . . . . the boys Was glad to leave Rocks And hills of Arkansas and South West Mo but for my Part I would rather have Staid there during the War for the people down there did not think themselves any better than a soldier if he was A fed and the excitement of the bushwhackers there suited me finely. And as for hardships we had got so used to them that we did not mind them Atall. Myself And four others concluded we would give the bushwhackers A Parting farewell before we left so the Evening before the boys left Neosho we started Just At Dark and went twenty five miles below Neosho down close to rutlege and Pineville to find out. . . . Wherebouts of Coffee and Men. we Played off Secesh And took the People in Completely As thay had No Idea of five feds beeing in that Country Alone. thay told us every thing thay knowed. we Passed ourselves for Livingstons men and the secesh was mighty glad to see us wee stoped at About 40 houses And found one union Woman. And wee went on at such a big rate . . . A telling her what we was gowing to do with the feds that we Left her About half Scared to death wee went to a Noted bushwhackers by the Name of hall . . . Wife came out . . . And we talked awhile and wee Acted Secesh so well and As good Luck would have it he was At home And After he found out that wee was All right he Came out and told A good many of his rounds.

Wee learned form him that that Coffee was in the indian Nation And while he was in the midst of his glory A telling us What he had done to the feds we put a few bullet holes through his head and Went on wee got back to Neosho Just at daylight after riding about 50 miles and overtook the boys at Newtonia. I will write again when wee get through . . .

yours

Henry C. & W. H Crawferd

Crawford Letters, Western Historical Manuscripts Collection, University of Missouri, Columbia.

PRIVATE DAVID ALLAN CARES LITTLE FOR
SUFFERING FARMERS IN SOUTHEAST MISSOURI

The people who lived in southeastern Missouri suffered as much from crisscrossing raids and retaliations as those who lived closer to the Kansas border. Their trials were less publicized because the raids were more sporadic and the bushwhackers not as well organized as the murderous gangs who operated farther west. Although southeast Missouri farmers offered less support for guerrilla activity than their fellows elsewhere, they still suffered punitive raids by federals. Moreover, both sides often pressed men into service. The writer of this letter, David Allan, describes the sufferings of southeast Missouri farmers toward the end of 1862. Allan mustered into service with the Twenty-ninth Missouri Volunteers in September 1862. He became a lieutenant in 1863 and rose to the rank of captain by 1865. Patterson is a small town in southeastern Missouri and the site of an important federal outpost that guarded the forts and depots farther north, including Fort Davidson at Pilot Knob.

Co. D. 29th Mo. Vols

Paterson Mo. Nov 17th 1862

Dear Mother

We left Cape Girardeau last Monday and have had no opportunity to write until now. we have been eight days on the roade and are now camped three miles from Paterson. Today and the day before we traveled all day in the rain. I have always slept on the ground but have been very well and am now in the best of spirits.

We could have moved faster but the teams could not stand travelling at such a rate.

We have had very little sickness considering the majority of the troops not being used to camp life.

The country we traveled through showed plainly the effects of civil war. Farm after farm laying idle and those which have been tilled are in a wretched condition. The inhabetants we found along the roade were generally poorly clad and appeared half starved and it is a mystery to me where they will get food during the coming winter.

We have lived very well this far as there are plenty of Hogs & chickens about.

If you will look in last years volume of Harpers Weekly you will find a pretty true picture of a foraging party in its descent on a farm house.

The following is a slight sketch of our March.

<u>Monday Nov 10th 1862</u> Left camp Peterson about 9 O'clock. Weather pleasant, arrived in camp about 4 O'clock this afternoon. The camp is called Camp Davidson in honor of Brig. General Davidson.

<u>Tuesday and Wednesday</u> we remained in camp nr Jackson

<u>Thursday Nov 13/62.</u> Left camp Davidson this morning and after a march of about 10 miles encamped on the banks of a creek near the ruins of a mill which was destroyed by Heckers Division on account of it being a source from which the rebels drew their supplies.

<u>Friday Nov 14th 1862</u>. Left camp Blair Jr this morning about 9 O'clock. After a march of about 12 miles came to a halt near the town of Dallas

<u>Saturday Nov 15/62</u>. Left Camp Peterson this morning Early. Passed through Dallas now deserted by all of its inhabitants except two or three women. The houses are all more or less destroyed, some being burnt to the ground. This place was a regular den of secessioners and last spring Hecker cleaned out the crew and destroyed their property. Halted this Evening after a march of 17 miles.

<u>Sunday Nov 16/62</u>. Travelled all day in the rain. Seen Pine trees for the first time. Halted after making 10 miles. This evening we halted on the Bank of the St. Francis River 3 miles from Patterson. Rain fell all day & roads muddy rendering marching very hard.

I have received no letter this week but will get one in a few days I suppose. Our movement from the Cape to this point of course disarranges our mail facilities. Direct your next letters to Patterson instead of the Cape.

Give my love to Aunts Sarah & Elizabeth and Alex Jim and Anna and retain a share for yourself.

When you write to Aunt Amanda and Uncle John remember me to them also to all my friends.

I will write again in a few days to Jim.

Write soon to
Your Affectionate Son
David Allan Jr.
To Margaret A. Allan
St. Louis
Mo

SARAH JANE HILL HELPS NURSE WOUNDED UNION SOLDIERS

By 1862, the U.S. Army west of the Mississippi urgently needed medical care for sick and wounded soldiers. As the war dragged on, women volunteered their services as nurses in hospitals in St. Louis, Cape Girardeau, and Springfield or on "floating hospitals" that ferried casualties from battles farther south. Sarah Jane Full Hill was born in England, immigrated with her family to the United States in 1850, and married Eben Marvin Hill, a successful builder, in 1858. Eben Hill served with the Army Corps of Engineers for the duration of the war, while Sarah volunteered as a nurse in St. Louis during the winter of 1861–62. She composed her Civil War memoirs some years after the end of the war, at the urging of her children, but the journal was not published until 1980. "Scraping lint" means scraping the surface of linen fabrics in order to obtain fuzzy, absorbent material for dressing wounds. Phoebe and Adaline Couzins ("Cozzens" in Hill's narrative) were the daughters of a prominent St. Louis society family. Phoebe later studied law at Washington University, became one of America's first female lawyers, and campaigned for woman suffrage.

. . . A large vacant block of stores on Fifth and Chestnut Streets was taken by the government for a hospital, and the store rooms on the ground floor were used as Headquarters of the Medical Corps. The three upper stories were used for the hospital. . . . At first there was little system or order in our work, each and every woman doing what she could, our main object being to help the sick soldiers, and we found plenty of work. Of course we were all giving our time and labor to the cause. The doctors and surgeons availed themselves of our help, and every day we women gathered at the rooms and scraped lint, tore and rolled bandages, knitted socks. We solicited donations of delicacies for the sick. Many boxes were packed and sent to the soldiers in the field hospitals. We were called on to assist the surgeons in their operations and to nurse the patients. There were no regular nurses then and volunteer nurses were scarce. There was much confusion and lack of system in the hospital work, I might almost say ignorance at first. To illustrate, Mother spent much time making soups, broths, and dainties, for she had had much experience in cooking for the sick. My sister and I would visit the hospital three or four times a week, always carrying a well-filled basket of broth and delicacies. These we would distribute ourselves among the patients who had come under our notice. We were not forbidden and there was no protest from anyone against it. Many other women did the same thing. The boys watched eagerly for our coming and I will say that we were careful to feed only the convalescents. My sister often accompanied me and we were known as "the two women in black." Beside that personal work, I was placed on the hospital visiting committee of which Mrs. Cozzens was the chairwoman. Her daughter, Phebe, was also on the same committee and I grew to know them very well. They were a fine family, the father being chief of some civic department. There were three daughters, all beautiful girls. Phoebe was the most brilliant and intellectual, with great executive ability, she was a valuable aid to her mother. In after years she became distinguished as a lawyer and lecturer. At this time she was engaged to a young officer in the army, and was to be married in the Spring, but they had a lovers' quarrel. He was on detached service in St. Louis at the time, but after the quarrel he rejoined his regiment and was killed at Fort Donelson. Being of an intense temperament, she was completely prostrated, for she truly loved him and his death greatly changed her.

But to return to our hospital work, we were frequently called on for nurses, for there was great lack of help in that line. Many days and nights of that winter I spent beside the beds of the sick, wounded and dying, assisting the surgeons in their gruesome work. They said I had good nerves and was not afraid of the sight of blood. The use of anesthetics was little known, and the doctors often called for me. They said I was quiet and efficient and obeyed orders and understood quickly.

After the battle of Springfield where the brave Gen. Lyon was killed and where Frémont's bodyguard made a brilliant charge, a number of the wounded were brought to our hospital. Several of our Committee were up all night after they arrived, helping the doctors attend to their needs. One young fellow I well remember, a splendid specimen of young manhood, had a badly shattered right arm, which the attending surgeons declared must be amputated at once. He protested and fought most vigorously against it, and would not consent to the operation. He said he was not going through life with one arm, that he was going to fight the rebels till they killed him, and if he could not use his saber he could still shoot. He was so insistent and determined that finally the surgeons yielded and set to work to save the limb. He refused to take a sedative and lay there white and grim while the doctors probed and extracted splinters and pieces of bone from the shattered elbow. They were over an hour before they finally dressed and bandaged the wound. Twice he fainted and the cold sweat poured off his pale face, but he never made a moan. It was a wonderful exhibition of courage, and the poor fellow deserved to save his arm. I attended the doctors in this case, held the basins and towels and did what was demanded of me without faltering, but after it was all over and I reached home the reaction took place and the tired nerves made themselves felt. We women who were called on to go through such scenes, lived on our nerve in those days.

The next day when I went to the hospital, I found the young man greatly exhausted after the night's ordeal, but hopeful of recovery. He had a wonderful physique and was a clean blooded boy. At his request I comforted him by writing to his mother and sweetheart in Northern Illinois. He subsequently recovered and returned to the army, but was unable to be a cavalry man, for his arm was stiff from the elbow, the joint there being partially gone. This is one of the many experiences we were called upon to pass through in our efforts to assist as best we could. We helped to dress wounds, washed and bathed the sick, closed the eyes of the dying, attending to the last sad rites at the death-beds of many, wrote letters and read aloud to the convalescents, and never forgot a cheery presence and encouraging word or smile for our boys to whom the reality of war was so sadly being demonstrated.

Sarah Hill, *Mrs. Hill's Journal: Civil War Reminiscences*, ed. Mark M. Krug (Chicago: Lakeside Press, 1980), 51–56. Reproduced by permission of R. R. Donnelley.

CORDELIA HARVEY CARES FOR
WOUNDED AND SICK SOLDIERS AT CAPE GIRARDEAU

Cordelia Adelaide Perrine Harvey was the widow of Wisconsin governor Lewis P. Harvey. After her husband drowned in 1862, she decided to carry forward his work of caring for sick and wounded Wisconsin soldiers. She traveled to Cape Girardeau, Missouri, where she volunteered to nurse wounded and sick soldiers. According to her memoirs, she secured President Lincoln's approval for a change in policy that made it possible for sick soldiers to be furloughed rather than remain in military hospitals. Her memoir is a set of handwritten, undated notes. Harvey married Rev. Albert T. Chester in 1876.

In the fall of 1862 I found myself in Cape Girardeau, where hospitals were being improvised for the immediate use of the sick and dying then being brought in from the swamps by the returning regiments and up the rivers in closely crowded hospital boats. These hospitals were mere sheds filled with cots as thick as they could stand, with scarcely room for one person to pass between them. Pneumonia, typhoid and camp fevers, and that fearful scourge of the southern swamps and rivers, chronic diarrhea, occupied every bed. A surgeon once said to me, "There is nothing else there: here, I see pneumonia and there, fever, and on that cot another disease, and I see nothing else! You had better stay away; the air is full of contagion, and contagion and sympathy do not go well together."

One day, a woman passed through the uncomfortable, illy ventilated, hot unclean infected wretched rooms, and she saw something else there. A hand reached out and clutched her dress. One caught her shawl and kissed it, another her hand and pressed it to his fevered cheek; another in wild delirium cried, "I want to go home! I want to go home! Lady! Lady! Take me in your chariot, take me away!" This was a fair-haired, blue-eyed boy of the South, who had left family and friends forever; obeying his country's call, he enlisted under the stars and stripes because he could not be a traitor. He was therefore disowned, and was now dying among strangers with his mother and sisters not twenty miles away; and they knew that he was dying and would not come to him. Father, forgive them, they knew not what they did.

As this woman passed, these "diseases" as the surgeon called them, whispered and smiled at each other and even reached out and took hold of each others hands saying, "She will take us home, I know her; she will not leave us here to die," not dreaming that hovering just above them was a white robed one, who in a short time would take them to their heavenly home.

This woman failed to see on these cots aught but the human [beings] they were to her, the sons, brothers, husbands, and fathers of anxious weeping ones at home and as such she cared for and thought of them. Arm in arm with health, she day by day visited every sufferer's cot doing, it is true, very little, but always taking with her from the outside world fresh air, fresh flowers, and all the hope and comfort she could find in her heart to give them. Now and then, one would totter forth into the open air, his good constitution having overcome disease, and the longings for life as strong within him that he grasped at straws determined to live. If perchance he could get a furlough, in a few weeks a strong man would return and greet you with, "How do you do, I am on my way to my regiment!" Who this stranger could be, you would never imagine until reminded by him of the skeleton form and trembling steps you had so recently watched going to the landing, homeward bound. But, if as was too frequently the case he was sent to convalescent camps, in a few weeks he was returned to hospital, and again to camp, and thus continued to vibrate between camp and hospital until hope and life were gone. This was the fate of thousands.

On a steamer from Cape Girardeau to Helena at table one day when the passengers were dining, among whom were several military officers, I heard a young major of the regular army very coolly remark that it was much cheaper for the government to keep her sick soldiers in hospitals on the river than to furlough them. A lady present quietly replied, "That is true, Major, if all were faithful to the government, but unfortunately a majority of the surgeons in the army have conscientious scruples, and verily believe it to be their duty to keep these sick men alive as long as possible. To be sure, their uneaten rations increased the hospital fund and so enabled your surgeons generously to provide all needed delicacies for the sick, but the pay was drawn by the soldiers from the government all the same. Don't you think, Sir, it would be a trifle more economical," continued the lady, "to send these poor fellows north for a few weeks, to regain their strength, that they might return at once to active service?" The laughter of his brother officers prevented my hearing his reply.

Cordelia Adelaide Perrine Harvey Chester, "Recollections of Hospital Life, and Personal Interviews with President Lincoln" (n.d.), Abraham Lincoln Presidential Library, Springfield, Illinois.

A WOMAN'S SECRET CODE

According to a penciled note added to the bottom of this letter, this was a coded
message to sixteen-year-old Susan "Ludie" Dorsey letting her know that medicines
had been smuggled to Confederate soldiers. The letter is signed "Annie," but is
probably from her brother Caleb. The Dorseys were a wealthy slave-owning family in
Cuivre Township in Pike County. By "bosoms," the writer means dressy men's shirt
fronts, which were sometimes heavily starched and worn over a less expensive shirt.
While it is impossible now to decode this letter, there is a certain humorous irony in
the notion of making and sending shirt bosoms, which most people considered to be
flashy and in poor taste and which certainly would not have been worn by soldiers
in the line of battle.

Miss Ludie

I gave the bosoms to Miss Annie Lawrance yesterday morning. She was in
the store just as I finished them and twas such a good opportunity I sent them to
Jennie by her. Excuse Haste

& oblige yours etc

Annie

[added in pencil, in a different hand]
1862
Code note notifying me of medicines on the way to Confederate soldiers in
Missouri.

Lou E. Dorsey

Dorsey Family Papers, Missouri Historical Society, St. Louis.

WILLIAM KESTERSON WRITES HOME FROM AN ARMY HOSPITAL

William Kesterson was born in Tennessee but served with the Seventh Missouri
Cavalry in 1862 and later with the First Missouri Cavalry until he became ill in May
1863. He remained in the hospital at Springfield until 1865. He died in 1883 in Lafayette
County, Missouri. In the letter dated July 11, 1864, Kesterson refers to the "paw paw
malitia," which was a nickname for men belonging to the Enrolled Missouri Militia.
In July 1862, General John Schofield issued General Order No. 19, compelling all men
of military age to enroll in the state militia or to declare their sympathies (if they had
fought for the enemy) and surrender their weapons. Enrolled men could be called up at
any time to help guard forts and other installations. They were sometimes suspected of
pro-Southern sympathies—that is, of camping and hiding near the paw paw shrubs
common in the western part of the state.[15] It is impossible to identify the "McPheron"
(McPherson?) referred to in the letter.

General Hospital
Springfield Mo February the 17th 1864

Dear Brother

I take my pen in hand to inform you that yore letter of the 12th came to hand this day and I was glad to hear that yore health was some better than when you wrote before. I am fat and saucy and feel as independent as a pig on Ice and hope that when this comes to hand you may be in the same fix. I have nothing of interest to write. I have a letter from father since I wrote last he was some better he said the doctor said that if he would take good care of himself when warm weather come he would get better. I hope that he shall for I do want to see him again so very bad. The bushwhackers are as thick as ever our boys killed four some days before he wrote. Bill Hearlston was one of them. I hope they will kill the last devil of them. I have wrote to my wife to stay where she is a while longer if she can stay there in any peace it is better than to move to town. That is the worst place a family can go to. I dont know but I will go up to Lexington this spring if I stay here and I expect to stay here some time yet as I have not heard anything more of the Invalids. I supose that they have played out or got lost in the mud or some thing of that sort and I shant be much sory if they dont come. I aught to be well satisfied here but it seems as if I cant and I wish that I was away and then I get so that I dont care where Iam untill my time is out then I want to get somewhere where I can live in peace with my wife and children and where I can give them good schooling that will be my main object when I get out of the service is the schooling of them. My wife says they are as fat as pigs and talk about me all the time you can guess whether I want to see them or not. I am sory to hear that you are not likely to get a discharge but you have not got a great while to serve at any rate that is some consolation. I begin to feel like I would be free some time again although nine months is a good while yet. everything must have an end and I shall be glad to see the end of our time for serving uncle Sam come to an end. I hope the end of this war is close at hand but I fear it will be a long time yet and if you dont wach you will loose yore bet on peace being made by the first of May. Well Brother I dont know as I have anything more that will be of interest to you. I hope that I shall see you again but when that will ever be the lord only knows but I hope that through gods mercy it wont be long. Yet life is very uncertain and then the dread of the future hangs heavily on my mind some times and dashes what little worldly pleasure I see away from me my concience tells me that all is not right and that a change is nesesary to my hapiness in this world and in the one to come. I think a great deal of this . . . of late. I attend church every sunday and sunday night and prear meeting a thursday night at the church up in town. There is as a good a preacher preaches there as ever I heard we have a chaplain here he preaches every sunday but I dont go to hear him I dont like him for I dont believe that he has any more religeon than I have. I suppose that there is some good ones in the army but I have never seen one of them. Well I will come to close excuse my bad writing and write soon. So farewell dear Brother I remain yore afescionate Brother untill death

Wm H Kesterson

to

Joseph Kesterson St Louis Mo.

General Hospital

Springfield Mo. July the 11th, 1864

Dear Brother

I one time more take my pen in hand to drop you a few lines to let you know how I am a geting along. I am not very well at this time but I still keep my place a nursing and I dont think my health will be much better while I stay here for I dont think that it agrees with me. Yore letter of July the 7th came to hand yesterday and I was glad to her that you was still in good health and hope that you may still continue so. I have no news to write at this time that will be interesting to you there is not much war news astir and you hear that before I do. I got a letter from father two days ago he said that they was all well and that there was plenty of bushwhackers up there and that them and the feds had a fight every two or three days. I supose that all the feds that is up there is paw paw malitia or old Mcpherons [McPherson's?] rigament and they are no better than rebels. I don't believe that if there was a good regiment of men up there that the bushwhackers would be half as bad as they are. Well I see in the paper that part of my regiment has reinlisted and gone up home on a furlough. I supose that they will be in St. Louis about the 20th of this month. I did think that I would try and get down there by that time and go south with them but I am not well and the weather is so bad that I think that I will stay where I am a while longer. We are a looking for the paymaster every day but I dont know when he will be here. I would like for him to come for I have spent the last cent that I have. I expect that I shall stay here untill about the first of september if I have any health then I intend to try and get to my regiment. Well brother I must now come to a close for the present. Keep up a brave heart and dont let yore troubles weigh two heavily on you. And now dear brother if we meet no more on earth let us try and meet in heaven where there will be no parting so fare well my dear brother for the present I remain yore afectionate brother

W. H. Kesterson to

Joseph Kesterson

Kesterson Letters, Missouri Historical Society, St. Louis.

ARE PARTISAN RANGERS CONFEDERATE SOLDIERS?

John B. Clark represented Missouri in the U.S. Senate from 1851 to 1861 but was expelled during the secession crisis for taking up arms for the Confederacy. He became a senator in the Confederate Congress and later a brigadier general in the pro-Confederate Missouri State Guard. His correspondent, George W. Randolph, was secretary of war for the Confederate government. In this letter, Clark worries about the legal status of "partisan rangers"—a widely acknowledged euphemism for bushwhackers. The Latin phrase lex talionis *refers to international law regarding actions against foreign combatants or civilians in retaliation for mistreatment of one's own citizens, principles that had been accepted in spirit (though never officially ratified) by the U.S. government.*

SPOTSWOOD HOUSE, Richmond, July 15, 1862.
Honorable GEORGE W. RANDOLPH, *Secretary of War.*

SIR: I respectfully desire to know from you whether the several partisan corps of rangers now organized or that my be organized in the several States of the Confederacy are to be regarded as part of the Army of the Confederacy and protected by the Government as such. And whether if any of said corps are captured in battle or otherwise while in the line of their duty by the enemy this Government will claim for them the same treatment as prisoners of war which is now exacted for prisoners belonging to our Provisional Army. Are not all corps of partisan rangers organized by your authority emphatically a part of the Confederate Army, and will they not be regarded and treated as such? I consider that it is not only the right but the duty of every loyal citizen in the Confederate States to resist by all means in his power, even to the death if necessary, the attempt of the enemy in a body or singly to invade his domicile or to capture his person or that of his wife, child, ward or servant, or to take from him against his will any of his property, and if in making such resistance, whether armed or not, our citizens are captured by such invading enemy, have they not the right to demand to be treated by the enemy as other prisoners of war, and will not this Government exert all its power if necessary to the end that its citizens are thus protected and treated? This is a war waged against the sovereignty of the several Sates of the Confederacy and against the lives, liberty and property of every citizen yielding allegiance to the States and Government of their choice in which they reside. Such a war has no parallel in the history of Christian nations. I respectfully request you to give me your opinions on the several points in this letter in a form to be submitted to my constituents to enlighten them in regard to the extent of their rights and powers as viewed by this Government and how far their Government will protect them in the exercise

of those rights which to an intelligent freeman are dearer than life itself. Your
early answer is respectfully requested.

With great respect,
JOHN B. CLARK.

. . .

WAR DEPARTMENT, *Richmond, July* 16, 1862.
Honorable JOHN B. CLARK, *C. S. Senate.*

SIR: I have the honor to acknowledge the receipt of your letter of the 15th
instant and to reply that partisan rangers are a part of the Provisional Army of
the Confederate States, subject to all the regulations adopted for its government
and entitled to the same protection as prisoners of war. Partisan rangers are in
no respect different from troops of the line, except that they are not brigaded
and are employed oftener on detached service. They require stricter discipline
than other troops to make them efficient and without discipline they become a
terror to their friends and contemptible in the eyes of the enemy. With reference
to your inquiry as to the protection which the Government will extend to private
citizens taken in hostile acts against the enemy, it is not easy to lay down a
general rule. War as conducted by civilized nations is usually a contest between
the respective Governments of the belligerents, and private individuals remaining
quietly at home are respected in their rights of person and property. In return
for this privilege they are expected to take no part in hostilities unless called on
by their Government. If, however, in violation of this usage private citizens of
Missouri should be oppressed and maltreated by the public enemy they have
unquestionably a right to take arms in their own defense, and if captured and
confined by the enemy under such circumstances they are entitled as citizens of
the Confederate States to all the protection which their Government can afford,
and among the measures to which it may be needful and proper to resort is that
of the *lex talionis.* We shall deplore the necessity of retaliation as adding therefore
we shall act with great circumspection and only upon facts clearly ascertained;
but if it is our only means of compelling the observance of the usages of
civilized warfare we cannot hesitate to resort to it when the proper time arrives.

Very respectfully, your obedient servant,
[Indorsement.]

This being a rough draft without signature I have taken the liberty to interline in
pencil for your consideration.

J. D.

The War of the Rebellion: A Compilation of the Official Records of the Union and Confederate Armies, ser. 4, vol. 4, pt. 1
(Washington, D.C.: Government Printing Office, 1901), 818–20.

THE ST. LOUIS UNION CLUB "WILL NO LONGER DALLY WITH TREASON NOR COMPROMISE WITH TRAITORS"

Union clubs were private voluntary associations in St. Louis and other urban areas, whose purpose was to encourage enlistments, put down secessionist sentiment, and support the Union cause. George Eliot Leighton served as provost marshal in St. Louis from 1861 until the end of 1862.

Sir,

The following preamble and resolutions were unanimously adopted at a meeting of the Union clubs of St. Louis City and County held last evening at the headquarters, corner of Fifth and Olive Streets. . . .

⁓

Whereas, the time has come in the history of American treason, when the honor, safety, and defense, and even the very existence of our free institutions are imperiled alike by the audacity of traitors and misplaced leniency of patriots, and whereas the dictates of duty and self preservations call upon us for prompt and decisive action in defense of the Constitution and Union of our country, and a vigorous enforcement of the laws for the maintenance of all that we hold dear on earth; therefore be it resolved by the Union men of the city and county of St. Louis, that from this hour henceforth we will no longer dally with treason nor compromise with traitors, that forbearance has ceased to be a virtue and leniency has become a false humanity.

⁓

Resolved, that the cruel and relentless system of guerrilla warfare recently inaugurated in our state must be met by the stern voice of public justice and the swift sword of public vengeance, and that those lurking traitors in our midst who, while enjoying the protection of our laws, are aiding and abetting the inhuman system of warfare, deserve and should receive the execration of every honest man.

⁓

Resolved, that we recommend to all members of the Union clubs throughout the state to enroll and organize themselves into military companies and be ready whenever and wherever they can to put down guerrillas and assassins now committing murder and desolation trough the state.

⁓

Resolved, that all the members of the Union clubs in this city be enrolled into companies for the purpose of military drill. . . .

George Eliot Leighton Papers, Missouri Historical Society, St. Louis.

HOW I ROBBED A YOUNG COUPLE

Samuel McDaniel fought with General Mosby Monroe Parson's brigade in Price's army. After the war, McDaniel composed a handwritten memoir of his wartime experiences. Although he does not provide specific dates, the following excerpt recounts incidents that probably occurred in 1863, when McDaniel was serving as a courier in Missouri and Arkansas. When McDaniel left his young hosts, he was just a few miles from his father's home in Pettis County. La Monte is in the north-central part of the state, about halfway between Sedalia and Kansas City.

HOW I ROBBED A YOUNG COUPLE

After leaving Mr. Owsley's I was so very hungry, not having tasted food since I crossed the Osage, three days before. I was desperate. I came in the course of a few miles to a new place on the edge of the prairie, a one room house with a plank fence on all sides was before me.

The front door was open and the man and wife had just finished their evening meal and were yet at the table.

I rode clear round the yard to see how the land lay before getting down.

I hitched the mare at the Northwest corner of the yard and climbed over. I laid joice [a joist] ten by two, one end on the fence so I could, if need be, run up and leap on to the mare without stopping.

Carefully I crept up to the door, in the darkness, outside. The young, newly married wife was saying: "Now, Jim, do you love your wife?"

He: "Yes, I certainly do love you, and would give anything in my power to prove it. Do you love me?"

She: "I love you as no woman ever loved a man, before."

Rebel Soldier in the dark:

"Hold up your hands. And get in the corner, there, face to the wall," and walked in, with cocked revolver in my hand. Then I said, after my command was obeyed: "If you do as I tell you, you will not be harmed. I am a Confederate Soldier half starved and I am going to eat. Go on with your love making, while I eat."

Husband: "Mr., we are Southern people, and if you will, my wife will give you a good supper."

Rebel Soldier: "No Thanks, this is good enough. Just remain in your seats and dont disturb me." I then helped myself to Cornpone, fried chicken, green corn, new potatoes, fresh butter and good buttermilk, O, it was excellent, to me, at least, whose appetite needed no whetting to give it edge.

The wife tried to get me to let [her] wait on the table, but I was an old "stager" and didnt intend to be trapped. I ate all she had, and as I rose to back out, I said:

"Now, I am no robber, I will leave 25 cts. in silver here, Madam, as somewhat of a reward for this excellent supper. Now, as I bid you goodnight, please, remain seated and dont move till I whistle, then you can do as you like in regard to this enforced contribution to the Cause of the Confederacy."

I then backed out, with the revolver in my hand and backed to the joice and then ran up it and onto my nag and whistled.

Be it said to the girl's credit that she didnt want to take my silver quarter, or at least, she seemed to not want to take it. But, I left it on the table linen, by the plate.

I wish I knew who they were. But I've never heard of them from that day. I rode all night, till nearly day light. I was in a strange country and one full of Militia men, and was afraid to go further in the dark and waited, letting the mare graze.

When day came, I was close to the grading of the Mo. Pac. R. R. somewhere below Lamonte, but near the town.

I then felt that I knew the country and pushed on for my Father's home, I'd not seen nor heard one word from since that Saturday, three years before. My heart *was full* and I had many and strange thoughts as I rode on that day.

Samuel McDaniel, "Reminiscences, 1910," Missouri Historical Society, St. Louis.

ADAIR COUNTY PROVIDES FOR WIDOWS AND ORPHANS

Because so little federal or state aid was available to refugees or to the families of soldiers, especially those whose pay was delayed, some townships and counties instituted local relief efforts for the needy. Government officials often used existing political divisions, such as election precincts, to organize such drives. Adair County is in north-central Missouri, close to the Iowa border. This little broadside was printed on a four-by-seven-inch sheet of paper and probably was distributed widely to the residents of Adair County.

COURT ROOM OF THE
COUNTY COURT OF ADAIR CO.

Kirksville, Sept. 13th, 1864.

We, David A. Ely, Noah Stukey, Canada Ownby County Court Justice.

In consideration of the Patriotism manifested by the citizens of Adair county in responding to all calls for volunteers for State as well as National, to sustain the integrity of the Union cause, we would there recommend the citizens of each municipal Township in the county of Adair to meet in mass at their election precincts of their respective Townships on Saturday the TWENTY-FOURTH day of September next, and then and there appoint a committee of five as a committee of relief from that date until the 15th day of March next for their respective townships, to see to the wants of all families of our soldiers now in the field, and that provision for their comfort during the coming winter may be provided, and that no widows and orphans of their respective townships may suffer during the coming winter.

We would also recommend that the several township committees meet at Kirksville the Saturday preceding the second Monday in October and then and there consult with the several committees for the best means of relief of all destitute families of our county for the ensuing winter, and also at said meeting of said Townships to give expression as instructions to the County Court to the propriety of levying a tax or making and appropriating a county fund of relief.

D. A. Ely, Pres.

C. Ownby, Associate Justice.

N.B. Judge Noah Stukey [illegible]

Civil War Collection, Western Historical Manuscripts Collection, University of Missouri, Columbia.

REFUGEE CHILDREN

In 1865, the Missouri Republican *published an appeal to the citizens of St. Louis, asking them to aid the children of refugees in the southern and western areas of the state. From the beginning of the war, refugees had flooded into cities throughout the state as well as army hospitals and forts, such as Fort Scott near the Kansas border and Fort Davidson at Pilot Knob. Both private relief efforts, such as the one depicted in this newspaper appeal, and more organized endeavors by the Western Sanitary Commission strove to aid the starving refugees. Of particular concern were orphans stranded in the southwestern part of the state. Mrs. J. S. Phelps's plea speaks eloquently of the depopulation of that region.*

ONE MORE APPEAL TO THE GENEROUS CITIZENS OF ST. LOUIS, FOR THE RELIEF OF REFUGEE CHILDREN NOW CONGREGATED IN THE VICINITY OF SPRINGFIELD.

I have no doubt the word refugee grates harshly on the ear of every St. Louisan, it has been so often repeated. I hope I shall be excused for this allusion to the subject, and promise if the present appeal is responded to, never to disturb your sensitive organs again by a repetition of the same. I do not wonder this benevolent people think they have already done enough for this class of individuals. Your beneficence has been without an equal. Every day there is a call for some benevolent object, and every solicitor thinks the object par excellent, and urges it with great vehemence. But all will admit there is no object so worthy, so necessary, as taking care of the destitute orphan children of our brave soldiers, and especially those children who have been driven from their homes in rebel States because their fathers loved the old flag. . . .

Had I come to St. Louis immediately after the Wilson Creek battle, and asked of the good people of this city for aid for the wounded soldiers, every man who had a dollar would have vied with each other to see who should be first and the most liberal. We did not then need your aid. We had an abundance and to spare, and we freely divided with every sick and wounded soldier. We would do the same for their children, if we had the same means now we had then. It is not a pleasant employment to ask men for money for the relief of those who have no claims upon them. Did I say no claims? Every widow and orphan child, made so by this war, has a claim, a just claim, upon every man who has been permitted to remain at home and engage in pursuits by which he has made money.

Some say to me, "We have in St. Louis homes for orphans, refugee relief societies, and now we are getting up a Soldiers' Home, exclusively for their orphan children. Why not send these children here?"

I made inquiry of one of the ladies engaged in that institution, how many children could be accommodated? "Not over fifty at present," was her reply. We have over three hundred destitute children now with us, suffering for clothing, food and shelter.

We have several reasons for wishing to keep these children, and raise them in Southwest Missouri. In the first place, there are true and noble ladies, who have faced every danger, labored on the battle field and at home, day and night, and who are still ready to work until the end of this unholy war. They are not willing to shift their responsibilities upon the ladies of St. Louis. Another reason, and a good one (as every reflecting mind will see), we wish to place these children on a farm, and teach them to earn their own living. Nothing is more injurious to children than to supply all their wants, without their making an effort for themselves. We see the bad effects even among the rich, and what will it be to the poor orphans, reared in your city orphan homes? It will be like exposing hot house plants to the cold winds of winter. . . .

And another reason, we shall need these children for laborers. It seems to me that every merchant and the city at large, have felt the effects (in the high price of living), of the depopulation of so many districts in our State. It is for the interest of St. Louis to aid in the re-population and rebuilding of those districts, with loyal citizens, as speedily as possible; this Orphans' Home in the Southwest will do much for that section. . . .

We have made an estimate, and ten thousand dollars, with what we have collected at home, and what we will collect there, will purchase a farm, stock it, and put all the improvements now needed (as we shall purchase a farm with very good buildings), upon it. The institution, after one year, will be self-sustaining. . . .

Something must be done immediately. If the children are sent here to St. Louis you will have them to support, indirectly, by small contributions to fairs, and other ways. Give us the money at once, and that will be the end of calls from the Southwest for refugees. When we have a place for the children, we will set their mothers to work. Now is the time for rich men to show their liberality, by aiding us in a great and good work.

Donations: P. E. Blow and H. T. Blow, $100; Samuel Stillwell, $50; Ticknor & Co., $50.

Mrs. J. S. Phelps,
Planters' House.

Missouri Republican, February 23, 1865.

SIX

Bushwhackers, Jayhawkers, and Prisoners

*I*N AUGUST 1863, General Thomas Ewing Jr. had had enough of the guerrilla warfare that was raging across western Missouri. Ewing ordered that any citizens giving aid to William Clarke Quantrill and his men were to be arrested. Ewing soon detained thirteen women in the makeshift jail in Kansas City, Missouri. Among the detainees were Mary, Martha, and Josephine Anderson, sisters of notorious bushwhacker William "Bloody Bill" Anderson. When the building collapsed on August 14, killing four of the women and severely injuring many others, Quantrill's raiders vowed revenge. They chose as their target the city of Lawrence, Kansas, long a stronghold of free-state sympathizers and the home of Senator James H. Lane. Just after dawn on August 21, Quantrill and 450 men attacked the city, murdering between 140 and 190 men and boys in cold blood. They looted and burned most of the buildings, robbed the bank, and left behind a scene of horrific destruction.[1]

Newspapers around the country reported the massacre, prompting Ewing to strike again at bushwhackers and their supporters in the countryside. On August 25, 1863, Ewing issued General Order No. 11, which commanded everyone living in Jackson, Cass, Bates, and Vernon counties, as well as several other areas, to vacate their homes within fifteen days. The order did not discriminate between loyal and rebel farmers; all residents were to leave. The purpose of the order was to make it impossible for guerrillas to survive in the western counties of Missouri by removing any potential local support. In reality, the displacement resulted in widespread suffering. Many families—mostly women, children, and elderly people—fled to the larger towns, creating a serious refugee problem.[2] Moreover, because the order provided for the confiscation or destruction of grain supplies, the refugees (who included both Southern sympathizers and loyal Unionists) suffered from shortages. Although some charitable aid societies, including the Western Sanitary Commission, donated food and supplies to those living near the large cities, many of the thousands of people who had fled their homes had to live on government aid. The artist George Caleb Bingham was so outraged by what he considered to be the oppressive severity of General Order No. 11 that he was moved to paint his famous protest *Martial Law, or Order No. 11*, depicting the hardships wrought by the evacuation.[3]

Throughout 1863 and 1864, the violence continued to escalate despite the wholesale evacuation of the western counties. On September 27, 1864, Bloody Bill Anderson launched a horrific attack on Centralia, Missouri, looting and burning. Anderson's men murdered twenty-two unarmed sick and wounded Union soldiers who came in on a train, scalping some of them. In some parts of the state, 1864 brought the worst bushwhacking violence of the entire war. Men and boys were murdered, and women were often the victims of personal insults and abuse, especially if they were suspected of pro-Union sentiments. A number of black women suffered physical assaults and rape.[4] While the guerrillas distracted federal forces, General Price determined to take advantage of the conditions to attack St. Louis.

On September 19, 1864, three divisions of Confederate Missourians led by Joseph O. Shelby, John S. Marmaduke, and James Fagan, comprising more than twelve thousand men, entered southeastern Missouri from Arkansas. Their long-term goal was to capture the St. Louis Arsenal and, if possible, the city itself. Price's men had been conducting raids into Union territory for the past year and gathering valuable intelligence. He hoped that his raid into Missouri would also bring thousands of new recruits into his army. By mid-September, some of his men had reached Pilot Knob, where they fought a bloody battle with Brigadier General Thomas Ewing's force of about fifteen hundred troops. Union artillery was able to hold off Price's force, but by the evening of September 27, Ewing began to realize that he would not be able to withstand Price's superior numbers much longer. Muffling the sound of the wagon and caisson wheels with blankets, he slipped out of the fort, blew up the powder magazine, and secured the depot at the train station. Ewing had lost about 250 men (killed, wounded, missing, or captive), and Price more than 1,000.[5]

In the end, Price's plan to raid St. Louis failed, as well. Following the time-honored tradition of concentrating on capital cities and other vital geographic objectives, Price turned his attention to Jefferson City. Capturing Missouri's capital, he believed, would give him control over the entire state. The 1864 gubernatorial elections were approaching, and a victory at "Jeff City" might have allowed the Confederates to put acting Confederate governor Thomas C. Reynolds into office. But Price was disappointed by the very low turnout of recruits. Rebellion fever had burned out in central Missouri, even as Price was slowly making his way toward Jefferson City. General William S. Rosecrans, commander of the Department of the Missouri, reinforced Jefferson City with 16,500 men, leaving the surrounding countryside vulnerable to the guerrillas. Families packed up their children, their livestock, and their belongings and fled into the nearby woods.

The Confederates skirmished briefly with Union defenders at Jefferson City, but soon moved westward toward the Kansas border, through Boonville and Lexington, where they skirmished again with pursuing Union forces. At Boonville, Price met briefly with Bloody Bill Anderson and then headed for Kansas City. By the end of October, however, Anderson had been killed in an ambush. Price began a hopeless retreat back into Arkansas, during which General Marmaduke was captured and most of his army and weapons were lost. The last battle between organized military units in Missouri occurred on October 27, 1864, when a small Union force under the command of General James Blunt caught up with General Jo Shelby's command of Price's army near Newtonia, Missouri.

Bushwhacker violence continued until long after the war was over, though much of it was unconnected with political or military goals. In the end, the most notorious guerrillas died as they had lived: violently. Bloody Bill Anderson was killed in an ambush in 1864, and Quantrill, who fled first to Texas and then to Kentucky, was shot a year later. The few bushwhackers who survived the war surrendered to civil and military authorities. The James brothers and other former raiders, notably Cole and Jim Younger, would turn bank and train robbers in the late 1860s, but some of them (especially Frank James) reformed and settled into a staid old age.[6]

MARY ANN CORDRY TAKES THE OATH OF LOYALTY

The following is an example of a loyalty oath, signed by a woman who lived in Cooper County in central Missouri. When federal officials enforced the laws requiring citizens to take these oaths, they often engendered even greater hostility toward the Union government. Mary Ann Cordry was born in Howard County, Missouri, which is located in the heart of Little Dixie along the Missouri River.

I, Mary Ann Cordry, of Cooper Co, Missouri, do solemnly swear that I will bear true allegiance to the United States, and support and sustain the Constitution and laws thereof; that I will maintain the National Sovereignty paramount to that of all States, County or Confederate powers; that I will discourage, discountenance, and forever oppose secession, rebellion and the disintegration of the Federal Union; that I disclaim and denounce all faith and fellowship with the so=called Confederate Armies, and pledge my honor, my property, and my life, to the sacred performance of this my solemn oath of allegiance to the Government of the United States of America.
Subscribed and sworn to before me, this 21 day of May 1863.
C. S. Moore,
1st. Lieut. and Ass't. Provost Marshal.

Mary Ann Cordry [signature]
Union
Description: Age 43, Height 5 7, Color of Eyes Grey, Color of Hair Aubun, Characteristics [blank.]
Copy.

Cordry, Alphabetical Files, Missouri Historical Society, St. Louis.

GENERAL ORDER NO. II

General Thomas Ewing Jr. issued General Order No. 11. Although the order was approved by President Lincoln, it came under sharp criticism even among pro-Union factions.

General Orders,

No. 11

Hdqrs. District of the Border,

Kansas City, Mo., August 25, 1863

I. All persons living in Jackson, Cass and Bates Counties, Missouri, and in that part of Vernon included in this district, except those living within 1 mile of the limits of Independence, Hickman Mills, Pleasant Hill, and Harrisonville, and except those in that part of Kaw Township, Jackson County, north of Brush Creek and west of the Big Blue, are hereby ordered to remove from their present places of residence within fifteen days from the date hereof. Those who, within that time, establish their loyalty to the satisfaction of the commanding officer of the military station nearest their present places of residence will receive from him certificates stating the fact of their loyalty, and the names of the witnesses by whom it can be shown. All who receive such certificates will be permitted to remove to any military station in the district, or to any part of the State of Kansas except the counties on the eastern border of the State. All others shall remove out of the district. Officers commanding companies and detachments serving in the counties named will see that this paragraph is promptly obeyed.

II. All grain and hay in the field, or under shelter in the district from which the inhabitants are required to remove, within reach of military stations, after the 9th of September next will be taken to such stations and turned over to the proper officers there, and report of the amount so turned over made to district headquarters, specifying the name of all loyal owners and the amount of such produce taken from them. All grain and hay found in such district after the 9th of September next not convenient to such stations, will be destroyed.

III. The provisions of General Orders No. 10, from these headquarters will be at once vigorously executed by officers commanding in the parts of the district and at the stations not subject to the operation of paragraph I of this order, and especially in the towns of Independence, Westport, and Kansas City.

IV. Paragraph III, General Orders No. 10, is revoked as to all who have borne arms against the Government in the district since the 21st day of August, 1863. By order of Brigadier-General Ewing:

H. HANNAHS,

Acting Assistant Adjutant-General.

The War of the Rebellion: A Compilation of the Official Records of the Union and Confederate Armies, ser. 1, vol. 22, pt. 2 (Washington, D.C.: Government Printing Office, 1888), 473.

Alexander Hequembourg (*seated, left*) with two unidentified soldiers. Alex Hequembourg (1830–1911), served in Co. B, Fourth Regiment, United States Reserve Corps; became Captain of Co. G, Missouri Engineers; and served in the Fortieth Missouri Infantry under General John Schofield. He fought at Vicksburg, Franklin, Nashville, Mobile Bay, and at First and Second Bull Run. *Courtesy of Missouri Historical Society*

GENERAL SCHOFIELD COPES WITH THE
AFTERMATH OF GENERAL ORDER NO. 11

Like other federal commanders in border states, General John M. Schofield struggled not only with the many "shades of Loyalty" in the districts under his control but also with continual political attacks and criticism of his policies in Missouri. The following excerpts from Schofield's diary, kept while he was in charge of the Department of Missouri in 1863, reveal some of his frustrations and difficulties.

August 26, 1863

Received by telegraph first report from General Ewing of the burning of Lawrence, Kansas, and murder of its Citizens by Quantrell. Informs me that he has ordered all people to leave the border Counties within fifteen days, when he will move all forage and provisions from those counties. Says he has written me explaining the reasons for the order. I reply that his order coincides nearly, with one, the draft of which I sent him yesterday for his consideration. Genl. Ewing calls for more troops. . . .

Radical papers keep up a senseless howl about the conservative policy of the present Administration in Missouri. They willfully ignore the fact that my policy a year ago, and at present, was and is more radical and vigorous, than that pursued by Genl. Curtis. In 1862, Guerrillas were, under my orders executed on the spot when captured, and hundreds of sympathizers banished or imprisoned. But a short time before being relieved by Genl. Curtis I had obtained authority to send rebels South, and had commenced proceedings. But it was stopped on Genl. Curtis assuming command and not recommenced until a short time before he was relieved.

My assessment orders were suspended by the President because Genl. Curtis refused to become responsible for them himself or see that they were carried out justly by the boards appointed.

It is a simple fact that nearly all the severe and stringent measures which I adopted in 1862 were abandoned by Genl. Curtis. After a few months trial I have found it necessary to institute those measures again. I ordered Genl. Ewing to remove the Slaves of rebels from that portion of Mo. which is in his District, to Kansas, and to banish the families of persons engaged in guerrillas warfare. The immediate effect of this is the sudden collection of several hundred of these villains under Quantrell and their destruction of the town of Lawrence Kansas. Had these measures been adopted last winter when the State was fully under our controll and a large force here to keep down or drive out the guerillas, there would have been no inducement for them to return, and our present difficulties would have been prevented. Now that "radical" measures are being carried out at a time when most difficult, but when necessary because not done when it should have been, the radical press howl like demons at the legitimate consequences, and declare them the result of the "conservative" party.

Sept. 8, 1863

Went to Independence yesterday in company with Genl. Ewing - Ran and conversed with a considerable number of leading citizens of all shades of Loyalty. Found some diversity of opinion regarding the necessity and wisdom of Genl. Ewings order No 11. All seem willing to submit to it if it could produce the desired result. The chief objection was the great loss of property that must result from the rigid enforcement of the order. And it was urged that to destroy the forage and subsistence so completely as to starve out the guerillas is impracticable. Made a few remarks to quite a large assemblage of people, which were well received. Was followed by Genl. Ewing in an appropriate speech, which produced a good effect.

Have determined to modify Genl. Ewing's order, or rather he will modify it at my suggestion, so that no property shall be destroyed. I deem the destruction of property unnecessary and useless.

The chief evil has resulted form the aid given to guerillas in the way information conveyed by disloyal people, and by preparing their food for them. This evil is now removed. Forage and grain can not be destroyed or carried away to such extent as to materially cripple them. I will as far as possible preserve the property of all loyal people with the view of permitting them to return as soon as the guerillas shall be driven out. Property of known rebels will be appropriated as far as possible to the use of the army, and loyal people who are made destitute. None will be destroyed.

Had a long interview this morning with Mayor Anthony of Leavenworth and a number of influential citizens of that place. Anthony was arrested and sent to this place yesterday by a detective in the employ of Genl. Ewing. The arrest was without authority and Genl. Ewing promptly discharged the Mayor. The object of the citizens was to obtain a revocation of Martial Law in Leavenworth and come to a correct understanding as to the relation between the Military and civil authorities in that town, so as to prevent difficulty in future. The whole matter was satisfactorily arranged. The Mayor agreed to abstain from any interference with persons in the military service, while in the discharge of their duties, or for *acts* committed while in the discharge of their duties. Recognized the general principle that persons in the military service in time of war are answerable to military law and triable by military courts for all offences, and that the military authorities should have exclusive jurisdiction in such cases, if the Com'd'g Officer chooses to exercise it. And that he recognizes the will of the military command-ers as supreme. Upon this Genl. Ewing is to revoke his order declaring Martial Law in Leavenworth Co., and is to remove certain of his detectives, who are obnoxious to the Mayor. It is hoped no more difficulty will occur on this subject.

John McAllister Schofield, *Diary of Events in Department of Missouri, 1863,* box 1, John McAllister Schofield Papers, Library of Congress

"THERE ARE STRICT ORDERS AGAINST TAKING ANY MORE PRISONERS THAT IS FOUND . . . AS BUSHWHACKERS"

George Wolz was the son of a German immigrant family. He enlisted as a private in the Union forces in 1862. His letters, like those of many soldiers on both sides, betray the homesickness of the writer. Wolz seems to have had an easier time of it than many of his brothers in arms. Still, he was vividly aware of the bushwhackers plaguing the countryside. The first letter was probably written while Wolz was with the Third Missouri Infantry, Missouri State Militia, in Springfield, just after the battle of Wilson's Creek. By the time he wrote the second letter, Wolz was serving with the Seventh Missouri Cavalry, Missouri State Militia, in southwestern Missouri and northwestern Arkansas. He mustered out in April 1865 and died in 1924 in Trenton, Missouri.

Officers of the Third Regiment, Missouri State Militia, taken at Corinth, Mississippi, October 28, 1863. *Courtesy of Missouri Historical Society*

Springfield, August 11th, 1862.

Dear Father, Mother, Brothers and Sisters:—

It is with pleasure that I take the present opportunity of dropping you a few lines to let yo know where I am and how I am getting along. I am at Springfield at present & enjoying moderate health & hope that these few lines will find you enjoying the same blessings. We have been encamped twelve miles west of this place for the lat week until Saturday evening when our boys were ordered to march to Newtonia to relieve Major Hubberd who was there contending with overwhelming odds. Hubberd had only one hundred and fifty men and was fighting fifteen hundred Rebels and had been for two or three days. But the 4th Mo. was sent out to drive them North and when they found that retreat was cut off on the south and that they were perfectly surrounded they began to run north and met with our boys yesterday morning which formed into line of battle in a ravine and waited until the Rebels came up and then poured a deadly fire into their ranks which threw them into confusion & caused them to turn back when they almost instantly met Hubberd with the artillery and the 4th Mo and was completely carelled. So if reports are true the battle is fought, the victory is won and they are ours, and if we have got them we have two of the worst rebel leaders there is. They have been a terror to the southwest of this state and also to Northern Arkansas. The people here dread Coffee & Rains worse than they do Price for Rains & Coffee are the main leaders of the Guerilla Bands that is prowling through this country almost all times and every place. But that game is almost played out for there are strict orders against taking any more prisoners that is found in arms or as bushwhackers, but to leave them on the ground we found them on.

On last Saturday the paymaster paid us off and I have given Capt. Garvin thirty-five dollars to take to you, which he will do as soon as he can, but at present there is no passing of any trains between here and Rolla where he will have to take the railroad for St. Louis. . . .

August the 26, 186

Dear Father and Mother and sisters and brother.

I once more avail the opportunity of writing you and answer to your kind and welcome letter. It found me well. I hope and trust when these few lines come to hand they will find you all enjoying the same blessing. I am in camp in Saline Co. Mo. I am at the house where I board. I board with a dutch family. I have been here ten days. The bushwhackers burnt ten thousand dollars worth of property in this town. There is a taxes levied on the rebels fighting to pay the damages the bushwhackers done to We are a collecting the taxes from the rebels. There is a good many bushwhackers in this country. I am a seeing better times than I ever seen since I have been in the service. Have plenty of good bacon greece to and plenty of lager beer to drink. And the nicest of it is we have nice girls to look after us and all live like at home. We will stay here two weeks longer yet

It has been two months since I have been to my company. My company is at Warrensburg, Mo. I was on a boat more than a month. I havent got no pay since I left home. I guess we will get pay the first of the month. The officers say we will get on the boat and go up to Kansas City and get our pay the first of the month.

The bushwhackers have killed a good many women fighting in this country. This summer the weather is warm and dry here now. . . . robbed a great many here too. The health is good here. there has been a great deal of garilla fighting in this country . . . I remain your affectionate friend. Till death.

From George Wolz
To Conrad Wolz

Versailles, Mo.
Sept. the 31, 1863.

Dear Brother:

It is with the greatest of pleasure that I avail the opportunity of writing to you once more to let you know that I am among the living. I am well at present and I hope when these few lines come to hand they will find you enjoying the same blessing. The last letter I got from you was dated the 4ᵗʰ of Aug. I was glad to heart at you all was well, I have wrote to you three letters since I got the last money. I would like to hear from home a little oftener. I think you all might write oftener if you would try. Sister Mary and Elizabeth I want you to write to me. I love to see your hand write and read it. There is plenty of apples here and plums and peaches. We haven't much to do here but eat watermelons and dress up and chat the girls. The health is good in the company now. Abraham Wise has got the chills. He has had them ten days. There has been several speeches made in this town about the conventions they had in favor of general president. There isn't much trouble here. There is some stealing of horses. The weather is warm here now. it has been very cold until [illeg] but it is warm. I guess you know more about the war than I do. I want you to write as soon as you get these few lines. So I will bring this letter to the close. . . .

George Wolz
to John Wolz.

Wolz Family Papers, Missouri Historical Society, St. Louis.

A MISSOURI SOLDIER BURNS HOMES IN TENNESSEE

Private Benjamin Guffey served with Company I of the Eighteenth Missouri Volunteer Infantry, which was mustered into service in 1861 and served at Shiloh and Corinth. Throughout his service, he wrote anxious letters to his wife, Caroline, frequently admonishing her to "live religious" so that she would meet him in heaven. Yet by spring 1863, he had begun to worry that he was becoming "lukewarm" and in danger of "backsliding." The death of some of his friends and the bitter news from Missouri had hardened him.

Camp of 18th Regt Mo. Vols. Inft
Camp Sheldon, Tenn.
May 5th, 1863
Mrs. Caroline Guffey

Dear Wife it is with great pleasure that I take my pen in hand to address a few lines to you in answer to yours of the 22 of April which came to hand yesterday and was received with great pleasure and gratification. I was very glad to hear from you for it had been just been precisely two weeks since I received a letter from you and the time seemed very long for I haven't received a letter from any person except you for two or three months. Mrs. Caroline I am glad to inform you that my health is still improving. I am getting as fat and stout as a bear I feel as well as every I did in my life and I cincerely hope this will find you and Baby are enjoying the same blessing. You stated that you were reasonably well and I [suppose] from that that you are not very well. But a person can't expect to be well all the time but when you are not well write just how you are and what is the matter for no person ever gets to see your letters.

Caroline I haven't much to write this evening. The boys are all well and hearty and in good spirits. But it is with regret that I announce the death of two of our best soldiers and the capture of one of our lieutenants. But it was the Cols. fault for not sending out more men for he knew the demons was thick in the brush, for humans I can't call them. They have made it customary for the cavalry pickets to skout in the day and stand picket of a knight and on the first day of this month they started Lieut. Codington and eight men out on a skout or rather to patteroll the roads. They was riding a long the road. When all at once the guerrilla raised up from behind a log. They hollowed whoa and fired without giving our boys any chance to surrender. They killed two dead and wounded two others. Lieut. Codington dismounted or his horse throwed him and the rebles surrounded him immediately. But he made good use of his time for he shot three times and wounded one man mortally that we got and we don't know how many others and the others saved themselves by running. The boys that was killed was George Picket of Company E and John Brison of Company C. They was boath shot in the head. Brison was shot four times The death of these men is lamented by all of our boys for they faught nobly at Shilow and Corinth Then was murdered by the demons of Tenn. We have been skouting ever since. But haven't accomplished anything. Only burnt and distroyed a great many houses and distroyed considerable of property and we are going to start again in the morning. We haven't heard anything reliabl from Lieut. Codington but if they don't return him we have five of ther men as prisners and they will have to suffer in his stead for the Lieut. is well thout of by all the boys and officers. He was second lieutenant in Com. B until the Shilow battle where he faught bravely until he was captured and sent south where he remained for some time until a short time ago, and while he was at St. Louis he was promoted to first Lieutenant in Company [?]. But he is a prisner now in Dixie. When we are out skouting we give the citizens so long to get their plunder out and if they are slow we stick the match two the house and burn them all together. This looks hard but it seems hard to have innosent men murdered. We have been protecting them ever since we have been down here. But thankful we have a commander that will clean them out.

When they came to camp and with the boys that was killed Col. Miller went to the ambluence and looked at them and the tears rolled down his face in grait drops and when we start out he tells us to make our mark that when a person can't write their name he likes to see them make a big mark. And I have herd nothing today but the boys [marking] the women begging the men not to burn their houses. This man that was wounded was at a citizen's house and our boys carried him out and laid him on a bed in the out of doores and burnt the house.

This is a hard way of taking revenge but it is the only way to stop such proseedings.

Now Caroline I must bring this part of my letter to a close for it is geting very late and I am tired and sleep for farewell for to knight.

Guffey Letters, Western Historical Manuscripts Collection, University of Missouri, Columbia.

"I HAD NOTHING MUCH TO [LOSE] AND WHAT I HAD IS GONE"

Lizzie Brannock's letter to her brother, Rev. Edwin H. White, describes the depredations of guerrillas in western Missouri. Chapel Hill is a village near Lexington, not far from Kansas City. Lizzie had been born in England and was about thirty-two years old in 1864.

Lizzie E. Brannock to Rev. Edwin H. White

Chapel Hill Jan. 13th, 1864

Dear Brother Edwin,

. . . [T]hank God you are yet alive and prosperous; seemingly so at least, thus far you have survived in this most horrible reign of Terror which has been so long desolating our once happy land. I grieve for your losses and yet you know thousands have been left as you were though that is no consolation but rather doubles our own sorrows. I had nothing much to loose and what I had is gone—but most of all my dear husband—our comfort and support. I have two dear lovely children . . . No dear brother I care not for myself but for my little ones I fear. I could endure anything but to see my little ones suffer with hunger and cold for scant of clothing is what I dread. So far we have not really suffered but the days have been very dark. God has always opened the way for me and this winter finds us well clothed and in a comfortable home [at] my father in laws . . .

Our country is desolate, indeed almost entirely a wilderness, robbery is an every day affair so long as their was anything to take our farms are all burned up, fences gone, crops destroyed no one escapes the ravages of one party or the other; we will remain where we are this winter but this spring we shall be obliged to leave. Where I shall go, or what do; I do not know. . . . [In] spring 1862 we went into Cass Co on the farm of William Brannock he having gone to Kz [Kansas] but the Kansas troops would give us no rest anything that was in Missouri was to be destroyed and taken, yes Brother we are what is called Rebels. I do rebel against anything dishonest and cruel in any way and we have suffered every thing, from the most inhuman and barbarous set of men that could have been turned loose upon any soil or country. Bro. John made a mistake in saying Mr. Brannock was conscripted, he went voluntarily to that army which he conceived to be the *right one* rather than go into the militia he could stay at home no longer; . . . He . . . has been a soldier ever since an honest Christian soldier from principle and conscience . . . do not think that I became rebel because my husband was, for I was rebel at least 5 months before my husband but my deffinition of rebel is perhaps different from yours.—I call an *Abolitionist* a rebel.

Would to God Brother we could have the dear old government with all its rights and privileges. heaven smiled upon us then, all I ask or wish is for the Constitution to be held sacred as it was given and the good laws of a good administration to be carried out to the letter—but I thought when two parties could not live in peace and happiness together it was best to separate, tho it was not best I know in our case, and I did think it might have been arranged peaceably—there are gross and fearful faults on both sides and I hate war, could not believe it possible we would come to arms—and if we did I thought in this enlightened 19 century war would be concluded upon honorable principles but it seems no age of barbarism can show us such scenes of cruelty and plunder.— and God only knows were it will end. I think every man is entitled to his honest oppinion and no one has a right to interupt or disturb him for his sentiments . . .

[A]nd if I am a rebel, know Brother I do not look with any degree of allowance upon robbery, and driving honest people from their homes, or bushwhacking in any shape. if we have war let there be two armies and fight honorabley but could we have peace I would be glad upon almost any terms, Mr. Brannock would be willing to live as a Loyal Citizen if he could, but I am not willing he should take an oath that he desires the North to triumph over the South in this unhappy struggle . . .

[I]t [is] human nature to hate those who do us wrong and the party to which they belong yet know that the good on both sides do not uphold it more than we. [T]hree times we have been threatened to be burned out and five times plundered it would take a book to tell you of all troubles. . . . let us ever look with upward gaze to the golden City New Jerusalem and pray for the day when Lion shall lie down with the Lamb and a little child shall lead them—let us be wise as serpents and harmless as Doves keeping ourselves unspotted from the world. . . .

Your Loving sister, Lizzie E. Brannock.

White, Edwin H., Rev., Alphabetical Files, Missouri Historical Society, St. Louis.

"BLOODY BILL" ANDERSON THREATENS
THE WOMEN OF WESTERN MISSOURI

Shortly after carrying out several cold-blooded massacres of Union soldiers in the summer of 1864, guerrilla captain William Anderson traveled to Lexington. After

reading local newspaper editorials critical of his actions, Anderson dispatched
several letters to the editors, who obliged him by publishing them. A little more
than two months after these letters appeared in print, Anderson and his henchmen
murdered another twenty-five federal soldiers at Centralia, Missouri, and mutilated
some of the corpses. Within a month thereafter, Anderson died in an attack by
federal forces at Albany, Missouri.

JULY 7, 1864.

To the editors of the two papers in Lexington, to the citizens and the community at
large, General Brown, and Colonel McFerran and his petty hirelings, such as Captain
Burris, the friend of Anderson:

Mr. EDITORS:

In reading both your papers I see you urge the policy of the citizens taking
up arms to defend their persons and property. You are only asking them to sign
their death warrants. Do you not know, sirs, that you have some of Missouri's
proudest, best, and noblest sons to cope with? Sirs, ask the people of Missouri,
who are acquainted with me, if Anderson ever robbed them or mistreated
them in any manner. All those that speak the truth will say never. Then what
protection do they want? It is from thieves, not such men as I profess to have
under my command. My command can give them more protection than all the
Federals in the State against such enemies. There are thieves and robbers in the
community, but they do not belong to any organized band; they do not fight for
principles; they are for self-interest; they are just as afraid of me as they are of
Federals. I will help the citizens rid the country of them. They are not friends
of mine. I have used all that language can do to stop their thefts; I will now see
what I can do by force. But listen to me, fellow-citizens; do not obey this last
order. Do not take up arms if you value your lives and property. It is not in my
power to save your lives if you do. If you proclaim to be in arms against the
guerrillas I will kill you. I will hunt you down like wolves and murder you. You
cannot escape. It will not be Federals after you. Your arms will be no protection
to you. Twenty-five of my men can whip all that can get together. It will not be
militia such as McFerran's, but regulars that have been in the field for three years,
that are armed with from two to four pistols and Sharps rifles. I commenced at
the first of this war to fight for my country, not to steal from it. I have chosen
guerilla warfare to revenge myself for wrongs that I could not honorably avenge
otherwise. I lived in Kansas when this war commenced. Because I would not
fight the people of Missouri, my native State, the Yankees sought my life, but
failed to get me. Revenged themselves by murdering my father, destroying all
my property, and have since that time murdered one of my sisters and kept the

other two in jail twelve months. But I have fully glutted my vengeance. I have killed many. I am a guerrilla. I have never belonged to the Confederate Army, nor do my men. A good many of them are from Kansas. I have tried to war with the Federals honorably, but for retaliation I have done things, and am fearful will have to do that I would shrink from if possible to avoid. I have tried to teach the people of Missouri that I am their friend, but if you think that I am wrong, then it is your duty to fight. Take up arms against me and you are Federals. Your doctrine is an absurdity and I will kill you for being fools. Beware, men, before you make this fearful leap. I feel for you. You are in a critical situation. But remember there is a Southern army, headed by the best men in the nation. Many of their homes are in Missouri, and they will have the State or die in the attempt. You that sacrifice your principles for fear of losing your property will, I fear, forfeit your right to a citizenship in Missouri. Young men, leave your mothers and fight for your principles. Let the Federals know that Missouri's sons will not be trampled on. I have no time to say anything more to you. Be careful how you act, for my eyes are upon you.

Colonel McFerran:
I have seen your official report to General Brown of two fights that have taken place in Johnson and La Fayette Counties with your men. You have been wrongfully informed, or you have willfully misrepresented the matter to your superior officer. I had the honor, sir, of being in command at both of those engagements. To enlighten you on the subject and to warn you against making future exaggerations I will say to you in the future to let me know in time, and when I fight your men I will make the proper report. As to the skirmish I had with your men in Johnson, I started to Kingsville with fifty men to take the place, but before I arrived there I discovered a scout, fourteen or fifteen of your men, on the prairie some half a distant to my left. I immediately gave chase. They fled. There were not over eight of my men ever got near them. They did not surrender or I would not have killed them, for I understood that Company M were Southern men; they sent me that word. I ordered them to halt and surrender. I was astonished to see them refuse after sending me such word. One of their lieutenants even planned the assassination of General Brown and the taking of his headquarters but I refused to commit so foul a deed. But they refused to surrender and I had them to kill. I regret having to kill such good Southern men, but they are fit for no service but yours, for they were very cowardly. Myself and two men killed nine of them when there were no other men in sight of us. They are such poor shots it is strange you don't have them practice more. Send them out and I will train them for you. After that I came down near Burris' camp with twenty-five regulars all told, belonging to the

Kansas First, some of my first men. I understood that Burris was anxious to give me a thrashing. Not wishing to lose more than twenty-five men at one time, I thought I would try him with the aforesaid number, but while I was waiting for him to come out from camp, that I might devour him or be devoured, forty-eight of your men coming from Lexington with three wagons had the audacity to fire on my pickets, and very imprudently asked me to come out of the bush and fight them. I obeyed reluctantly. They dismounted and formed on a hill. I formed under their fire under the hill and charged. They fled and I pursued. You know the rest. If you do not, I can inform you; we killed ten on the ground and wounded as many more. Had all of my men done their duty we would have killed thirty of them. Farewell, friend.

To BURRIS:
Burris, I love you; come and see me. Good-by, boy; don't get discouraged. I glory in your spunk, but damn your judgment.

General BROWN:
General: I have not the honor of being acquainted with you, but from what I have heard of you I would take you to be a man of too much honor as to stoop so low as to incarcerate women for the deeds of men, but I see that you have done so in some cases. I do not like the idea of warring with women and children, but if you do not release all the women you have arrested in La Fayette County, I will hold the Union ladies in the county as hostages for them. I will tie them by the neck in the brush and starve them until they are released, if you do not release them. The ladies of Warrensburg must have Miss Fickle released. I hold them responsible for her speedy and safe return. General, do not think that I am jesting with you. I will have to resort to abusing your ladies if you do not quit imprisoning ours. As to the prisoner Ervin you have in Lexington, I have never seen nor heard of him until I learned that such a man was sentenced to be shot. I suppose that he is a Southern man or such a sentence would not have been passed. I hold the citizens of Lexington responsible for his life. The troops in Lexington are no protection to the town, only in the square. If he is killed, I will kill twenty times his number in Lexington. I am perfectly able to do so at any time.

Yours, respectfully,
W. ANDERSON,
Commanding Kansas First Guerrillas.
(Editors will please publish this and other papers copy.)
[Indorsement.]

Headquarters Central District Of Missouri,

Warrensburg, July 18, 1864.

Respectfully referred to Major-General Rosecrans, commanding Department of the Missouri, as a curiosity and specimen of a guerrillas chief's correspondence.

E. B. BROWN,

Brigadier-General of Volunteers, Commanding.

The War of the Rebellion: A Compilation of the Official Records of the Union and Confederate Armies, ser. 1, vol. 41, pt. 2 (Washington, D.C.: Government Printing Office, 1893), 75–77.

CYRUS RUSSELL IS TAKEN PRISONER DURING THE BATTLE OF PILOT KNOB

Pro-Union farmer Cyrus Russell and his son, Cyrus S. Russell, lived near Pilot Knob. Some time after the war, Cyrus Russell wrote an account of being taken prisoner by Sterling Price's men, and his son attached his own memories of the family's encounters with soldiers during the battle of Pilot Knob. On Monday, September 26, 1864, a portion of Price's army attacked nearby Fayette, Missouri, while other units ranged through the country looking for recruits.[7]

A PRISONER DURING PRICE'S RAID
BY CYRUS RUSSELL.

It was Monday, September 26, 1864. I was making sorghum Molasses in the back yard, when my wife came running to me and said, "The Rebels are coming!" I drew my purse from my pocket and gave it to her, which she hid in her dress and I followed her into the house. There was no time to escape to the Fort, two miles away, for the Confederates had surrounded the house; so I went upstairs and lay down on a bed. I had been sick for a long time and was not able to go into the army. It was not long before the house was filled with soldiers, and they soon found me and demanded my surrender. Resistance was useless.

As they led me out of the house, one of them struck me over the head with the butt of his pistol. I had on an old felt hat with the crown tarred, but the blow was so heavy that it cut through the hat and made an ugly gash in my scalp. He turned to a comrade and said, "This is a damned, black Republican. Strip the house and put fire to it." They found that I could not walk as fast as they wanted to have me, so as we were passing my brother William's house, they took one of his horses and put me on it. We marched down to their camp of the night before, at the St. Francois River, eight miles east. There we had to sit all night in the rain, on the rocks in the woods. Next day we were taken into an old sheep pen where the mud was ankle deep, and we had to stand there all day and one night, not able to sit down. There were about seven of us in all—Andrew and William Tong, "old Man" Means, John Ake, and two of their own men. We had nothing to eat until the next morning. I asked one provost officer if they were not going to give us anything to eat. He said he did not know. He had had nothing himself since the morning before.

They brought us each a pint of flour and about two ounces of bacon. We made a dough of the flour with water and no salt, rolled it on a stick and cooked it and the bacon before the fire.

About ten o'clock on Wednesday, the 28th, we were started on the march twenty-six miles north. We stopped three hours in Arcadia, and as we passed my home I was allowed to stop and get some medicine and say a few words to my wife. We reached camp after dark. We sat on rocks in the rain again that night. The next morning we had another pint of flour and I stole an ear of corn from a mule and roasted it in the fire. For drink we had water out of the creek where the horses had been through and washed their feet until it was pretty highly colored and strong enough.

Thursday morning we were taken before General Cabell, who inquired of each one, "Are you a Union man?" I told him I always had been and always expected to be. Some of the other prisoners were taken on farther, but William Tong and I were released, for they did not care to be encumbered with sick prisoners, or to conscript men whose guns would have been more ready to shoot backwards than forwards, and we reached home before sundown that evening.

CIVIL WAR EXPERIENCES.
BY C. S. RUSSELL.

. . . The people were advised to repair to their homes and the men after leaving their families safe, to report to the Commander at the Fort. I well remember my father, dressed in his Sunday best, with his double barrelled shotgun, as he rode away on his grey horse "Mack."

It was two hours later, perhaps when he returned with the news that it was a false alarm, that some scouts near Frederictown had heard General Marmaduke was on his [way] to attack Pilot Knob, but they had no definite information. Everyone slept as soundly that night with a feeling of security, as though not a Confederate soldier was in the State of Missouri.

The next day being Monday, wash day in all well regulated households, everyone was engaged in their usual occupation. Father was busy making sorghum molasses, assisted by the orphan boy "Dick," and an old German. My older sister Julia and I were allowed to go to visit our cousin Bert, who lived less than a quarter of a mile away with instructions to come home at a specified time. It was probably about two o'clock when we started for our weekly exchange of visits. Our homes were on the State Roed from Ironton to Fredericktown and lay well to the eastern part of the Valley, about two miles from the Shut-In through which the road ran. The first clear view of Pilot Knob, Ironton and the Valley was possible only from the rising ground near our Uncle's home.

About half way between the homes which lay on opposite sides of the main road, a side road from the south was almost hidden by a high Osage orange hedge. As we neared the corner of our father's farm we saw a group of mounted men who did not look like regular soldiers but several were dressed in army blue. My sister at once became suspicious, but I called her attention to the fact that they were blue. When we neared the men they spoke kindly and told us to hurry on to the next house for there would be some shooting pretty soon. We obeyed and I doubt if they would have allowed us to return to our own home. These men were intently looking toward town and probably wore the blue to allay suspicion when seen at a distance. When we reached our Uncle's house, our Aunt hurried us indoors, telling us they were rebels, and had shot at our Uncle who was on his way to the Fort to give the alarm. Soon we saw them advancing in a large body over the hill on which the Baptist Home for the Aged is now located. For the first time in our lives we saw the Confederate flag and the soldiers forming in battle line.

Our Aunt now thought it time to take refuge in the cellar, so she called us to follow her and soon she had us, her own two children, the orphan boy, Wash and the black girl, Mag safe behind a solid stone wall. We could hear the sound of rapid firing to the west of us where evidently they had been met by the Federal soldiers, and were engaged in a brisk skirmish. . . .

As darkness came on the skirmishing grew fainter tell we could hear only the tramp and noise of passing soldiers. Mother gave each of her children a slice of bread, butter and honey. We were too frightened to relish our food and huddles about the cheery fire in the fireplace and were glad of the light of the lamp which took away a little of the [gloom].

Mother's sister had gone with the other aunt in that dangerous trip across the fields, so that Mother was alone with her children and the fourteen year old orphan boy who lived with us. An officer came to the door and said, "I will place a guard at your door, Madam, and you will not be disturbed." His protection did not extend to the kitchen and we could hear men prowling around in search of something to eat.

Mother put all of the children to bed and too tired to do otherwise they all slept till morning. Daylight came and with it a drizzling rain. Looking from an upstairs window we could see a row of cannon in our Uncle's yard, and men behind them ready to begin a battle. There was no firing however and soon the cannon were moved nearer the Fort. An officer sat on his horse in our woodshed which adjoined the kitchen, the rain dripping off his butternut suit, and he freely asked and answered questions with Mother.

The officer assured Mother they had 35,000 men, part of them had gone by way of Farmington.

There was no cooking that morning for there was nothing [to] cook nor to eat. As the day advances the Confederate Army which had been firing at intervals, began their fighting in earnest. The cannon in the Fort sent shells over the house with that peculiar whistling shriek that once heard is never forgotten. The shells burst in front of the house and a fragment killed a horse near by. News of the battle came back from time to time and now and then a wounded man as he was able to ride. . . .

. . . A little later we had another surprise. When a squad of soldiers guarding prisoners came into the yard, Father was allowed to speak to us for a minute only and to tell us they would be taken on with the army. It was a joy to know that he was alive even though he must still be a prisoner. His shirt was caked with blood from the wound on his head where a brutal captor had struck him because he could not walk fast enough because of his lameness. Another soldier during that march was more merciful and placed him on a horse which they had stolen from his brother's stable. The prisoners were marched about sixteen miles farther and after an examination by officers a few were released, given passes through the Confederate lines, and allowed to return to their homes, while some who claimed to be in sympathy with the South were required to go into the ranks. On the way home they were frequently halted by stragglers, and on one acxasion they attempted to take the shirt off the back of one of the returning men. The road was strewn with calico and other goods taken from store in Ironton and Pilot Knob and other stuff for which they had no use. . . .

Russell, C. S., Alphabetical Files, Missouri Historical Society, St. Louis.

"THE MILITARY FORCE LOOKED MISERABLY INSUFFICIENT TO SUCCESSFULLY COPE WITH THE ENEMY"

Prolific author Richard J. Hinton was a stonecutter and printer who emigrated from England to New York in 1851. Becoming firmly convinced of antislavery principles, he left for Kansas as a "free state settler" in 1854 and quickly became involved in free state politics there. He was active in recruiting black men for the First Kansas Colored Infantry Regiment in 1862 and became its lieutenant in 1863. After the war, he served as inspector general of the Freedmen's Bureau. The following excerpt was taken from his 1865 description of Price's Missouri raid.

While east of the Mississippi River success crowned our arms during the entire current of the eventful year 1864, west thereof we were generally defeated: two splendidly equipped armies almost routed, each only saving themselves by a great loss of material, as well as of men. At the same time, in a portion, at least, of the Trans-Mississippi region, over which our rule had most successfully re-established, by reverses to our arms the rebels succeeded, if not in reinstating themselves, at least in rendering our control precarious, and confining the Federal garrisons within the limits of their posts. . . . Price had about 10,000 veteran troops, well armed, equipped and clothed. Jackman, Dobbins, Brooks, and others were busily engaged bushwhacking and conscripting in all sections of Arkansas, except the immediate vicinity of the posts held by General Steele. During the summer he succeeded in conscripting about 8,000 men, a large number of whom were boys and old men, unfit for and incapable of withstanding the fatigues and hardships incidental to all military service; but especially so to that of the Trans-Mississippi Confederate armies with their ill-supplied quartermaster bureau. From the spoils of Red River and Camden, General Price received a good share of transportation, clothing, small arms, several Parrott guns; . . .

For months rumors were rife in sympathizing circles, and among the bush-whackers in Missouri that "Pap Price" (as the general is familiarly known by his admirers) would soon be in the state with a large army. It was generally credited by our troops stationed on the river and elsewhere in Arkansas, that the rebel general intended an advance northwards; yet this was hardly deemed possible by the distinguished soldier [General Steele] commanding at St. Louis. . . . As for General Curtis, in command at Fort Leavenworth, fully occupied with the important duties entrusted to his inadequate forces, it is not surprising that he should have deemed it both monstrous and impossible that a rebel army could march unchecked in the slightest degree, for over two hundred miles beyond our advanced lines, into the very heart of our territory; not only without resistance, but almost unknown to the commanding officer of the department immediately concerned.

In Kansas, the military force looked miserably insufficient to successfully cope with the enemy, so soon to threaten the security of that state. . . .

Lieutenant-General Sterling Price, C. S. A., crossed the Arkansas River at Dardennelles, a village in Pope county, Arkansas, about equi-distant from Little Rock and Fort Smith, the two principal posts occupied by our troops. It is a position of military importance, and before the spring campaign of '64, was held by the 3d regiment Arkansas Volunteers. . . .

Their operations showed the rebel army consisted, at the time of crossing, of about 18,000 armed men, nearly all of whom were mounted. Some three or four thousand recruits and conscripts were added in Northern Arkansas.

This force was organized into three divisions, under the command respectively of Brevet Major-Generals Fagan, Marmaduke and Joe Shelby. . . .

Shelby's division was composed mainly of the old bushwhacking, raiding force of Southern Missouri, increased by a rigorous conscription in Northern Arkansas.

The notorious partizan leader, Jeff. M. Thompson, commanded Shelby's old brigade, and the infamous guerilla, Colonel Jackman, commanded another. . . .

The route of this army in Northern Arkansas was through the counties of Pope, Van Buren, Searcy, Izard, Fulton and Lawrence. The rebel movements were unmolested and conducted in the most leisurely manner.

The contradictory intelligence which for two or three weeks reached St. Louis and Little Rock, served only to confuse Generals Rosecrans and Curtis. General Steele, who had been largely re-inforced by several thousand infantry, does not seem to have been very active. The rebels showed great activity in the neighborhood of our posts in Western Arkansas, and by demonstrations in the vicinity of Forts Smith, Gibson, at Cane Hill, Clarksville, Fayetteville, and along the supply route in the Indian Territory. General Gano moved along the latter line with two brigades of cavalry, one of Texans and the other of Indians, under Stand Waitie, the rebel Cherokee leader. The rebels, Colonel Brooks and Major Buck Brown, whose operations in Washington and Benton counties, Arkansas, had kept our troops at Fayetteville on the alert all summer, were reported at Clarksville, while other forces, marauding parties mainly, were reported at Cane Hill, Crawford county. By these means and this activity, our intelligence was confused, and the attention of our officers directed from the rebel line of march.

Richard J. Hinton, *Rebel Invasion of Missouri and Kansas, and the Campaign of the Army of the Border against General Sterling Price in October and November, 1864* (Chicago: Church and Goodman, 1865), 13–14.

THEY RECEIVED CONFEDERATE FRIENDS WITH SMILES AND TEARS

James Kennedy worked as a telegraph operator for the Morse Telegraph Company at Parkville and Kansas City, Missouri. He joined the Confederate army, serving in Searcy's battalion, Tyler's brigade, and made the march with Price during his failed attempt to capture Jefferson City and St. Louis in 1864. Kennedy was able to look back on his service without regret; he wrote his twelve-page memoirs of the events of 1864 sometime in the early 1910s.

. . . As soon as we crossed the Missouri line guns were heard on both flanks as well as in the front the woods were full of Bushwhackers styled Union men and Mounted Militia on fine Horses Kept in front of our Column burning houses and destroying the property of all Southern sympathizers and especially of the Noble Women whoes husbands brothers and sons had left Missouri to join the Confederate Army It was sad to see the Noble Women both old and young looking on the destruction of there homes Furniture and cooking utensils Beding Clothing. Notwithstanding they received there Confederate friends with smiles with tears as well as blessing

The Malitia was not allowed to carrey out this cruel way of doing business very long Two hundred picked men were sent after them with orders never to stop until they were driven off killed or captured. . . .

If the student of history will read the report . . . he can come to no other conclusion than this raid in Missouri was one of the boldest most daring raids made by the troops of any command during the war. He will see that an army of not more than 8,000 men weighted down with 4000 unarmed men invaded a country filled with troops well armed and equiped. With no supplies or Depots to draw from with no Rail Roads or steam boat transportation with no clothing or ordinance stores to supply the needs of the troops compelled to obtain supplies for the men and Forage for the Artillery and Cavalry horses and mules from the country and that in the presence of a large Army well trained well fed well clothed well mounted 8,000 Cavalry in our rear 6,000 well armed well clothed Infantry on our left and an Army of at least 20,000 well armed well equiped and organized well mounted state troops from Missouri Kansas and Colorado in front that we marched from South Arkansas crossed the Arkansas River through North Arkansas filled with Federal troops through the state of Missouri from South to North to Kansas fighting skirmishing every day and night taring up R Roads destroying Bridges R Road Depots Clothing and Subsistence depots Capturing more artillery . . . Not withstanding the fact that we failed to accomplish all we started to do and that our losses were great and our suffering great and the Student of history will be compelled to say that no greater valor was ever displayed. That no braver no truer Southern patritotism and no greater self denial was ever shown by any command during the war. The number of brave Southern patriots buried far from home on the raid in Missouri will prove this to be true. . . .

James Kennedy Papers, Missouri Historical Society, St. Louis.

"STRANGE TO SAY—WE DID NOT FEEL AFRAID"

Eliza Ward Hammond lived in Jefferson County, Missouri, near the Mississippi River. Her letter demonstrates the unpredictable nature of military raids; Hammond and her sister took some precautions to ensure that they would be able to maintain themselves with wood and food if they were raided, but they suffered few depredations. The Frissells were a slave-owning family in Jefferson County.

St. Louis, December 11th, 1864.

My dear Margaret:—

I received your letter and should have answered it immeadiately. I have been very sick with a very bad cough which redeuced me so much that I had to keep to my bed the greater part of the time. I am better under Homeopathic treatment and hope soon to be well. I am staying with Mary this week. Eliza is moving to her ould home and would not let me stay for fear I would get more cold and take a relapse, so I am here until she gets settled and my room is fixed for me. I hope they will be done with moving and that they will be content in their ould home. People never know when they are well off.

Well, you wish to know how we, I mean your Mother and family, got along during Price's raid. Well, we were as happy and a merry as could be. We did not see a man or boy except the Rebels on Fayeta [Fayette?] for a week. Did just as we pleased. Everything went on as smoothly as could be. At night each one gathered in their share of wood. Caroline fed the hogs at daylight and sorted them. We had no trouble. She kept the gates all tied. We had plenty to eat. Cooked when we pleased and ate when we pleased. I do not know when I was ever more full of fun. I am sure Cat was so full of spirits she laughed at everything—and strange to say—we did not feel afraid. Lay down and sleep sound all night. We hid everything except enough to be comfortable on. It is a mystery to me why they did not rob us. Your Father did not lose one cent by them. They took about fifteen hundred dollars from George La Beaume. Broke him up entirely. He has nothing left but his house and land. They took all of his clothes except what he had with him. A good many of Zoe's also. Cut up her stair carpet for saddle blankets. She went as soon as she found they were there and she gave them a piece of her mind. They said that if the ladies had stayed at home that they would not have taken more than they needed. It made them mad to find the houses deserted. They did not take any of her bedding or destroy any of her furniture. I suppose her going home and staying there saved it. Enough of Price's Raid. I am sick of hearing and talking about it. They did no more than our army would do in their country.

Ella Drake is to be married in February to Mr. Cresen a Philidelphia gentleman. She will do well. She will go there to live. Anna was quite sick when I left home. The rest are all well and Austin is at Paduca on Staff duty. Lou Tompkins said she would not move out home with us. Tompkins is up the river on a boat. George and Zoe are with us and will remain all Winter. He was drafted and had to pay a substitute. He is going on the river, for he is flat broke, losing so much and having to pay so much for a substitute. The draft is going on in Jefferson County. I suppose your brothers will be taken. They were disbanded three weeks ago. I got a letter from Cat last week. She has been suffering with her hip, and head. There was a doctor from St. Louis there to examine her and he said he can cure her if she is sent up and gets medicine. They had a Thanksgiving dinner. Mr. and Mrs. McFarland, Simpson and daughter, and I do not know how many more. Your Mother had gone on a visit to Mrs. Lear when Caroline wrote.

William Hurst is married to Miss. McCulloe. Caroline is more happy than she was. I think she is coming to her senses. Sophy Tatum is married to Dr. Casey of Potosi. I suppose you knew him. I suppose you have heard of Mason Frissells death. I suppose you do feel lonesome away from your family and ould friends but you must make the best of everything and if your husband is spared to you and escapes the draft you ought not to complain. I have no doubt that you will be very happy if you all have your health. Always contrast your situation to hundreds of others, that are driven from their homes and lose everything. Mrs. Sweet and Mary send their love to you, as do all of the rest of your cousins. Tell Willie Grandma has not forgotten him and his many kindnesses and kind acts he did for me, nor the many cool drinks he brought me. I hope he is a good boy and he learns his books. My best regards to Mr. Muse. I often think of him and the pleasant Summer we spent together. And now, dear Mag, excuse this badly written letter for I am quite weak yet. Write me whenever you can. My love to you and yours,

Eliza W. Hammond

Frissell Papers, Missouri Historical Society, St. Louis.

THE SUFFERING CONDITION OF THE PEOPLE

Starving and destitute refugees and freedmen received federal assistance at various places throughout the state, including Cape Girardeau, Cassville, Pilot Knob, Rolla, Springfield, and St. Louis. Army appropriations were never enough to feed and clothe the hundreds of people gathered at the forts, however, so newspapers often printed solicitations for private aid from citizens. The army chaplains generally took responsibility for distributing charitable donations to the refugees.

SUFFERING CONDITION OF THE PEOPLE.

Office of the Superintendent of Refugees,

Pilot Knob, Mo., APRIL 21, 1864

Editors Missouri Democrat:

Will you permit me, through your paper, to give some painful facts respecting the condition of hundreds now flocking to this post for protection In Ripley county, especially just now, there is a most deplorable state of things. Three or four families a week have been arriving from that region for several weeks, driven by the merciless guerrillas from their homes, some of them taken from beds of sickness and thrust out during this inclement month, robbed of even their wearing apparel and bedding. With their half starved cattle they started in the night, having had but two or three hours' warning. Their cattle died on the road from starvation, and they made their appearance here nearly starved and chilled with cold. Twenty more families are on the way, and will be here in a day or two. Two families arrived this morning, their teams nearly dead. The balance of them were obliged to stop—their teams having given out. These are loyal families and when they come here must have food and clothing. Shelter there is none for them and no tents can be obtained. Many of them are sick and need some of the comforts of life. The great question is, what can be done for them? The rations supplied by the government are not half enough for a family and there is but very little food in the country. In many places not a pound can be bought at any price. Many farms in this region will be untilled this summer. The teams that are left will be unable to plow. The young men are in the army, and altogether the future looks dark. I wish some one of the Sanitary Committee of St. Louis would visit Pilot Knob and become acquainted with the real wants of the refugees. I am [sure] if they were to understand the distress among these families those having in charge the Sanitary Fair to be held in St. Louis would aid them, for I do not see that their condition will improve during the summer, as far as food is concerned. The families are large and helpless, the men being old or in the service or their husbands and sons, who were their sole dependence, have been killed or have died in the Union army. Soldiers in the army, many of them are thoughtless about their families at home, and fail to send them money when they might; others are in hospitals far away; some are prisoners at Richmond and other places and some so far away that they cannot if they would send them [any].

Some of the citizens of St. Louis have been exceedingly liberal, and their private donations of shoes and clothing have done much for their relief. The Western Sanitary Commission, the Union Ladies; Aid Society, at St. Louis and Carondelet, and the Freedmen's Relief Society, have also aided us very much. But clothing soon wears out, as the women and children have to carry their wood a long distance, which is very hard on clothing and shoes. The Western Sanitary Commission has just sent me a gill of medicines, and a humane physician is attending upon the sick gratuitously. A large number have been quite ill during this month, and many have died. Never was summer more warmly welcomed than the coming sunny days will be by those who, through a long winter, have suffered untold privations.
A. WRIGHT,
Chaplain and Superintendent of Refugees.

Daily Missouri Democrat, April 5, 1864.

THE *JOURNAL OF WESTERN COMMERCE* REPORTS RISING PRICES IN MISSOURI

In 1864, Missouri newspapers began reporting on the alarming rise in the prices of commodities. The Kansas City, Missouri, Journal of Western Commerce

*carried weekly columns explaining to its readers that the effects of the war,
higher transportation costs, rising price of gold, and the shortage of labor made
it increasingly difficult to buy basic needs for homes and farms. Price inflation
and shortages of goods were problematic enough for people living in towns and
cities, but for refugees driven from their homes, the economic problems proved
devastating. As a point of comparison, here are the prices for a selected group of
basic commodities, reported on August 27, 1860. Note that the paper did not always
specify the unit of measure; for most items, the figure given probably refers to price
per pound or yard.*

Flour—$3.00 to $3.15 per sack
Sugars—8 to 8½ cents
Coffee—16½ to 17 cents
Cheese—11½ to 12 ½ cents
Oysters—$5 to $6 per dozen (probably per dozen cases)
Hides—9 to 10 cents according to quality
Tobacco—No. 1, 30 cents; No. 2, 20 cents; common, 15 cents.
Candles—18 to 20 cents per lb.
Soap—5½ to 6 for yellow, 7½ for white.
Rice—6½ to 7 cents
Brown sheetings—6½ to 7½ cents
Kentucky jeans—18 to 25.
Brooms—$2.25 to $2.50 per dozen.

*The following editorial discusses the various reasons for rising prices of commodities
but does not mention that prices for labor were also rising at this time. All men of
military age who were not already in uniform were required to join the Enrolled
Missouri Militia; those who were able to avoid impressments were therefore able
to command high wages. The symbol @ probably stands for the Latin word ad,
meaning "to."*[8]

HIGH PRICES IN MISSOURI

It is altogether an error to suppose that the high prices now prevailing, are
due wholly to the rise in gold. If such were the case we ought to find the prices
of other things enhanced only as much as the price of gold, which is not the fact.
Gold at 100 per cent. premium is an advance of 100 per cent., or just double its
price at the commencement of the war. But many articles have risen in price from
200 to 500 per cent. Coffee which we used to purchase at 12½ cents per pound,
is now worth 50c, an advance of 400 per cent. The price of cotton has advanced

still more. Were other things no higher, proportionately, than gold, they would be much cheaper than they are now.

One of the chief causes, doubtless, of the rise of prices, is to be found in the scarcity of labor, and the diminished productions of industry. During the war, not less than three millions of able-bodied men, north and south, who were previously engaged in productive industry, have been withdrawn from the sphere of labor and production. Hence, there is an absolute scarcity of labor, especially among skilled workmen. Hence, too, there must be a great falling off in production. The great rise in cotton is due, in good part, to its absolute scarcity.

If we take some article, such as real estate—land—which is not capable of increase or reduction, we shall find that the rise in the prices of other things has affected it but slightly. The price of land has advanced somewhat, but nothing to compare with the prices of other things.

So, too, the prices of some of the great agricultural staples have not increased much beyond their standard in ordinary times. Thus, wheat is quoted in New York at only $2.25@$2.30 per bushel, prices which have often been exceeded in times when gold and currency were on a par.

A little study and reflection will show us that the increase in prices may be traced mainly to these causes: First, to an absolute scarcity of the article, as cotton; secondly, to the scarcity of labor, as in the case of most kinds of handicrafts and skilled labor; thirdly, to an excessive demand created by the war for some articles, as in the case of iron manufactures; and, fourthly, to high taxes and the difficulties of foreign importation, as in the case of liquors, tea, coffee and tobacco.

Gold itself has become scarce, owing to its being extensively hoarded and to the immense amount of it shipped out of the country to pay for foreign goods.

The redundancy of the currency is not nearly so great as is popularly supposed. At the present time the money market is "stringent," and in some of our larger cities money commands two per cent. a month.

We believe the great mistake, if he made any at all, of Mr. Chase's financial scheme, was the inauguration of the National Banks. There should be no currency authorized in any nation except that issued by the government itself. No bank should ever be allowed to issue a single dollar of currency. There never was so favorable a time for inaugurating this sweeping but most necessary and beneficent reform, as during this great war. Had Mr. Chase "made war upon the banks" until he had driven every one of them out of existence, so far as the issuing of currency is concerned, and given us nothing but greenbacks, he would have conferred an inestimable blessing upon the country.

Western Journal of Commerce, July 8, 1864.

WEEKLY REVIEW OF THE MARKET

Our quotations are still on the advance. Markets have been very unsettled, owing to sudden and violent changes in the price of gold, tightness in the money market, &c., &c. Congress having adjourned and the tariff and excise bills being finally settled, prices will probably soon settle down to more permanent rates.

OFFICE JOURNAL OF COMMERCE,
FRIDAY, JULY 8, 1864.

DRY GOODS.

Spragues	32@33c
Other good styles	28@30c
Denims, according to quality	40@75c
Striped Shirtings	30@50c
Check Shirtings	25@65c
Brown Sheetings, according to quality	30@63c
Brown Shirtings,　　"　　　　"	28@55c
Bleached goods,　　"　　　　"	25@55c
Cotton Flannels	35@50c
Woolen Flannels	50@1.00
Kentucky Jeans	50@85c
Satinets	75@1.25

GROCERIES.

SUGARS—New Orleans, 25@26c; Clarified "O" in sack, 30c; Crushed, 31@32c.

COFFEE—Prime Rio, 50@52c; St. Domingo, 48@50c.

FLOUR—$4.50@$5.50.

SOAP—Superior Family, 11c; Palm, 10@11c; Oline Oxide, 12c@13c; German, 11c; Castile, 20@30c.

CANDLES—Star Candles, 30c p lb.

TOBACCOS—No. 3, 65c. No. 2, 75c. No. 1, $1.00; Natural Leaf, $1.40; Smoking Tobacco, 20@30c p lb, owing to quality; Laclede, $6.50@$7.00 per box.

NAILS—We quote $8.50@$9.00, owing to size.

HIDES—Dull, 15c for dry flint.

SALT—Sacks, $4.50; Onondaga in bbls. $4.50@$5.00.

TEAS—$1.25@$2.50 p lb.

CANDIES—Assorted, $7.00; Hoarhound $8.50.

RAISINS—New M. R. $6.75; Layer $7.25.

SODA—English 12 ½ c; American 11 ½ c.

CHEESE—W. R. 18@20c.

WHISKY—$1.75@$3.00.

WOOL—We quote, Mexican, washed, 32@35c; unwashed, 30c; American, fine, washed, 55@75c; unwashed, 40@45c.

Western Journal of Commerce, July 8, 1864.

WEEKLY REVIEW OF THE MARKET
OFFICE JOURNAL OF COMMERCE, FRIDAY, MAY 19, 1865.

Business during the past week has been moderately brisk. The farmers are generally very busy planting so that trade from the country round about is rather dull. The Southern Kansas trade is increasing rapidly. We notice goods for that section of the country going out almost daily. The demand from that section for agricultural implements is very heavy, indicating farming operations on an extensive scale. Several new houses are about opening in this city. Building has not commenced extensively yet, though considerable will be done in that line as soon as brick can be burned.

The quotations for goods are almost without change in our market. The process of reduction in prices goes on slowly. The last quotations of gold in New York are 130¼.

DRY GOODS.

Sprague's Prints	22@25c
Other good styles	20c
Denims, according to quality	25@35c
Striped Shirtings	25@40c
Check Shirtings	25@50c
Brown Sheetings, according to quality	12 ½ @25c
Brown Shirtings, " "	15@30c
Bleached goods, " "	12@20c
Cotton Flannels	25@35c
Woolen Flannels	35@75c
Kentucky Jeans	40@65c
Satinets	50@1.00
Hampden and Glasgow Ginghams	25c
Hamilton Delaines	25c
Other	15@20c
Debases and Hamala cloths	12 ½ @20c

GROCERIES.

Sugar, common N. O. p lb	16@18
Crushed and Powdered sugar	24@25
A Sugar	21@22
B Sugar	20@28
C Sugar	19@20
Coffee	34@36
Salt, p barrel	$4.75
Rice	16@17
Star Candles	24@25
Soap	11@13
Soda	11@13
Nails, p keg	$6.50@7.00
Tea, best Imperial	1.75@2.50
" 2nd qualities	$1.65
Can Fruits, p case	$10.00@11.00
Oysters, p case	$11.50@12.00
Brooms, p doz.	$3.50@4.00
Dried Currants	28
Dried Apples	15
Blackberries	48
Cherries	35
Raspberries	50
Wooden Ware, No. 1 tubs p doz.	$17.00
" " , No. 2 "	15.00
" " , No. 3 "	13.00
Three-hoop Pails	4.75
Two-hoop Pails	4.25
Wash-boards	5.50
Golden Syrup, p keg	$19.00
Belcher's Syrup	14.50
N. Y. Molasses, p gall	1.25

SUNDRIES—Pepper, 50c p lb; cloves, 60c; nutmegs, $2.25; Sardines, qr box, 42c; S. S. Almonds, 35c; Filberts, 30c; English Walnuts, 30c; Coal Oil, p gall, $1.25; Indigo, $1.50@2.25.

Western Journal of Commerce, May 19, 1865.

DR. HOLMES CARES FOR HIS FELLOW PRISONERS

The highly eccentric Dr. Joseph McDowell headed the medical department of Kemper College but moved to a new location at Ninth and Gratiot streets to found the famous medical college that bore his name. Known as an ardent anti-Catholic, anti-immigrant, and prosecession physician, McDowell eventually ran afoul of General William S. Harney, who commandeered the medical college and turned it into the Gratiot Street Prison. The prison was infamous for its overcrowding and unhealthy conditions. Note that one of the men who aided the author of the following letter, a surgeon named William Duncan, was most likely a Catholic belonging to the order of Christian Brothers.

McDowels Colege, St. Louis, Mo. [n.d.]
Dr. T. Holms

Dear sir

I am a prisoner in this place with several Hundred others some citizens others from fort Donaldson but the most of them from the Pittsburge fight. Through the influence of a Mystic Brother I was transfered from the common to the officers department of this extensive prison where I enjoy some privaliges and many comforts I could not otherwise do. Since the arival of the Pittsburge Prisoners my services as Surgeon and Physician have been brought into requisition.

This morning in passing through the hospital department your son approached me made himself known and requested me to write to you. He was and had been sick His clothes much worn and dirty without money with the conviction on his mind that if his situation was not soon aleviated he would soon die. You can see I have embraced the first oportunity to comply with his requests.

Should you attempt to assist your son either by letter or by visit I would sugest caution or you might be detained From the prison yourself. I would sugest an application for the assistance of the kind angels who are in the habit of visiting us to learn our wants for the purpose of aleviating them to whom I have represented your sons case. I shall send this letter through their hands with the request thay send you their adress.

Since I see the amount of good I can do The sufering my limited means permits me to aleviate I hardly regret that I am a prisoner. The providence of heaven may so have disposed of me for that purpose and I submit without another murmer. In haste I subscribe myself your friend

Wm H. Duncan

William Duncan, letter, n.d., Missouri Historical Society, St. Louis.

HOW A YOUNG LADY GOT INTO GRATIOT STREET PRISON

Colonel Joseph Darr Jr. was provost marshal general in St. Louis in 1864. The provost marshal's records indicate that over the course of the war, several hundred women were arrested and held in Gratiot Prison, usually for such activities as feeding bushwhackers or writing to rebel soldiers. Many were released upon taking the oath of allegiance. Whether "Fannie Smith" represents an actual person is uncertain; Darr's records indicate that an eighteen-year-old woman with "fair hair" named Fannie Little was arrested in August 1864, but no other women on his list fit the description given in the following article. Still, the fact that the Missouri Republican, a staunch Democratic paper, reported this case reveals that sympathies for Confederate prisoners were at a low ebb.

HOW A YOUNG LADY GOT INTO GRATIOT.—

On Sunday afternoon, November 6, just after the long train of rebel prisoners had passed down Fifth street, on its way to prison, a fair and elegantly-dressed young lady of seventeen or eighteen tripped up the stairs leading to the headquarters of the Provost Marshal General, and entered the first door that was open. At a desk sat a stern-looking gentleman engaged in writing, of whom the fair young damsel at once inquired: "Is this Colonel Darr, sir?" "Yes," was the response. "My name, Colonel, is Fannie Smith, and I have called to have a little conversation with you about those poor Confederate prisoners. [Here the Provost Marshal General ceased writing and raised his head.] They looked so very tired and cold and hungry, I thought I would make a little coffee for them, but my ma said I had better get permission of you to give it to them first, and I know, Colonel, you are too kind-hearted a gentleman to refuse that." . . . "Miss Smith, I am always glad to see young people cultivate benevolent feelings. Now, did you ever do any thing or express any sympathy for our Union soldiers?" The young lady replied, hesitatingly, and with some trepidation, "Well, no, Colonel, I can't say I ever did. But I thought the Government took care of them." "The Government takes care of its prisoners, too," said the Colonel, "and as you have no desire to give sympathy to those who are protecting you, I shall not let you encourage our enemies. Therefore, you will not be allowed to give coffee or anything else to prisoners."

. . . It was well-known to the Provost Marshal General . . . that the Smith's were rebels and, after Miss Fannie's doleful departure from his office, he directed a more careful *surveillance* to be kept over the entire family.

In just two weeks from that time he found it necessary to place the eldest sister in a safe place, as she was actively engaged in assisting and secreting the worst of the rebel spies and smugglers. Orders were accordingly issued for her arrest.

The mother followed next, having been caught in the same business with her daughter and the spies . . . A few days after the loss of her amiable mother and gentle sister, Miss Fannie appeared at Col. Darr's desk . . . On arriving at her destination, smiling and happy, her heart was electrified at Col. Darr's warm welcome and his saying: "Now Fannie, I have sent for you to write me a nice little letter, asking me to release your mother."
[She wrote the letter in pencil as he had asked.]

. . . [T]he Colonel told her he guessed she could go down and visit her [mother] awhile, at the same time giving directions to confine Miss Fannie in Gratiot till further orders. As she left the room the Colonel said, with some feeling, "that is the last of those infernal snakes."

It now turned out that Miss Fannie had been corresponding with the rebels in arms, and, under her amiable appearance, cloaked her character as a spy. It seemed almost impossible, but there was one of her letters which had been captured by the squadron near the river and forwarded here. It was in Fannie's own hand, signed with her own name, written *in pencil*, full of useful information to the rebels, bitter against the Government, and contained a few lines about Grant's reverses, Lincoln's tyranny, and the anxiety of the people of St. Louis to be "delivered from the most damnable despotism in the world."

The fair but bitter hypocritical young rebel, had she had the slightest idea of the capture of the treasonable correspondence, would have written her *pencil* note in a very different state of mind. Under some circumstances, and in some countries, she would have been placed in irons and finally hanged.

Missouri Republican, November 26, 1864.

ONLY EIGHT IN THE GUARD HOUSE

Unruly soldiers continued to be a problem for officers of both sides until the end of the war. William Patrick received a resigned letter from a friend observing that "only" ten men had to be disciplined after being paid, presumably because they had spent their money on alcohol. William Patrick enlisted as private in the Third U.S. Reserve Corps and later served as assistant provost marshal for the Department of Missouri. His correspondent, Lieutenant Colonel James F. Dwight, served with the Eleventh Missouri Cavalry, under the command of Colonel W. D. Wood, in Missouri and Arkansas.

I've got camp quiet at last after the row caused by the distribution of your funds. Reduced only 2 non-commissioned officers & 8 in the guard house . . . that speaks well for the sobriety of the Regt. Take my horse "Yank" if you can; he is not to be harnessed to drive. Have had the damndest storms for a week. . . . yesterday the gale carried away my flag pole & uprooted two trees at full leaf.

P.S. Wood has resigned . . . If you can see Gov. Fletcher or can influence him, suggest the propriety of commissioning me Colonel, although I can't be mustered, the regiment not having enough men.

William K. Patrick Papers, Missouri Historical Society, St. Louis.

SEVEN

~

First Steps toward Emancipation

*B*EFORE THE WAR, a majority of Missouri voters supported the institution of slavery, but this attitude did not automatically translate into support for secession. Conservatives—like Provisional Governor Hamilton Gamble, Democratic senator John B. Henderson, and Missouri State Convention delegate Samuel M. Breckinridge, for example—had always believed that slavery would be safeguarded under the Union and the Constitution, and they trusted President Lincoln's assurances that he had no intention of interfering with slavery in the loyal border states. Such men remained steadfast as long as the Union cause was winning in Missouri and the slaves remained on their owners' farms. But by the middle of 1862, Missouri slaves were beginning to flee toward Union marching lines and bivouacs, across the Kansas border, or into towns and cities. What Missouri slave owners had always feared had finally come to pass, and their slave property was no longer quite secure. Furthermore, many white Missourians—especially those living in the larger towns—had begun to change their minds about the institution of slavery. The ongoing guerrilla violence, the threat of disloyalty among the secessionist element, and the fact that President Lincoln was beginning to urge border state representatives to consider local emancipation schemes loosened loyal Missourians' commitment to slavery. Even some conservatives gradually came to realize that human bondage was doomed, and they began to look for a way to make the end of the institution less costly for slave owners.[1]

Change, however tentative, had been in the air since the beginning of the war, no doubt influenced by the German presence in St. Louis. In January 1861, for example, a public protest at the courthouse steps in downtown St. Louis broke up what proved to be the last slave auction ever to take place in the city. The fact that public officials in the city did nothing to halt the protest, and indeed allowed it to put a decisive end to slave auctions, suggests that the times were ripe for transformation. Yet few white Missourians, even those in Republican-dominated St. Louis, advocated radical or immediate action on the issue of slavery. When General John C. Frémont proclaimed martial law in the state in August 1861 and announced the freedom of every slave owned by individuals in rebellion against the Union, his action, though overturned by Lincoln, created a sensation in Missouri and beyond. While abolitionists throughout the nation applauded this move, regarding it as a precursor of general emancipation, loyal conservatives in Missouri were less enthusiastic about the prospect, even as they praised the general's harsh measures in dealing with rebels in arms.[2]

Emancipation was highly divisive in Missouri. Provisional Governor Hamilton Gamble made it clear that he had no intention of interfering with the institution of slavery. On August 3, 1861, Gamble issued his own proclamation, stating unequivocally that "[n]o countenance will be afforded to any scheme or to any conduct calculated in any degree to interfere with the institution of Slavery existing in the State. To the very utmost extent of Executive power, that institution will be protected."[3] Gamble's message reassured Missouri's conservatives, but by the end of that year, most of them had come to recognize that the institution of slavery had no future in the state. When the Thirty-seventh Congress reconvened in Washington in early December 1861, it proceeded to pass laws that freed slaves in particular localities (in the District of Columbia, for example, and in the territories) and permitted the enrollment of black men in the Union armies.

Lincoln usually took a stance less radical than that of many congressional Republicans, and he had always favored state action on the issue of emancipation. He was firmly convinced that emancipation had to begin in the border states.[4] But as the only Northern states that still permitted slavery, the border states were in a terrible bind. Because the U.S. Constitution still protected private property, Congress could pass no laws emancipating the slaves within loyal states without paying just compensation. So by the spring of 1862, Lincoln was determined to persuade the congressional delegations from the four border states to come to some agreement on freeing the slaves. Under his plan, emancipation in Delaware, Kentucky, Maryland, and Missouri would come gradually and would include some compensation from Congress. Lincoln insisted that emancipation had to come through state action, not through congressional legislation. Lincoln chose to address legislators in Washington because he hoped that they would be able to influence their constituents to support gradual, compensated emancipation in their states. On March 6, 1862, Lincoln met with representatives of all the border states to ask them formally to consider his proposals. Although Senator John B. Henderson (who was becoming far more progressive on the issue of emancipation) and Congressman John W. Noell agreed, the rest of the Missouri delegation refused, as did those of the other border states.[5]

The political climate in Missouri, however, was changing. The test oaths that kept disloyal residents from voting increased the number of antislavery members in the General Assembly and in the Missouri State Convention. Slaves took advantage of the chaotic conditions spawned by the war and escaped, causing a severe labor shortage in the northern and central counties. Fugitive slaves found

work in St. Louis, near refugee camps, and along the Mississippi River. The eager-
ness of these fugitives to work reassured some white residents that freeing the
slaves would not cause the devastation and violence they had always feared.[6] Even
supporters of slavery found stability within the state more desirable than the prof-
its of bondage and were willing to reconsider their commitment to the peculiar
institution.

Even as Missourians prepared themselves to face these changes, they still had
to determine *how* to eliminate slavery within their state. Provisional Governor
Gamble had always been a proslavery political moderate, and in 1862 he asked
the legislature to develop a plan of gradual emancipation. State representative
Charles P. Johnson, of St. Louis, chaired a committee whose task was to examine the history and future of slavery in the state; the committee issued a lengthy
and detailed report that included many pages of statistics showing the economic
backwardness of the state in comparison to her free neighbors. The report recommended amending the Missouri state constitution to permit legislation on the
elimination of slavery, preferably in a gradual manner and without compensation
to slave owners. Gamble agreed with the recommended course, disappointing
radicals, who demanded not only immediate emancipation in the state but also
equal political and social rights for black people. That went too far for most Missouri moderates. Radicals were best represented among the German populace,
particularly in St. Louis, and their growing irritation with the governor's moderate
policies soon led them to work against him. Radical newspapers published harsh
criticisms of Gamble, even blaming him for the ongoing guerrilla violence and
military setbacks. The pro-Union element in the state became ever more divided
as conservatives stressed a slow emancipation process with no increase in rights
or equality for black people, while the radicals pushed harder and harder in the
opposite direction. Extremists on both sides blocked the efforts of moderates to
reach a compromise. But for the time being, the radicals were successful in keeping the proslavery element out of power.[7]

According to historian William Parrish, most Missouri voters, even conservatives, wanted to face the issue of slavery squarely rather than avoid or ignore it as
their representatives in Washington did. On April 2, 1862, for example, delegates to
the Missouri State Convention debated a resolution whose purpose was to inscribe
within the state constitution a process of gradual and compensated emancipation.
This highly controversial measure garnered a great deal of support among the
antislavery convention delegates but was voted down after much heated debate.
Still, by mid-1862, radical Republicans (especially delegates from St. Louis) had
gained enough seats in the General Assembly that by the end of the year, they
were able to introduce several resolutions for gradual emancipation. Ultimately,
however, they adjourned without taking action.

Lincoln had laid plans for preliminary emancipation before he met with border state conservatives in 1862. But when the border state men rejected his proposals, the president moved ahead without them, effectively leaving Missouri out of the process. Although the Preliminary Emancipation Proclamation, issued on September 23, 1862, did not free slaves in Missouri or other loyal states, it did set in motion a profound commitment to end slavery in the nation and state. White Missouri voters began to support antislavery candidates. Both black and white abolitionists in the midwestern states labored hard to make emancipation a reality. In 1863, midwestern and border state antislavery activists called a Slave State Freedom Convention at Louisville, Kentucky, for the purpose of finding ways of effecting the abolition of slavery through political action. Similarly, the Equal Rights League, composed mostly of free black Missourians, met to advocate for political rights for African Americans and an end to discrimination.[8] Black men also joined the Union army.

The first battle in which black men fought took place on Missouri soil, at Island Mound on October 29, 1862. More than eighty-three hundred black men from Missouri served in the Union army, although many initially had to volunteer for regiments in other states, including Illinois, Iowa, and Kansas, because Missouri refused to recognize the recruitment of blacks. There were four regiments in all: the Sixty-second, Sixty-fifth, Sixty-seventh, and Sixty-eighth U.S. Colored Troops Infantry. Many in these regiments were former slaves from Kansas and Missouri who had run away or been taken by Union forces. Like their counterparts in other regiments, Missouri's black soldiers fought heroically, even though they faced discrimination, harsher punishments for infractions of military rules, and substandard medical treatment.

Because the General Assembly had proven itself incapable of reaching a consensus on the fate of slavery, Provisional Governor Gamble recalled the Missouri State Convention into service in June 1863, charging the delegates with taking a stand on emancipation. According to historian Dennis Boman, a majority of the members of the Missouri General Assembly had expressed antislavery sentiments, but they were inexperienced and unable to overcome the uncompromising stance taken by ardent proslavery members. The convention, on the other hand, had served the state well during the early years of the war, so it seemed logical to call on it to cope with this most intractable of issues. On July 1, 1863, the convention issued an ordinance of gradual emancipation, which provided for the abolition of slavery by July 4, 1870, exemption of slave property from taxation, and apprenticeship of younger slaves. Radicals, however, continued to demand speedier emancipation as well as political and civil rights and educational opportunities for the freed slaves.

HENRY T. BLOW ASKS PRESIDENT ABRAHAM LINCOLN
TO PASS AN EMANCIPATION EDICT

Staunch Unionist and antislavery activist Henry Blow drafted a letter to President Abraham Lincoln asking for the removal of General John M. Schofield, who had been placed in charge of the District of Missouri in February 1862 and whom radicals considered far too moderate. The Blow family had purchased and freed Dred Scott in 1858. Henry T. Blow was married to Minerva Blow (see her letter to daughter Susie in chapter 2).

Willards Hotel
Washington Aug 12, 1862.

Sir:

. . . .

It may not be entirely becoming in me, President Lincoln, in this connection to urge on you a certain view which I hold in common with millions of devoted Americans but I do not deem this a time for any patriot to withold [*sic*] his convictions from those in authority and therefore address you freely.

It is this! "I am of the opinion that the masses of our country men including our noble Army, and a majority even in the border states, feel *that we are unequal to the task of putting down the Rebellion while we protect slavery.*

You can order your Generals to lead on the new hosts, and sacrifice more precious lives than have yet been wasted on this unholy rebellion, but the result will be the same; Military science with all the boasted wealth of this great country and pretension on the part of those who consider their Generalship as of more importance to the Nation than a great living and enduring principle, will still fail to subdue the states banded together to *uphold that institution we have not yet dared to assail, and which is the main support of the Mighty armies that have so often been hurled against our inferior numbers*. . . .

Pardon me, sir, for writing so plainly, we have no future with the institution of slavery perpetuated while we will ensure a destiny more brilliant than imagination can conceive, if we are faithful to the *great idea* of the Revolution. . . .

With sentiments of the highest esteem
I am Sir, Your Obt. Svt
Henry T. Blow

Blow Family Papers, Missouri Historical Society, St. Louis.

A MISSOURI LADY DREADS WINTER AMONG "INSOLENT NEGROES"

The full name and precise location of the author of this letter is unknown. S. F. Craig complains bitterly about her slaves, as well as depredations committed by soldiers from both armies. Craig wrote this letter to a young woman named Stephanie (Fannie) B. Carr, whose family originally came from Lexington, Kentucky, and settled in St. Louis before the Civil War.

Susa. Oct 21st 1862

My Dear Fannie

. . . I am bitterly disappointed in having the prospect of a winter among these insolent dreadful negroes, but I will try to endure it as long as I can and help [my husband] bear up in these sore misfortunes. I can but die at the worse, and perhaps something may turn up to brighten the now gloomy prospect before us. The country looks dreadful, not a soul to be seen except a few marauding soldiers who are prowling around destroying every thing in the country. A few days since a train of twelve waggons drove to the Gin and tore it all to pieces—took off the weather boarding—broke down the doors & window sash with all the most expensive fixture of every kind and carried them all off. The Mill house also has been destroyed in the same manner, and several other building[s] near and about the Gin. . . .

The soldiers *stole* [my husband's] horse from him to day again—but I begged the Capt so hard for him he made the man give him up—they stole all the bedding in the overseers house & the Hospitals and broke into the cellar and got the milk—fortunately the butter jar was hid or I should have lost that. The negroes lost their clothing and bedding to a considerable amount likewise.

The pillaging is renewed again and unless something is done we will lose all we have in the house I fear. . . .

May God have you all in his holy keeping & bless you & yours is my earnest prayer.

yours truly S. F. C.

Carr-Zimmerman Collection, Missouri Historical Society, St. Louis.

EDWARD BATES WARNS PROVISIONAL GOVERNOR
HAMILTON GAMBLE OF POLITICAL INTRIGUES

Edward Bates moved to St. Louis in 1814, studied law, and became a prosecuting attorney of the northern circuit in the Missouri Territory at age twenty-four. A leader of the Whig Party in Missouri until its collapse in 1854, Bates later served as attorney general of the United States from 1861 to 1864. He remained friendly with his brother-in-law, Provisional Governor Hamilton Gamble, throughout the war. By the autumn of 1862, however, radicals in Missouri were already aligned against Gamble because they detested his moderate policies on slavery. Like most moderate Republicans, Bates supported gradual emancipation but believed that freed slaves should be colonized in Africa or other tropical climates. The phrase "verb: sap:" most likely means "verbum sat sapienti," or "a word to the wise suffices."

Attorney General's Office
Washington, Sept. 11, 1862 (Night)
Excy. H. R. Gamble
Gov. Mo St. Louis

Dear Sir:

Today, the Sec. of War promised me to send, without delay, to the ordnance office at St. Louis, subject to your order, 2700 Garibaldi Rifles, with ammunition. . . .

. . . Without having my suspicion fixed upon any one in particular, I cannot help suspecting that there are persons in Mo, sustaining some relations with the government here, who are seeking to undermine your influence & power for good, by secretly insinuating doubts and suspicions, if not downright lying. Within the last week, two different members of the government, (who I know, have no malice against you) asked me, with an air of concern, "have you full confidence in Governor Gamble?" I answered each, promptly & emphatically— "Yes sir, quite as much as I have in you." And both of them seemed pleased and satisfied with my answer. But, *verb: sap:* If we ought to be as harmless as doves, still, our safety consists largely, in being as wise as serpents. Watch them at that end of the line & I will keep a lookout at this. . . .

Your attached friend,
EDW: Bates

Bates Family Papers, Missouri Historical Society, St. Louis.

"HE TALKS OF NOTHING BUT EMANCIPATION"

James O. Broadhead was born in Virginia and, like many of his peers, combined a firm commitment to the institution of slavery with equally staunch Unionist ideals. He was a well-respected lawyer whose many correspondents valued his advice and political influence. One of them was Missouri senator John B. Henderson—soon to become one of the leading lights of the emancipation movement—who hoped to persuade Broadhead to enter his name for the state senate contest in the upcoming fall elections. Instead, Broadhead served as provost marshal. Louisiana was Henderson's hometown; Ashley was a nearby village, also in Pike County. Democrat Robert A. Campbell was a St. Louis politician who became lieutenant governor of the state in 1881.

Louisiana Missouri
Oct 23 1862

Dear Broadhead.

I am just recovering from a long and somewhat exhausting spell of sickness—been in bed since I last saw you in St. Louis. . . . I see you are on the ticket for Senate and I have been told you are indifferent about running. Indeed I was told you would not run. This you should not do. You ought to run and go to the Legislature—Now is the time for you to do something for Missouri if ever you intend anything and I know your *intentions* are good. We want some cool, quiet, determined, clear headed men in the counsels of this state at present, for it really seems that between the rampant secessionists and the radical destructionists we shall lose all.

We are in a bad fix here and most unexpectedly so. I am astonished at the course of Bob Campbell. I don't know exactly at what he aims but I have my suspicions. I care nothing about his opposition to me personally, but the speeches he is making are of the most injurious sort.

The questions of emancipation, negro equality, abolition army in Missouri, bad treatment towards our Southern men, &c., are his themes. What it will lead to I cannot tell—perhaps to a war at the polls. Such is now anticipated. . . .

They have cut up a furrow of excitement and many people are shuddering over negro insurrections and the terrible outrages of negro freedom. At Ashley they are running their men on the local issue and the Union men will vote for them, because our candidates are from Louisiana . . . If you can in any manner influence Bob Campbell and think he is inclined to act longer with the Union party I hope you will do so. But I will see you when I come down.

Yours truly
J. B. Henderson

Samuel T. Glover was a prominent St. Louis lawyer and, like Broadhead and Henderson, a conservative Unionist. By "perpetuationist," he means those men who wanted to preserve the institution of slavery.

St. Louis June 4 / 62

Dear B.

I have yr welcome note of the 2nd. I am greatly gratified to learn that you contemplate taking the ground mentioned on the emancipation question. The form in which you put it is a good one to draw out the Kindliest consideration of the convention. It will not pass. Of course not. There is a pro-slavery party in Mo yet and tho' it would seem to be thinking now: it is not. It is feeling most intensely. And it is not long till we see the *bitterness* of it. We can not compromise now any more than formerly because with it *slavery* is every thing. How would it do provided your propositions are voted down to have this voted on by the convention, a joint resolution to be approved by the governor "Slavery ought not to be perpetual in Mo." As stated the potent objection *"not at this time"* would be flanked and gentle men compelled to vote or leave the hall. Nothing will more certainly test the anti slavery feeling of the convention than a vote if you have one on the disfranchisement of the rebels. The perpetuationists will all look to the rebels for sympathy and support. I have never seen a *perpetuationist* who was a loyal man.

Yr friend

S T Glover

Broadhead Papers, Missouri Historical Society, St. Louis.

MISSOURIANS REACT TO THE EMANCIPATION PROCLAMATION

Proslavery Missourians denounced the Preliminary Emancipation Proclamation. For example, the Democratic editor of the Conservator, *a paper published in Platte City, freely voiced his opposition. Platte City is very close to the Kansas border, just south of Kansas City. Even the most loyal residents of Platte City were likely to retain some bitter memories of the Union army's policies toward civilians. On December 16, 1861, Colonel W. James Morgan, in command of the Eighteenth Missouri Infantry, had burned the courthouse and most of the city to the ground in an effort to capture bushwhacker Silas M. Gordon. The editorial was somewhat mistaken, however, as to the scope of the proclamation; slaves owned by Missourians or by residents of any other loyal border state were not freed by the document. In another column, the paper gave the full text of the proclamation under the headline "Mr. Lincoln's Proclamation. The Niggers To Be Set Free!! 'The End of the Beginning.'"*

THE EMANCIPATION PROCLAMATION.

President Lincoln has on several occasions intimated that the abolition element with which he had to contend, the assistance of which he considered indispensably necessary for the restoration of the Union, would probably compel him, eventually, to proclaim some new dogma in behalf of the African slave; that interference with the institution of slavery *might* be necessary. We have believed, however, that President Lincoln was too wise a man to ever take such a step; and that his intimations of such a policy were only for the purpose of appeasing the howls of the abolition party. We had flattered ourselves that the President was prosecuting this war for the preservation of the Constitution as well as the restoration of the Union. But, alas! we are forced to admit that such is not the case.

We fail to see any good that can result from the President's Proclamation; but we can see much harm that is inevitable. The rebel leaders who have always insisted that the great object of the Federal Government was to completely annihilate the institution of slavery, will lay hold upon this and prove thereby, that their prophecies are being fulfilled, and thus, establish themselves as wise and far-seeing men, meriting the confidence of the people; and at the same time discourage loyal citizens living in the rebel States.

According to the proclamation, it matters not how loyal a man may be himself, if, on the first day of January, 1863, he shall be a resident of a State, of which a majority of the citizens are in rebellion against the Federal Government, if he be a slave holder, his slaves shall be free. Not as a penalty for his own deeds, but the deeds of his neighbors. Is there any justice, or anything statesmanlike in such doctrine?

We think the "outside pressure," to which the President alluded some time since, has finally overcome him.

We have no negroes to lose, and therefore, have no personal interest at stake, but we intend to oppose with all our strength, *any* abolition scheme, come from whence it may. If it be an act of Congress, an order of a military commander, or a proclamation of the President, we will oppose it. Because we feel sure that no greater calamity could befall the American people than to have four million of ignorant Africans turned loose among them. And because we *know* that no constituted authority, whether it be legislative, executive, judiciary, or military has any *right* to interfere with negro slavery. And when they do it they violate the most sacred principle guaranteed by the Constitution, the right of the people of a State to regular their own domestic affairs. . . .

Platte City (Mo.) *Conservator,* September 27, 1862.

By early 1863, thousands of Missouri slaves had already fled from bondage. The ongoing guerrilla warfare convinced many Missourians that "the bone of contention," slavery, had to be removed from the state in order to achieve peace. The following editorial, from the Republican Weekly Central City and Brunswicker, *placed the blame for emancipation on secessionists. Brunswick is in Chariton County, in the northwest part of the state. The word "pressing" refers to "impressment," or the seizure of goods, livestock, or people by force.*

EMANCIPATION.

Considerable excitement exists in this county on the subject of emancipation; and a great diversity of opinion exists in regard to the plan best calculated to relieve the State of the "peculiar institution." Our readers will bear in mind that we took the position even before the outbreak of the rebellion, that if Missou[ri] raised the standard of disunion and rebellion, it would be the means of destroying slavery in our State. We were denounced, for that declaration, as an abolitionist and negro thief, and our press threatened to be thrown in the river.—The rebellion was inaugurated in our State upon an extensive scale, and Union men were in many instances driven from their homes and families, and their property seized by the rebels for the purpose of waging war upon the Government. All these outrages were committed to in open day in every neighborhood and town in this portion of the State, and those rebels who did not participate in this bold system of theft and robbery justified it—calling it by nickname, pressing. Now these are grave charges against rebeldom, hereabouts, but we can prove them all, in any court of Justice. It is true, many men who at first commenced this shameful conduct, soon abandoned the foul party, and took an honest and form stand for the Government. They had created a party that they fear[e]d themselves. Union men, everywhere, were denounced as negro thieves, and the Germans were classed lower than negroes, and enemies to God and humanity. As we predicted a strong and dominant party has been organized in Missouri unfriendly to negro slavery. That party will wage a war upon slavery until it is driven from our State. The secessionists are indebted to no other party than themselves for the destruction of slavery in Missouri. Emancipation is inevitable, and no plan, that we have seen proposed, suits our views so well as immediate emancipation, with compensation to the loyal owners. Then the bone of contention will be forever removed, and peace restored to our State. No man in Missouri, of ordinary intelligence pretends to believe that slavery can be preserved in our State. Even should no scheme of emancipation be adopted the "peculiar institution" will very soo[n] flicker out.

Weekly Central City and Brunswicker, January 29, 1863.

DEED OF EMANCIPATION

Samuel B. Wiggins signed a deed of emancipation for Mary Epps and her son James Young Epps some months before the newly elected governor, Thomas Fletcher, issued his general proclamation in 1865. Wiggins must have freed or sold most of his slaves by 1860. The 1850 slave schedule in the Missouri census indicates that he owned thirty-nine slaves, both male and female. By 1860, he owned a total of six female slaves ranging in age from four to thirty-five.

DEED OF EMANCIPATION

I, Samuel B. Wiggins, of the City and county of St. Louis and State of Missouri, moved by feelings of humanity, and in consideration of the faithful services rendered me by my slave Mary Epps, do hereby emancipate from slavery, and forever set free the said Mary Epps, a negro woman, of black color, aged about forty years, marked with the small pox, and weighing about one hundred and fifty pounds. I do also hereby emancipate and forever set free from slavery, an infant male child, of the said Mary Epps, emancipated above, aged about two months, now at the breast, named James Young Epps born the 7th October 1863.

> In Witness Whereof I have hereunto set my hand and seal, this the 23rd day of November A.D. 1863.
> Samuel B. Wiggins [seal]

Witnesses
Samuel N. Holliday
D. Robt. Barclay
   In St. Louis District Court September Term 1863
        November 24th 1863
State of Missouri
County of Saint Louis

Be it remembered that on this twenty fourth day of November A D Eighteen hundred and Sixty three in open Court came Samuel B. Wiggins who is personally known to the Court to be the same person whose name is subscribed to the foregoing deed of Emancipation, and he acknowledged the same to be his act and deed for the purposes therein mentioned which said acknowledgement is entered on the records of the Court of that day = In testimony whereof I hereto set my hand and affix seal of Saint Louis Circuit Court at office in City of Saint Louis the date last above written. Stephen Rice clk

Wiggins, Alphabetical Files, Missouri Historical Society, St. Louis.

A UNION SOLDIER DEPLORES
LINCOLN'S EMANCIPATION PROCLAMATION

Columbus Bryan hailed from Caledonia, Missouri, a village in Washington County near St. Louis. His sentiments against emancipation were probably not typical of residents of the heart of wine-growing country, which was mostly populated by Germans. Indeed, by the time Lincoln issued his proclamation, U.S. soldiers serving in Missouri were gradually beginning to favor emancipation in their home state. Still, Bryan was not a "Dutchman" and probably would have voted Democrat. With his brother Bennet, Bryan served in the Thirty-third Missouri Infantry in southern Missouri and in Arkansas, where he died of disease.

Helena Arkansas
Jan 30th 1863

Dear Brother

As I have a few leisure moments I thought I would write you a few lines to let you know we are still in the land of the Living & enjoying good health.

We recd your letter a day or two since we were exceedingly glad to hear from you. We had about come to the conclusion by your not writing you did not care whether the School kept or not.

Well Bob when Bennet wrote Home last we were a board of a Boat expecting to go down to Vicksburg but that order has been countermanded & we ar again on land. . . .

Bob there is one thing I do know that is the Soldiers here are becoming very much Demoralized on account of Lincolns Proclamation and I would not be Surprised if there would be a general burst up in about a month. Our Regiment to a man Say they are going home as soone as they get their pay.

Bob I am afraid the Union is about played out. What think you.

One Regiment in our Brigade stacked their arms the other day but were prevailed on by their Col. to take them again. They say they are going home the first March.

Bob I want you to write to me and tell me what the opinion of the people is around in Belleview on the Negro question for it is all the talk here amongst the Soldiers.   They all sware they will not fight to free the negro. I hope Lincoln will Revoke his proclimation if he dont dear knows what will become of us.

I will have to close my remarks for the present. Give my Love to all.

Bob when you read this you had better burn it. Columbus

Write soon

Columbus

Bryan, Columbus and Bennet, Letters, 1862–1863, Western Historical Manuscripts Collection, University of Missouri, Columbia.

PRIVATE WILLIAM R. DONALDSON CRITICIZES
THE RECRUITMENT OF BLACK SOLDIERS

William R. Donaldson served as a private with the First Missouri Light Artillery and was later promoted to corporal of Company H. The First Missouri served at Shiloh and Corinth and with Sherman's Atlanta campaign. William frequently wrote to his father, Isaac, while he was stationed at Pilot Knob, and like many other young Democrats, he resisted the recruitment of black men for the Union army. "Three cheers and a tiger" was a customary way for Union soldiers to celebrate good news: it consisted of shouting "hurrah" three times, followed with a ferocious growl.

[The] 1st Mo. Arty. is the best regiment or amongst the best in the service and take the *battles* they have been in—as *batteries* and as a regiment and there aint a flag in the United States that the names of the battles could be put on. That is making the letters the usual length—such as are placed on the colors of Regmts in honor of battles and placing these letters and words on the white stripe——I knew of about 20 Battles the Regmt and batteries have been in not counting small battles—Bully for the 1st Mo—three cheers and a tiger-r-r-r-r-r—

As far as the Negro Regiments are concerned. I for one will not go into it. I wrote to know if you would be willing I should go—not that I had any ideas of going—Adjutant Genl Thomas made a speech here this afternoon or this morning did not go to hear him myself as I was busy in the office. Heard something about it though. Was the same as the rest of this speeches made while down in this part of America. "Arming the negroes"—and from what I heard to day (from a person who was present) he intimated that *"negroes* would make better soldiers tha[n] white men." I will say nothing about that—but could I see you, would tell you of a little nice dust that occurred during his speaking. That but few know of—which will no[t] do to put on paper—my ideas about the negroes fighting are the same as yours. We agree on this question precisely.

Donaldson Papers, Missouri Historical Society, St. Louis.

"IF THEY WANT ANY OF THEIR FAMILY, THEY CAN ARM THEMSELVES . . . AND TAKE THEM"

Although many U.S. soldiers and officers were sympathetic to the plight of slaves and offered aid to runaway slaves seeking to free their families, others continued to treat slaves as property and refused to shelter them. Greer M. Davis, a relative of Missouri state representative Lowndes Davis from Cape Girardeau, was clearly worried about the problem of freed or runaway slaves attempting to rescue members of their families from bondage.

Jackson Mo. Feby 24 1863

My Dear Lowndes

. . . The ghost of old John Brown is still marching along, we had a visit last night in the shape of two negroes, demanding me to open the door requesting a nights lodgeing. I did not discover they were negroes till they said they wanted Caroline, on my refusal, they said the soldiers would come and take them, I replied, I would go and see the Col. and they left. They tried to pass themselves off as soldiers. . . . We are in a bad condition about negroes. A large number are congregated at Cape Girardeau, if they want any of their family, they can arm themselves, go with a few soldiers and take them; and they can with the same facility take any other property we have, as we have no weapons. I will ask the Col. today for a revolver, to keep at least as long as he remains here. Two negroes & some soldiers went to old Mr. Poe's about two weeks since, and took five in open day light. So long as the Government permits negroes to remain at the Cape, & the citizens of that place take no steps to have them removed, no one in the country is safe in person or property . . . .

Most affectionately
Your father
Greer M. Davis

Civil War Collection, Missouri Historical Society, St. Louis.

MISSOURI STATE REPRESENTATIVES ARGUE ABOUT EMANCIPATION

Charles P. Johnson chaired the legislative committee that drafted the report recommending gradual emancipation. Johnson later became governor of the state. Appended to the thirteen-page committee report is a brief, two-page minority report signed by the more conservative Thomas H. Allin, of Lafayette County.

REPORT.

Mr. Speaker:

The Special Committee, to whom was referred that part of the Governor's message relating to the subject of Emancipation, appointed at the commencement of the present session, have had the same under consideration and beg leave to submit the following report:

The State of Missouri applied for admission into the Federal union in the year one thousand eight hundred and twenty. The violent controversy that ensued upon such application and subsequent admission is a well known matter of history. It was a controversy that shook the Republic at the time to its very centre. . . . She was the first slave State formed out of new territory—Kentucky being originally a part of Virginia, and Tennessee a part of North Carolina. The southern portion of Louisiana territory was settled as a French colony, with local usages and customs differing from other parts of the country. The wild district to the North was new territory, and the central question involved in that celebrated controversy was whether it was right and expedient to make new slave States. . . . Suffice it to say that Missouri was admitted as a slave State, and has continued to exist as such to the present time, given over to slavery and the slave power, when in all that territory ceded by France to the United States, under the name of Louisiana, lying north of thirty-six degrees and thirty minutes, . . . slavery and involuntary servitude, except for the punishment of crime whereof the party was duly convicted, was and has been prohibited. Looking back now to the period of her admission, and viewing the national history up to the present time, . . . your Committee is convinced of the commission of a fundamental error upon the part of the framers of our State Constitution, in engrafting slavery thereon. It has proved anything but beneficial to our State. . . . The fact of being surrounded and immediately contiguous to territory in which slavery was prohibited and free labor fostered, out of which new States have arisen, has offered strong and unanswerable proof. . . . From that territory, blessed no more by the advantages by of nature—for Missouri possesses them in full fruition—have come noble and ambitious rivals that have followed, overtaken and passed her in the race of civilization, progress and empire. Illinois, Wisconsin, Iowa and all the Western and North-Western States, have far excelled her in their increase of population, agricultural developments, wealth, education and their attendant blessings. . . .

Thus it has been shown that previous to the breaking out of the present deplorable civil war, slavery was detrimental to our best interests, to our advancement in every thing that makes a State great and noble. If we now look at its efforts since the advent of the war we find it the source of unnumbered woes. So perceptible have been the ruinous consequences of its existence, that in a little over two years the loyal people of the State have undergone a complete revolution in opinion upon the question, and have spoken at the ballot box in favor of the immediate initiation of a policy of Emancipation. . . . The adherents of [the Confederate] government—rebels and rebel sympathizers—in our midst, in connection with those sent from the South, have used every endeavor, regardless of the dictates of justice and humanity, to place her in the possession of the traitorous Confederacy. . . . A number of times has an invading army crossed our border, and attempted to wrest the State from the Union. On each invasion, the attendant horrors of war, following in the track of armies, have not been the only evils brought upon our State. Rebel emissaries and sympathizers, have come among us, and have arisen among us, and by their reckless and utter disregard of all civilized usages, have so worked upon an excitable portion of those living in our midst—fanatics in the cause of slavery—as to inaugurate a system of warfare repugnant to the civilized world. Nor has such system of war existed only on invasion, but it has been carried on, in many different parts of the State, long after invading armies had been defeated and driven back. Guerrilla bands have been formed throughout the State, and waged a vindictive and sanguinary warfare upon all citizens who professed an adherence to the Union, and it has been found, in all instances, that those engaged in acting the guerrilla, the robber and the assassin, profess to fight against our Government, and against all law, human and divine, because, as they claim, the

Government of the United States intends and is engaged in depriving them of their slave property, and destroying the institution of slavery. . . .

Such have been the effects of slavery in our State in times of rebellion, and it behooves us to examine well into our condition, to view it as legislators, and use all wise and necessary means to reinstate and reinvigorate our exhausted energies, and start forward in a new career of usefulness and prosperity. . . .

The most important question, therefore, for you and the people of the State of Missouri to consider, in the opinion of your Committee, is, how can this be brought about? Your Committee are fully convinced that EMANCIPATION IS THE ONLY REMEDY. Slavery abolished from the State, or a policy of emancipation initiated, would, we feel confident, exercise an incomparably beneficial effect upon the State. It will induce immigration to our midst, a main requisite—the source of wealth and advancement. We cannot expect to be able to induce labor and capital from abroad under existing circumstances. Since the civil war commenced, no security has existed for that already possessed, and much of it has been driven away. And to your Committee it is a self-evident proposition, that neither capital nor labor will go where there is no security afforded them. There is no doubt that the impression exists in the free States and the countries of Europe, from whence we must accept all accessions of these valuable auxiliaries to advancement, that slavery is the cause of our past evils, and a source of disadvantage and insecurity for the future. . . . Nor can we expect, as in times past, to secure any accession of labor and capital from the cotton or border slave States, for the difficulties as we have shown, have rendered alike all property insecure, slave, no less than any other. . . . Immigration is still going on, suppressed somewhat by the national troubles, avoiding us and peopling surrounding States. How rapidly has been the advancement in population and wealth in Illinois, Wisconsin and all the Western and North-Western Free States, as before referred to, in comparison with Missouri? . . .

Your Committee are convinced that the initiation of a policy of Emancipation will bring to us labor, capital and population, and fill our State with enterprise, wealth, and activity. It will develop our mighty resources. It will afford the means of freeing ourselves from the burdens of an enormous debt that bids fair to dishonor our State with repudiation. It will increase the value of our property, and turn the tide of immigration into its legitimate channel. Those great enterprises contemplated previous to the rebellion will be undertaken. The artificial arteries of commerce will reach from her borders to the Pacific; and bring to us the productions of Kansas, Colorado, New Mexico and California, and pour into our metropolis the riches of the East. It will cause Missouri to reach the proud position to which she is entitled by her resources—the Empire State of the Valley of the Mississippi. . . .

MINORITY REPORT
OF
SPECIAL COMMITTEE ON EMANCIPATION.

To the Honorable Speaker of the House of Representatives:

The undersigned, from the Select Committee on Emancipation, respectfully submits the following minority report: . . .

Whatever may have been the purposes of those who inaugurated the rebellion, it must be admitted by all candid and unprejudiced minds, that if it was designed to protect and foster the "peculiar institution," it has signally failed of its object. On the contrary, . . . the slavery interest has sustained great loss, and much depreciation of the slaves remaining. . . .

Nothing should be left undone that would tend to preserve the relation which Missouri now sustains to the Federal Union. Every cause of irritation and excitement should be removed. We should sustain the President in "all his constitutional and legal prerogatives," and sustain the Federal Government in its efforts to put down the rebellion, with a view and for the purpose of restoring the Government, and for such purpose should sacrifice everything that conflicts with that object.

While it is true that a large proportion of the slaveholders have sympathized with, or directly or indirectly given aid and comfort to the enemy: yet it is equally true that a large number of the most intelligent of the slaveholding class, high in position, socially, morally and politically, have most earnestly opposed this rebellion from its incipiency. We should be careful in any legislation deemed necessary, not to compromise these our friends any farther than shall appear to be absolutely necessary, to secure the peace and prosperity of the State. The *loyal slaveholders* have proven themselves patriots, and would doubtless cheerfully give up the last slave, if deemed necessary to preserve the Government to maintain the integrity of Missouri as a member of the Union. . . .

From the best information at hand, it is believed that a large majority of the loyal people of the State will acquiesce in a liberal system of gradual Emancipation. Many of them, however, will be slow to perceive the necessity of proceeding more hastily upon this subject, than did many of the Northern States, for the following amongst other reasons.

1. We are in the midst of a revolution which has already seriously embarrassed our industrial relations.

2. The white labor of the State is now in a great degree enlisted, either in the Federal or State service, producing a great deficit in the industrial element of the State.

3. Our sister loyal States are suffering from a like defiency produced by the same cause, and we cannot therefore borrow labor from them.

4. We are about being subject to heavy rates of taxation to sustain both the State and Federal Governments, and to this end should require the active exercise of the whole laboring strength of the State.

5. In the midst of revolution colonization would be impracticable; whereas under a gradual plan, the people of the State would, in due time, inaugurate some judicious system of colonization, *consulting at once the interest and comfort of both master and slave.*

There appears to be no good reason why Missouri should not adopt a gradual system similar to that adopted by Pennsylvania and other Northern States, limiting the service of children born of slaves then in being, to a term of years. . . .

Missouri, General Assembly, *Journal of the House of Representatives of the State of Missouri at the 22nd Session of the General Assembly* (Jefferson City: James Lusk, 1863), 244–60.

REPUBLICAN ISIDOR BUSH IMPLORES
THE PEOPLE OF MISSOURI TO TAKE A STAND ON SLAVERY

Isidor Bush, a prominent Republican politician who represented St. Louis in the Missouri State Convention, delivered a speech on June 29, 1863, demanding that the state finally take decisive action on the issue of slavery. Bush had fled Prague after the failed revolution of 1848. He served in the Missouri State Convention called by Governor Claiborne F. Jackson in 1861 and worked to defeat secessionist forces in the state. Bush was well known as an ardent abolitionist and a leading light of the Jewish community in St. Louis. He battled mightily with the ultraradical politician and abolitionist Charles Drake in the 1865 convention.

MINORITY REPORT

AND

MOTION TO ADJOURN "SINE DIE."

SPEECH

OF

ISIDOR BUSH,

OF SAINT LOUIS,

DELIVERED IN THE MISSOURI STATE CONVENTION, JUNE
29, 1863.

The people of this State have to take a stand on one side or the other. To place ourselves on the middle ground between the contending parties, is to be destroyed by both fires. When they decided to stay in the Union, to fight with the North in this struggle to maintain our national existence, this question was virtually decided. You had only to draft the deed and to acknowledge it. You ought to have declared simply that we will *cheerfully* sacrifice the institution of slavery, whose value has *already been destroyed by this rebellion,* to our country, and the people would execute the deed, thus showing to the South as well as the North, on which side Missouri will forever stand.

On the other hand, I find, from the admission of loyal slaveholders themselves, that the value of slaves has been destroyed by the rebels; and while they are chargeable with the loss, it is not for the loyal people (who did nothing to damage it) to compensate the owners for the same.

If another throws down this tumbler [referring to the glass of water before the Speaker] breaking it to pieces, and I remove the worthless, injurious fragments, am I to pay you the damage? . . .

It is further a fact established by proof and experience, which cannot be denied, that the wealth and general prosperity of the State would be so much increased that it is not only proper that the interest of the individual should give way to the interest of the whole, but that it must also benefit the former slaveowner. He, the slaveowner, is at the same time, almost without exception, also a landowner and it is admitted that the . . . *value* of lands cultivated by free labor, exceeds the capital represented by slaves. . . .

Now, sir, as the abolishment of slavery in Missouri cannot be avoided, as you believe you have the right and power to do it, and as it would be to the great advantage of Missouri, in general, while it would prove but a small loss to the slaveholder; the question seems to be now only whether slavery shall cease in 1876 or in 1866.

But even this is by no means in reality a question. Does any gentleman on this floor really believe that in the present state of our national affairs, slavery can exist until 1876 or even 1870? . . .

The great majority of the people are in favor of Emancipation. Most of those even who were opposed to it a short time ago, acknowledge that we cannot avoid it even if we would; that Emancipation is an unavoidable necessity of this war. I might almost say in the Lincolnian style, that "as we cannot remove anti-slavery we must remove slavery." *Still you hesitate.* . . .

Now, gentlemen, the "let alone" policy—to use a common but expressive phrase—the let alone policy is played out. The very call of this Convention, for purposes which one year ago you decided to "let alone" by an overwhelming majority, is but one of the many proofs of the fallacy of your system. An early decision by the people at the ballot box is the only way to close agitation, is the only means to give any action of yours force and stability. . . .

African American Pamphlet Collection, Library of Congress.

NEGRO HUNTING

On July 31, 1863, an editorial appeared in the Daily Missouri Democrat *(a Republican paper) mocking the outcry for "law and order" among rebels who defied their government and hunted escaped slaves. Potosi is a small community in southeastern Missouri. General Order No. 35, issued on Christmas Eve 1862, required provost marshals in Missouri to issue certificates of freedom to slaves who had escaped from disloyal masters.*

NEGRO HUNTING—THE FUGITIVE SLAVE LAW AT WORK IN MISSOURI.

POTOSI, July 26th, 1863

Last Saturday we had an example of what it means to have regard for "law and order." I mean one of those old fashioned negro hunts. Some half a dozen slaves, who had deserted their rebel masters and were in possession of their regular protection papers, issued by a Provost Marshal, under General Order No. 35, Department of the Missouri, were hunted down like wild deers, handcuffed, and on a wagon hauled to jail in Potosi. This whole section of Washington county was alive. All the law and order men were out and busy. You could see men who never show their faces except on an occasion of this kind. By "law and order men" I understand that class which hold only as law the fugitive slave law, the black laws of the State of Missouri and the laws of the Confederacy; they don't consider the laws of our Congress as binding on them. It has come to a nice state of affairs in Missouri. Men who by their true loyalty and good faith toward the Government have shown their regard for "law and order" and have sacrificed everything to save this country, are stigmatized as "Revolutionists" and Radicals and are now at the mercy of men who have done everything to ruin this country and who only enjoy their freedom by forbearance of the Union men. There is not a Union man in Washington county, when he goes to bed at night does not fear that the may be murdered before morning. A band of about twenty-five bushwhackers is in this county and declared only last week that Potosi could not hold a Union man. A Union man, Rev. Wilson Adams, who was worth some $12,000 to $15,000, has been shamefully ruined by them—been compelled to take refuge in Potosi with his family. The rebels are in possession of his place. They took all his horses, and in fact everything is at their mercy, and then we see the rebels prowling about the country declaring that they are going to run this machine now and the Union men tremble for their lives because they don't know how it comes that these rebels get in power. The way they intend to run this machine we have seen last Saturday. For the purpose of "law and order" they set all law aside. We will see what our Provost Marshal does in the matter. These negroes are promised in their papers the protection of all officers of the United States, but he thinks perhaps he don't belong to the Untied States officers, being in the Missouri State Militia.

After having spent one hundred millions and given innumerable valuable lives, not to speak of the suffering and desolation of our homes, we have just come again to the barbarous state of affairs where we were at the beginning, and near the end of the nineteenth century, in the midst of a civilized community, we see enacted before the eyes of children scenes, which make the blood rush to every true man's face. Human beings are treated like beasts; children only 5 years old separated from their parents for the purpose of keeping them from running away; husbands separated from their wives, in fact we don't know if we are dreaming or if it is reality. Who is responsible for this state of affairs? We Union men have proven that we have regard for law and order; but if these rebels think that we will submit to their rule they may find themselves mistaken.
JUSTINE.

Daily Missouri Democrat, July 31, 1863.

RECRUITING SOLDIERS OF AFRICAN DESCENT

By mid-1863, the U.S. Army had begun enrolling black soldiers. In early fall of that year, Adjutant General Lorenzo Thomas traveled through the border states of Maryland, Missouri, and Tennessee to recruit black men for the Sixty-second U.S. Colored Troops Infantry Regiment and for several other out-of-state regiments. Black men who fought for the Union armies gained their own freedom as well as the liberty of their wives and children.

HEADQUARTERS DEPARTMENT OF THE MISSOURI,
Saint Louis, September 29, 1863.
Col. E. D. TOWNSEND,
Assistant Adjutant-General, Washington, D. C.:

COLONEL: I inclose herewith a copy of a letter received on the 26th instant from Brigadier-General Thomas, Adjutant-General, asking me to afford facilities for raising another colored regiment in Missouri, and my reply. I have thought it advisable to transmit these to the Honorable Secretary of War with a few additional remarks for his consideration and such instructions as he may be pleased to give.

In July last General Thomas, at my request, gave Colonel Pile authority to raise colored troops in Missouri subject to the approval of the Governor of State. The Governor gave his consent with the condition that the laws of Missouri should not be violated—a very difficult condition to comply with.

It was, however, observed as far as practicable, and a regiment was soon raised, mustered in, and sent to Helena. Colonel Pile then obtained permission to raise another regiment to rendezvous at Keokuk, Iowa. Recruiting officers were appointed, by whom I know not, and sent into Missouri, bearing copies of the authority I had given to those engaged in raising the regiment in Saint Louis, together with a similar one from General Thomas. These recruiting officers went through the northern part of Missouri with armed parties of negroes, enlisting all who would go with them without regard to the loyal of their masters, and in some instances, I am informed, forcing them away. Of course this could not fail to produce intense excitement, and I was compelled to put a stop to it.

General Ewing has authority, given by the Secretary of War at my request, to raise one regiment in his district. He has been able to make but little progress so far, but I have no doubt will raise the regiment in time.

The first regiment raised absorbed all the negroes fit for military duty who had been collected at the various posts in Missouri, and which included nearly all those at that time remaining in the State who were unquestionably entitled to their freedom under the confiscation act.

Nearly all those now remaining in the State belong either to loyal men or to men who cannot be proven to have committed any act of disloyalty since the 17th of July, 1862. If it be admitted that a man who was to any extent disloyal before that time may be a loyal man now, it is impossible to decide without judicial proceedings whether the act of July 17 applies or not in a large majority of cases that arise. Moreover, under the confused notions as to what constitutes loyalty which now exist, the officers engaged in recruiting are about as likely to decide one man to be disloyal as another.

I believe the able-bodied negroes in Missouri will be worth more to the Government as soldiers than they are to their masters as laborers, and that this is the general opinion among slave owners in the State. Moreover, I believe it would be a great benefit to the State as well as to the negro to have him transformed from a slave into a soldier.

I respectfully suggest that it might be wise policy to enlist all able-bodied negroes in Missouri who may be willing to enter the service, giving to their masters receipts upon which those who established their loyalty may base a claim upon the Government for the value of the services lost. Those masters whose loyalty is undoubted might perhaps be paid immediately out of the substitute fund, and the doubtful cases left for future settlement.

If the Government decides to adopt such policy, I shall be glad to carry it out.

Very respectfully, your obedient servant,
J. M. SCHOFIELD,
Major-General.
[Inclosure No. 1.]

MEMPHIS, TENN., September 21, 1863.

Maj. Gen. J. M. SCHOFIELD,

Commanding Department of the Missouri:

GENERAL: It is very desirable that another regiment of African descent should be organized with as little delay as possible in the State of Missouri. I have therefore to request that you will give such facilities to recruiting officers in your department as will hasten this object, and that you will instruct the officers of your respective staff departments to furnish without delay all supplies that may be called for on proper requisitions.

I am, general, very respectfully, your obedient servant,

L. THOMAS,

Adjutant-General.

The War of the Rebellion: A Compilation of the Official Records of the Union and Confederate Armies, ser. 3, vol. 3 (Washington, D.C.: Government Printing Office, 1899), 847–48.

AN AMBUSH AT POISON SPRINGS

The First Regiment Colored Kansas Volunteers was composed primarily of former slaves from Missouri and Arkansas, and it was the first regiment mustered into service by jayhawker Jim Lane. Major General Frederick Steele of the U.S. Army had sent about six hundred men, four hundred of whom were black soldiers from the First Kansas, into Camden to forage for food. Steele had been careful to restrain his men from plundering private homes, and he ordered the setting of guards to protect the townspeople. Brigadier General John S. Marmaduke commanded about twelve hundred Arkansas troops and seven hundred Choctaws. He launched an attack on Steele, which turned into an outright massacre when the First Kansas retreated. Wounded black soldiers were hunted down and killed, even as they attempted to surrender. Colton Greene's report does not mention the massacre, reporting instead a gallant fight with cheerful insults hurled at a retreating enemy. Poison Springs is a town in southern Arkansas near East Camden.

Poison Springs, Arks. Col. C Greene's Report.

Head Qrs, Marmaduke's Brig.

In the field, Apr 20, 1864.

Major.

On the morning of the 17th, whilst bivouacked in front of the enemy near the junction of the upper and middle Camden and Washington roads, my scouts reported that a train of twenty wagons, escorted by 200 cavalry was moving on the upper road. I immediately ordered the 3rd regt commanded by Lt Col Campbell to get on the rear and attack it. A short time after the regiment had marched, my scouts again reported that a large train had joined the other: that it numbered 200 wagons, and was guarded by one regiment of cavalry and two regts of negro infantry, with three pieces of artillery. I at once placed the regiment in ambush and reported the facts to the Brig Genl . . . .

On the morning of the 18th inst, leaving Kitchins regt and a detachment of the 3rd to cover our front and flank, I marched with Greenes Regt commanded by Lt Col Campbell, Burbridges Regt commanded by Lt Col Preston, a small detachment of Jeffers under Capt Cobb, and Harris' battery—numbering in all 486 men. I came on the enemy in rear of Cabell's Brigade at 9½ oclock, dismounted, and placed Harris' battery in position on the extreme right of our line. At 10 oclock this battery opened on the enemy: the remainder of my command was held in reserve.

The enemy heavily engaged our left & centre, and at 10¾ oclock I was ordered to its support. Moving rapidly for an half mile through a thick forest, we tore down a rail fence: formed in an open field under a heavy fire of musketry: and advanced steadily across it, passing another fence. The left centre was hotly pressed, when I advanced at the double quick with loud cheers, passed the line, delivered several well directed volleys, and charged the enemy through burning woods and a dense smoke. He gave way, closely pressed, but reformed under cover of his train. Upon this position we advanced firing: charged the train with great slaughter to the enemy, who abandoned his artillery on the field, and again formed behind the huts, fences and timber of an adjoining plantation. With cries of "heres your mule" and cheers for Missouri his line was again broken by our advancing forces. Once more he rallied in the thick brush beyond the plantation, through the bare fields of which we charged and drove him in confusion. Again another stand was made, on the crest of a steep hill, which was as quickly carried at the charge. No further resistance was now made to our victorious line, which scattered and drove the enemy in every direction: until by your order the pursuit was stopped: the command rallied and moved by the left flank across the roads to cover the removal of the captured train, animals, artillery and arms. Towards sunset we remounted, brought up the rear, and marching all night reached the position left in the morning at daylight. In this action three of my regiments were absent.

Where all behaved so gallantly, it is difficult to determine upon whom to bestow praise. Every man did his duty: there was no straggling, no plundering. For eighteen days we marched and engaged the enemy and notwithstanding the loss of sleep for three nights previous to this action the men bore themselves with cheerfulness and fortitude. . . .

I am Major, very respy
your obt svt
Colton Greene
Col cmdg Brg

Marmaduke Papers, Missouri Historical Society, St. Louis.

EIGHT

~

Reconciliation and Promises

$\mathcal{B}$Y LATE AUTUMN 1864, General Sterling Price's dream of a Confederate Missouri had ended. The state was safe in the Union and free from the burden of slavery, but still tormented by guerrilla and criminal violence. Refugees who had fled or been forced out of the western counties were slowly beginning to return, but they faced severe hardships due to the missed planting season and depredations committed on their livestock and food supplies by traversing armies. Money was scarce, prices were high, and some agricultural industries, such as hemp and tobacco, had nearly died out. In addition, because so many men had left to fight and so many slaves had fled to St. Louis or across the border to Kansas, there were labor shortages throughout the state. The urgent need for labor proved to be a benefit to some; the freed slaves who had left the northwestern farms and plantations often found paid work near cities and along the rivers. Economic problems were less evident in cities like St. Louis, where contracts for warships and other military matériel kept the economy lively. It was the subsistence farmers who faced the toughest challenges.[1]

Farmers still remained on the front lines of guerrilla attacks. Many Missourians believed that the solutions to the ongoing problems of criminal gangs and their sympathizers were tied to the future of slavery: the destruction of slavery, they reasoned, would bring an end to the war. These economic, military, and political problems forced Missourians to recognize that their long-standing desire for neutrality and moderation on controversial issues was simply no longer realistic. War-weariness, fear and grief over continuing brutalities, and internal divisions over the issues of equality and civil rights for black people made it necessary to consider new ideas. Missourians were willing to

General Sterling Price. *O'Neill, steel engraving. Courtesy of Missouri Historical Society* accept changes that would have seemed far too radical only five years earlier. Then, moderates such as Provisional Governor Hamilton Gamble and General Henry Halleck had been popular and respected in Missouri because they were reasonable men who understood the people. But Gamble had died, under sharp (and often unfair) criticism by radicals, and Halleck was back in the eastern theater of the war.

Another important factor in postwar politics in Missouri was the effective silencing of the conservative opposition, which included not only those who had favored the Southern cause but also loyal Democrats and even some moderate Republicans. The 1864 state elections had been a stunning victory for the radicals, at least in part because the name of the Democratic Party had become tainted with treason and the test oaths prevented many Missourians who might otherwise have opposed radical policies from voting. Democrats decided to keep quiet and wait—what historian William E. Parrish called "playing possum"—until internal divisions in the Republican Party brought about its downfall. As a result, the radicals enjoyed great success in politics for at least five years after the end of the war. They gained control of Congress as well as a majority in the Missouri state legislature and local government offices.[2]

When Thomas Fletcher entered the race for the governorship in 1864, he ran against the unfortunately named Thomas L. Price (who actually had no connection with the Confederate general). Because of his military record and staunch dedication to the cause of emancipation, Fletcher won an easy victory by a margin of more than forty thousand votes. Historians attribute the sweeping radical victories to war-weariness, the previous year's increase in bushwhacker violence (the worst since the beginning of the war), and the general sense that Gamble's moderate policies had not kept Missourians safe from the guerrillas' murderous rampages.[3]

It was true that the Democrats, or Conservative Unionists as many of them began to call themselves, commanded little influence in Missouri's political arena. But the Republicans were also divided. Those called Liberal Republicans proposed a progressive program that included votes for black people, education reform, and a moderate policy toward former rebels. They also believed in measured progress for black people, but not immediate political and social equality. After Lincoln's death in 1865, the liberals supported President Andrew Johnson's moderate Reconstruction policies. They believed that their divided state's only hope of recovering peace and prosperity lay in the reconciliation of former enemies. Those known as Radical Unionists wanted not only to enfranchise former slaves but to ensure their complete political and social equality. At the same time, their ideas about former rebels were punitive and often vindictive. They knew, for example, that they had the test oath to thank for some of their political victories, and they distrusted the former rebels, who had supported a traitorous government. In 1864, a "Charcoal" (a nickname for radical abolitionists in the Republican party) named Charles Drake made a bitter speech that denounced earlier moderate policies and revealed the depth of ill will against those who had opposed the Union. The war, he declared, had been waged not only to reestablish the Union and the Constitution but also to exterminate his former enemies. Henceforth it was to be a war fought "for the absolute, unconditional and permanent subjugation, aye and if need be, for the complete extermination of the rebels in arms—and above and beyond these, a war for the utter overthrow and final extirpation of southern slavery."[4]

At the end of 1864, many young men who had so confidently joined the Confederate army or marched with the Missouri State Guard were disheartened and tired of bad food, ragged clothing, and military defeats. They began making their way back to their farms and families and were no longer interested in continuing the struggle. Some die-hard Confederates refused to accommodate themselves to the changes. Governor-in-exile Thomas C. Reynolds, along with Generals Sterling Price and Joseph Shelby, for example, left for Mexico to fight on Emperor Maximilian's side against Benito Juarez, and a number of other rebel soldiers followed them. But when that effort failed, the erstwhile Missouri rebels returned to their home state. Many others took the oath and joined local Missouri militia units. The enrollment laws remained in force for years after the war to cope with continuing bushwhacker violence, so some former Confederate soldiers stayed on, although they never abandoned their loyalty to the Confederacy. For example, a Rolla newspaper reported that when a Dent County militia unit elected two former rebel soldiers as officers, the two men were so elated over their success that they "got drunk and rode out of town shouting for the Southern Confederacy."[5] Most others, though, put their rebellion behind them and quietly returned to their former lives. The divisions between European ethnic groups such as Germans and Irish gradually disappeared, perhaps because the political arena provided plentiful opportunities for all. In the first ten years after the end of the war, the sharpest divisions in Missouri politics revolved around equality of voting rights for black people and the punitive provisions in the constitution.

Missouri's new governor, Thomas C. Fletcher, a radical Republican, officially proclaimed emancipation in his state: all slaves became free on Saturday, January 14, 1865. Despite the "Charcoal" influence in Missouri politics, however, the right of suffrage for black men proved to be a difficult proposition. There was simply too much opposition from both conservatives and moderates, especially in the northern and western counties of the state. Although the black community in St. Louis strongly urged the passage of such proposals and on January 31, 1865, submitted a petition signed by thousands of citizens, voting rights for black people remained elusive until after the Civil War.

In spring 1865, Jefferson City celebrated Lee's surrender to Grant in Virginia, while the Missouri State Convention met for the fifth and final time. The convention's aim was to end slavery, to shore up rights for black citizens, and above all, to destroy the last remnants of secessionist sentiment. The convention that met in the Mercantile Library in downtown St. Louis quickly (and with very little opposition) abolished slavery in accordance with Governor Fletcher's recent proclamation to that effect, issued a provision streamlining the government, and instituted economic reforms. The convention also deliberated a new constitution for Missouri. Charles Drake became the dominant figure in that convention, particularly because he helped draft this radical (and extremely punitive) constitution, which soon came to be known as the "Drake Constitution." The radicals achieved important reforms. They worked hard to establish rights for black people, made it easier to charter corporations to finance and build railroad networks throughout the state, and passed bills to improve and reform education.

But some of their more vindictive measures only exacerbated the political divisions and factional hatred in the state. The punitive elements of the new constitution included a provision for an "iron-clad" oath, which required voters, officeholders, lawyers, teachers, jurors, and clerics to swear that they had never sympathized with or aided the Confederate cause. The Drake Constitution also contained an "ousting ordinance" (an "ordinance," in the usage of the time, was a legal provision) that dismissed judicial officers who opposed radical measures. Although the test oath and the ousting provisions were undemocratic and even unconstitutional, the radical program of which they were a part brought significant improvements to the lives of Missouri's black people. They effectively disfranchised many of the men who would have halted some of the progressive reforms, such as helping freed slaves to establish even minimal political rights. The punitive clauses would prove difficult to dislodge in later years, however, and their restrictions kept alive old resentments and divisions and denied a significant number of Missouri's voters participation in the shaping of policies.

In 1865, leaders of the black community in St. Louis gathered at a local church to form the Missouri Equal Rights League. Speakers at the first meeting emphasized that although black Missourians had been "released from chains, lashes, bloodhounds and slave marts," they could not feel secure in their liberty until they enjoyed the same rights to which every other American was entitled: the free "exercise of the right of suffrage."[6] At the same time, Missouri's Bureau of Refugees, Freedmen, and Abandoned Lands, later known simply as the Freedmen's Bureau, helped the former slaves find work, negotiate fair labor contracts, and establish schools. However, Missouri's freed people continued to suffer abuses and discrimination; there was simply not enough manpower to protect them. After 1868, the Ku Klux Klan gained adherents in the state, mostly in the bootheel counties, and terrorized both black and white people in southeast Missouri until Governor Benjamin Gratz Brown called out the state militia again in 1871.[7]

Still, in spite of continued discrimination and segregation, Missouri's black population continued to make strides through the end of the decade. In 1870, African American citizens met in Jefferson City to discuss education and progress toward equal civil and political rights. The Equal Rights League presented petitions to the General Assembly demanding schools for black children and voting rights for black men; by 1870, they garnered more than three thousand signatures. Although all attempts to pass a voting rights law failed in Missouri, the ratification of the Fifteenth Amendment to the federal Constitution granted the franchise (at least in theory) to black men of legal age.[8] After the end of the war, the black population in Missouri had dropped slightly from prewar levels, from just under 9 percent to 6.9 percent of the total. While many freed blacks suffered severe discrimination, others were able to make a decent living in the Jefferson City and St. Louis. Perhaps their most important achievement was the development of educational opportunities. Before the war, black children had been denied education by the 1845 Negro and Mulatto Law (see chapter 1), but now educators busily founded schools and academies for black children. Black people would continue to struggle against discrimination and segregation for decades, but at that moment, the improvements were real and visible. Frederick Douglass published a letter that he had received from a former St. Louis slave describing some of the positive changes. Claiming that the Fifteenth Amendment was "working wonders," the writer explained that now "streetcar conductors cannot tell whether you are black or white. I take a look in my glass sometimes to see if by some hocus pocus I have turned white, but it gives back the same old face, and tells me I am a citizen and not a chattel now. It used to be Old Pen, but now it is Mr. Pentalpha."[9]

By late 1869, some moderate Republicans had joined with Democrats to form the short-lived Liberal Republican Party. This party gained enough national prominence and support from well-known opinion leaders that it was able to influence the 1872 presidential election, but after that the party disappeared. For a few years, progressive reform in Missouri brought about an interest in wider rights for all citizens. Women who had dedicated their time and energies to the war effort—exemplified by the brilliantly successful Western Sanitary Commission—had gained the respect of Missouri's citizens. The idea of women's rights, however, was too far-reaching even for radical Missourians. Some of the women who had been especially active throughout the war years, such as Phoebe Couzins, tried to enter new professions or to gain equal rights. Couzins, for example, entered law school and in 1871 became the nation's third female law school graduate. Later she continued to agitate for women's voting rights, though by the end of her life she had reverted to opposition to women's political activism. Virginia Minor risked arrest and prosecution by attempting to vote at the St. Louis courthouse, though all her efforts failed. Women would have to wait for a national constitutional amendment in 1921. More successful was Susan Blow, who founded the first public kindergarten in the United States, because education had been seen as a more acceptable venue for women's activism.

The end of the Civil War in Missouri brought prosperity and progress, though some promises would take a long time to fulfill. The horrific violence between neighbors and the repeated attacks by paramilitary and criminal gangs had created problems unparalleled in any other state. But the Missouri economy recovered quickly after the war, especially in the cities, which drew in large numbers of Americans and Europeans. According to the 1870 census, these new immigrants raised the state's population by nearly 50 percent.[10] Within a generation, soldiers who had fought on opposing sides had largely forgotten their differences. Some of the survivors of Quantrill's gang, such as the Jameses and the Younger brothers, continued to rob trains and banks in Arkansas, Kansas, Missouri, and Texas into the late 1860s. But even many of the former bushwhackers and members of criminal gangs found their way back into respectable society, some participating in reunions for decades. The wounds finally were healed, even to the extent that an old soldier who had served under Price and sustained an injury in battle would eventually be granted a pension by the government he once had fought against.

"THE RUINOUS . . . CONSERVATIVE WAR POLICY"

The Missouri Statesman *was a Republican paper that reported legislative news from the state capital. By 1864, the editorial policy of the paper had become thoroughly committed to the new Radical Union platform of abolitionism and severe policies against pro-Southern civilians. The same issue that carried the following editorial also contained endorsements for the 1864 presidential and gubernatorial contests, supporting Abraham Lincoln and Thomas C. Fletcher for the "Radical Union Ticket" as well as Colonel Joseph W. McClurg for Congress. McClurg would later serve as governor. The phrase "allies not in the brush" probably refers to civilians who supported bushwhackers by hiding or feeding them.*

. . . Time has shown the ruinous effects of a conservative war policy. The work which should have been accomplished at the earliest day possible, still remains to be done; and the delay has been productive of the most disastrous consequences. The problem of restoring law and order in Missouri, is today of more difficult solution than at any previous time since the breaking out of the rebellion in the State. The difficulties which presented themselves at first, and which could then have been successfully grappled with and overcome, have become so magnified that Radicalism itself regrets the work that is now forced upon it. A firm and decisive policy towards the rebels when the Radicals demanded it, would have made them humble and submissive now. The loyal people, but little subjected to wrong and outrage, would have been more tolerant and less vindictive. Both sides would have been more tractable, and the peace of the State far more easily preserved. Now, when social breaches have become widened, when personal animosities have become intensified, when immunity to treason has made many actively disloyal who would otherwise have avoided openly identifying themselves with rebellion, Radicalism is called upon to do its work. Who now preaches anything but extermination to bushwhackers, and who dreams of exterminating them except by destroying their allies not in the brush? No loyal man. Did Radicalism ever demand more? Certainly not. It would have accomplished by timely penalties much that can now be performed by the bullet only. Where then is the humanity of conservatism? And where was the inhumanity of radicalism two or three years ago? The alarming condition of the State now is an answer to both questions. Conservative warfare has proved to be nothing but three disastrous years of procrastination, at the expense of the loyal people of the State. It required no great wisdom to foresee this result; and the men who advocated the conservative policy which has been followed, have either lost all claims to intelligence or honesty—It has been done with sinister intent, or through a stupidity scarcely less criminal. It now appears plain to all, that a rebel life in time would have saved the lives of nine Union men, and who can blame the loyal people for bitterly execrating the men who refused to perceive this self-evident fact, in time? . . .

Missouri Statesman, August 27, 1864.

"FREEDOM AS THE WATCHWORD OF OUR NEW LIFE"

Lawyer, newspaper editor, and politician Benjamin Gratz Brown was one of the leading lights of the Republican party in St. Louis. A cousin of Frank P. Blair Jr., he served as senator and later as governor of Missouri. He had founded and edited the Daily Missouri Democrat *before the Civil War and was chiefly responsible for endowing it with its Republican point of view. Indeed, he was one of the founders of the Republican Party in the state. Brown raised a regiment in the Fourth U.S. Reserves and served as its colonel until 1863. Throughout his wartime political career, Brown was tireless in promoting emancipation. In November 1864, Brown wrote a letter to the editor of a local newspaper; this letter was also published as a circular, or pamphlet.*

LET US HAVE GENUINE FREEDOM IN MISSOURI.

St. Louis, November 15, 1864.

To The Editor of the Cosmos:

. . . The returns which are as yet incomplete, nevertheless make it sure that Missouri by an overwhelming majority has declared in favor of our cause. Governor, State officers, the Legislature, a Convention, all elected upon unequivocal pledges, and all charged as their first duty to extirpate slavery from the soil of our commonwealth,—these are the first fruits of our victory. Nor is this all. A clear recognition of the fatal influence which any form of human bondage exerts upon society has gone along with this judgment of the people, inducing everywhere the choice as representatives of those avowing the extremest liberal views, recognizing in all the outgrowths of opinion or the promptings of sympathy an identity betwixt slavery and rebellion, and connecting the franchise with freedom as a corelative [sic] term to be enforced as such in any reorganization.

A more absolute, unqualified decree was never rendered by any community upon any matter of great public concern, than has been delivered by the citizens of this State upon the fundamental basis that should characterize the recasting of our Constitution.

Let all friends of radical freedom be vigilant then in this hour of triumph to see that full expression is given by those appointed to the task, to the will of the people thus declared. It is the past with its slavery, its inhumanity, its retardation, its sterility, its substitution of classes and castes and masteries for that simple faith of the equality of all men before the law, which is to be obliterated. A future is to be inaugurated that shall be blurred by one of the disfigurements of bad passions taking the shape of oppressive enactments against the weaker members of society—none of the old prejudices of the slave code founded on color, done up into new idols to be worshiped by the ignorant and blushed for by the good and brave. Let us have a charter of liberties, that will not require to be apologized for whenever cited, that will carry on its face guarantees of freedom to all—freedom in its ultimates as well its surface showings—freedom that is to be a reality and an evenhanded justice, not a mockery and a sham. . . .

Without undertaking to amplify the positions thus presented, it may be sufficient to state in brief the requirements at the hands of our new Convention on this head. They are—

1. Protection of the purity of elections by a registry act that shall identify the person and the ballot.

2. Elimination of slavery from the State, not only in its present constitutional guaranty, but in all those recognitions which go to its support, and enable it more or less directly to control the suffrage.

3. Opening up the franchise to the attainment of all save the criminal— amongst whom must primarily be classed those whose sympathies led them to foster rebellion.

4. Facilitating the modes whereby popular expression may accomplish constitutional reform as the only complete assurance of future progress.

. . . Trusting that our noble State may yet be the first to pioneer the way of deliverance from former afflictions, and that in establishing here freedom as the watchword of our new life, we may be paralyzed with no halting performance, but declare and set forth with undaunted faith the equality of all men before the law,

I remain very truly yours,

B. GRATZ BROWN.

William K. Patrick Papers, Missouri Historical Society, St. Louis.

PRIVATE SOLOMON B. CHILDRESS SWEARS VENGEANCE ON COLUMBIA

Solomon B. Childress served as a private with the Eighteenth Missouri Volunteer Infantry. Born in Indiana, he moved to Missouri in 1857, where he grew corn and reared four children with his wife Lydia. His service record describes him as 5'11" with blue eyes and fair hair. He left behind a 172-page journal describing his wartime experiences and camp life. When General William T. Sherman marched through Georgia and the Carolinas in late 1864 and early 1865, he took with him several brigades of hard-bitten western soldiers, many of whom came from Missouri. In late November 1864, just after Sherman's famous march to the sea had begun, his soldiers heard about the conditions at the infamous Andersonville prison camp. The descriptions of thousands of starving prisoners so enraged Sherman's men that they swore to take bitter revenge on the South Carolinians. Many federal soldiers blamed the state for the rebellion, and after four years of bloodshed, they were ready to make an end of the war.

February the 15th 1865

Wednesday morning the company agane is in the column marching in the direction of Columbia S.C. at 8⁰⁰ Aᵐ in the advance of the division and senter Division of the Corps and at 11⁰⁰ Aᵐ there was heavy Artilery heard in the direction of Columbia with the 15th Corps and the Enemy and at 9:00 Pᵐ the Column came to a halt and went in to camp distance marched 10 miles

February the 16th 1865

Thursday morning the company and regt was on Gard Garding the Waggon train while the column moved on and at 12⁰⁰ Pᵐ assended a high summit on the Southside of Columbia and had a fair view of the City which was in the Enemys hands and the column Baring to the Left up the Saluda river went in to camp at 9⁰⁰ Pᵐ distant marched 8 miles

February the 17th 1865

Friday Morning the company with the command lay in camp on the Enemys old parade ground whair somany of our soldiers had ben kept in the dirt prisons and

whair there graves is a memorial of there suffering and our armey is Swaring
Vengence on the Grate Capital when permitted to Enter her Gates. an at 1^{00} P^m the
column took up a line of march and crossed the Saluda river. And marched to
Brod river and crossed on the pontoon and at 7^{00} P^m the company with the command marched through the city with Colors flying and Bands playing and at 8^{00}
P^m went in to camp the company was detailed on picket there is abundence of
wine in the place and soon the most of the boys is prety well drunken and at 11^{00}
P^m the City is on fier and the aufulest seen that ever was witness takes place the
burning of Buildings the screaming of woman and children turned in the streets
destitute of homes or food or rament but such is the fortunes of war and nothing els better can be expectin from an outraged armey who have premeditated
revenge for rongs done to our soldiers

February the 18 1865
Saturday morning the company is relieved from picket and at 8^{00} A^m was
marched in to the city and viewed the smouldering remains of the once butiful
City of Columbia which is nothing but a heap of broken bricks the company and
regt. went to tairing up the railrode track and at 12^{00} P^m the job was don and still
the fier is rageing in the outer parts of the city the main part being alredy con-
sumed and at 2^{00} P^m the company marched with the command and at 6^{00} P^m went
in to camp 8 miles from the once city of Columbia on the railrode
the day is past and all is quiet.

February the 19th 1865
Sunday morning the company and regt with the 27 Ohio & 64 Illinois under
command of Genl Mower marched up the railrode . . .

February the 20th 1865
Monday morning the company marched with the command at 7^{00} A^m in the
advance of the command and skirmishing with the enemy and still the black
clouds of smoke assends upwards from the burning of cotton and plantations
of disloyal citizens of the country and at 5^{00} P^m the command came to a halt and
went in to camp near Elkin Station on the railrode
distance marched 10 miles

February the 21st 1865
Tuesday morning the company and regt. was detailed for train gards and
marched from camp Near Elkin Station at 8:00 AM and after marching through
swamps and building several miles of Cordroy Bridge came to a halt near Wines-
boro S C and went in to camp
distance marched to day 12 miles

Solomon B. Childress Journal, Civil War Collection, Missouri Historical Society, St. Louis.

WILLIAM B. NAPTON FEARS THE CONTROL OF RADICAL REPUBLICANS

William Barclay Napton kept a diary throughout most of his political career. The Missouri State Convention that met in 1865 passed (as part of its efforts to revise the state constitution) an ordinance that allowed the removal of justices and court officers—ostensibly for refusing to take the "iron-clad" loyalty oath, but in practice to prevent them from overturning emancipation and civil liberties clauses in the new state constitution. Napton had served as a state supreme court justice since 1838 but was removed in 1865 as a result of the so-called ousting ordinance. Shortly after the war, he expressed his bitterness and despair over the state of affairs in Missouri.[11]

October 14, 1865.

. . . [T]he reign of radical absolutism promises to be indefinitely protracted. . . . The government is gradually settling into a consolidated despotism. . . . The whole machinery of government is in the hands of the Radical party, and although destitute of any talented leaders, they have so completely taken possession of all the avenues to power that without some revolutionary effort all attempts to dislodge them will be fruitless. . . . Constitutional liberty, such as we once thought to be indispensable to American life, has ceased to be regarded as among the practicable desiderata of citizenship. We resemble the French after the Revolution and its attendants and consequents had worried them for twenty or thirty years, and would hail with satisfaction the absolutism of some respectable leader—but none such seems destined to appear here for many years to come and the hydra headed monster yet has sway—King Numbers—that is, at the north, where all the real power of the government is now fixed and fixed forever. The South and West are mere outlying provinces, governed directly and indirectly at Washington.

Diary, William Barclay Napton Papers, Missouri Historical Society, St. Louis.

THE *DAILY MISSOURI DEMOCRAT* CELEBRATES THE END OF SLAVERY IN MISSOURI

A joyous editorial from Benjamin Gratz Brown's newspaper celebrates the end of slavery in Missouri.

LET US CELEBRATE.

Missouri is free. Emancipation, real, genuine, radical emancipation is achieved. This is a victory equal to any event won upon the field of battle, and as such deserves to be commemorated. We feel like celebrating the event for which we so long have labored, and doubt not that such is the universal feeling among the liberty loving people of this community. The deliverance of the State from slavery ought not to be passed over as an ordinary occurrence. There should be some public manifestation of rejoicing, in which all the people will be invited and permitted to participate. We make the suggestion—who will take hold of the matter and give it effect?

MISSOURI FREE.

The work is done. After a struggle extending through long years, and contested with all the force and bitterness which Slavery could muster beneath its banner, Freedom has triumphed, and Missouri, the battle ground, is redeemed. The eleventh day of January, A. D. 1865, is made memorable in the history of the State forever. Through the bright period of prosperity which, we believe, has now dawned upon our Commonwealth, long dishonored by oppression and injustice, and repressed in its development by the cruel and ruinous system of slavery, the anniversary of that day will bring gladness to the hearts of thousands and of millions. It has introduced a new era, the brightness of whose glory will extend through all time.

We have so long labored to impress the advantages of emancipation upon the people of Missouri; so long urged the arguments of freedom, that we do not now deem it necessary to go over the entire ground, and gather up the trophies of the victory won. It is enough to know that liberty and right have triumphed. Missouri takes her place in the ranks for the Free States, and as the long line moves on in the grand march of progress, of civilization and of loyalty, her steps will be with the foremost. The chains, the lash and shackles of slavery no longer belong to Missouri. They were carried out of sight forever on yesterday—the Eleventh day of January, 1865.

Daily Missouri Democrat, January 12, 1865.

COUSIN JIMMIE DESCRIBES EMANCIPATION ON THE FARM

James W. Clemens, a physician, wrote a somewhat contemptuous letter to his young cousin Alice describing the reaction of the family's slaves to the news of emancipation in Missouri. The Clemens family came from Kentucky in the mid-eighteenth century and settled in Ste. Genevieve, Missouri.

St. Louis, Jany 15, 1865

My Dear Alice,

. . . [T]he State Convention passed a law setting free all the slaves in the State, so now Missouri is a free state. It is said up home that Aunt Harriet, when she heard the news jumped up and cracked her heels together three times and cried "Bress the Lord"! What a clattering of dry bones there must have been, for Harriet is so old & dried up there is scarcely anything left but bones. Westly is talking of leaving and going to driving Hack. Cassa, I suppose will remain, as she is too lazy to go away. . . .

Don't forget Cousin Jimmie but believe that he is very fond of Coz. Alice and always will remain with much love, her affectionate Cousin Jimmie.

Clemens Family Collection, Missouri Historical Society, St. Louis.

GEORGE CRUZEN MUSTERS OUT OF THE
CONFEDERATE SERVICE AND EMIGRATES TO MEXICO

George Richardson Cruzen participated, willingly or not, on all sides of Missouri's war. He fought with a pro-Southern force to drive the federals out of Saline County, was captured and impressed into service with the Enrolled Missouri Militia, and finally left to join Quantrill's men in 1864. His memoir, "The Story of My Life," details his experiences until the end of the war, after which he emigrated to Mexico. This excerpt picks up the story at the end of his service under General Sterling Price in 1864.

We camped near Cane Hill beside of a fine orchard full of splendid apples. Stayed there two nights. We ate apples raw and roasted and I had near ½ bushel in a sack when we left. We got two days rations there so had one when we left. When that gave out we done with out or most of the men did and horses the same. We went southwest into Indian Territory. My horse died about two days after we left Cane Hill. I put my saddle clothes and blankets into one ambulance. There soon was quite a company afoot with me. I got something to eat most every day as Ikie had a good horse he was able to scout around and kill something most every day but most of our men went hungry. Co. H had a fine colt following its mother one of the boys was riding. They killed and ate it. I saw men kill horses that gave out and cut meat out of them to cook and eat. Dave Ferrill was one of them walking and one day he saw Gen. Price coming in his hack. He said now boys watch me. He picked up a stick got his crooked legs out of shape and was hobbling along. Gen. Price stopped said my dear man get in here one crippled like you should not walk. He rode with the Gen. for several hours got to camp thanked the Gen. got out gave a yell and walked as straight as anyone to his camp. Gen. Price laughed and said that was one on me. . . .

We crossed the Arkansas River above Fort Gibson went up the South Canadian River one days march went in camp grazed horses on the cane killed hogs and cattle and oh how we did eat had no salt or bread. We jerked the lean beef so we had something to eat as we went but Gen. Price sent some wagons with meat to meet us from Baggie Depot. When we got there an old friend of Col. Blackwell told him if I come to his house next day he give me a horse. So I started on Col. B.'s negro's old mule but I could not talk Indian nor could I find where he lived.

I finally found a negro woman and her son. They said the party did not live near there. I was hungry and asked if I could get a bite to eat. They said shure we have corn bread and venison and hominy. While eating they said if they had gun caps the boy could kill all the deer they wanted so I gave him 15 or 20. My how glad he was to get. I started back to Baggy Depot met two confederate Indians. All I could understand was trade. They were leading a nice pony and I traded a blanket for it. I took my saddle off the mule put on pony mounted and rode on they pleased to get a good blanket and me to get the pony. . . .

We marched slowly down the Red River . . . The next morning Gen. Shelby told us he expected to go to the west coast and would disband us. So ended the last organized Squadron of Confederates. He said tomorrow we sell our wagons mules and supplies to the highest bidder and divide what we get as before.

Col. Elliott came to me that night said Dick are you going to stay with Col. Blackwell. I said probably not. I want to get near the coast so I can get out of the country when I care to. He said here I have a man from California he has been in a Texas Regt. he talks reads and writes Spanish and come from Mazatlan. He will guide us there and be interpreter for us if we furnish what he and horse eats. I said Col. that sounds good to me. He said see some of your friends and I do same. If we can get 40 we buy a wagon 6 mules and a lot of grub at our sale in the morning. So I saw Gil Snaling and Capt. Nixon Luther Isom—John Isbell—Mose carpenter and we formed our mess that night. I also saw several others and before we slept organized a company of 44 men under Col. Elliott and another company of 20 was formed under Col. Dorsey. The next day at the sale both Cos. bought wagons and teams and supplies. It took about $18 of each of us to pay for what we bought but got $27 back out of our share of the sale.

The next day I think July 4th 1865 we crossed the Rio Grande but as we came off the ferry boat were told that we must leave our guns under a guard in their armory but could keep our pistols. We soon were scattered all over the town most of us buying something to eat or drink. An old German who could talk but little English walked up to Ben Rudd a few feet from me said this is my horse it has my brand and with him was a Mexican witness and the mayor. He said get off of my horse he had gotten one before. But I said no doubt you give up your horse. . . . Gen. Shelby heard us and galloped to us said get on your horses boys we lick the whole lot. We began to get in line and we heard their bugle sound assembly at their barracks. One of the Mexican Governors who could talk to us said Gen. Shelby for God's sake don't let your men go meet those Mexicans. I go turn them back and you please get your guns and go out of town and camp and we did that but that settled us joining the Mexicans.

George Richardson Cruzen, "The Story of My Life" / Reminiscences, circa 1930, Missouri Historical Society, St. Louis.

WILLIAM MURPHY PLEADS FOR RELEASE FROM GRATIOT STREET PRISON

William Murphy was from New Orleans and appears to have been involved with
Confederate sympathizers who burned boats and destroyed government property in
St. Louis. Eventually, he came forward to give evidence against them. Murphy's letter
refers to Colonel James H. Baker, provost marshal of the Department of Missouri,
who compiled reports on boat burners in St. Louis. In April 1865, Baker had arrested
Edward Frazor, considered the ringleader of the Confederate boat burners, who also
was being held in Gratiot Street Prison with Murphy. The details of Baker's report
can be found in the Official Records of the Rebellion. *Murphy's desperate letter is*
confirmed by some details in Baker's report, which indicates that Murphy should have
been released after turning over his evidence. Murphy's friend John Clarke served with
Company I of the Thirty-first Missouri Infantry and mustered out of service shortly
after receiving this letter. Murphy's fate is unknown.

Gratiot Prison July 4th 1865

Mr. Clark Dear sir, if Col Baker would write to the authoritys at Washington
and State my case to them just as it is I think I would be Released from this
prison. I was promised protection [by] Col. Baker when I first went to him and
deposed & gave my evidence against frazer and his gang of St. [Louis] Boat
Burners he also knows that it is dangerous for me to walk the streets of Saint
Louis I stated to Col. Baker the object of my going Back to mobile but I dont
think he beleived me. All I can give is my oath that I told the truth. I hope he will
write to Washington in my behalf

Yours with Respect
W[m] Murphy

John T. Clarke Papers, Missouri Historical Society, St. Louis.

TO ALL WHO WERE REBELS, TRAITORS, SYMPATHIZERS AND THEIR FRIENDS

The "L. & U. A. A.," a pro-Union club in St. Louis, published this angry circular
shortly after the end of the Civil War, revealing the deep bitterness still remaining
between the warring factions. The precise name of this association is unknown.

CIRCULAR.

TO ALL WHO WERE REBELS, TRAITORS, SYMPATHIZERS AND THEIR FRIENDS DURING THE WAR:

WE, THE L. & U. A. A. OF THE STATE OF MISSOURI IN GRAND COUNCEIL
ASSEMBLED, MAKE THE FOLLOWING PROPOSITIONS:

Whereas, You madly plunged the country into a fratricidal war of unparalleled severity, without cause or provocation, to perpetuate a system of human bondage more diabolical and revolting than anything world ever saw before; and

Whereas, You drove from the Southern and border States, tarred, feathered and murdered hundreds of innocent men who had never interfered with even a pretended right of yours, merely on account of a supposed belief, and

Whereas, You carried on the war on your part with the most atrocious and fiendish brutality that ever disgraced a conflict of arms, culminating in the absolute starving to death in the slaughter pens of Belle Isle, Andersonville and Saulisbury of a hundred thousand of our gallant comrades in arms, whose only crime was their patriotic zeal for the welfare of their government and willingness to die in its defence; and

Whereas, You have made an indebtedness of over $2,000,000,000 to hang like an incubus upon the energies of the nation, resulting in an inexorably burdensome taxation; and

Whereas, You have made a hundred thousand widows and five hundred thousand orphans dependent upon the cold charities of the world for the necessaries of life by the late war; and

Whereas, Since you were fairly whipped in the field, and the government gave you the most magnanimous terms ever extended to a beaten foe, you have continued to persecute, drive from their homes and abuse Union men, who chanced to reside where you were in the majority, killing men in Missouri, Kentucky, Arkansas and all the Southern States, frequently with the most atrocious barbarity, butchering and burning innocent women and children in Memphis and New Orleans;

THEREFORE, This Circular is published to notify you, your friends, and all concerned in this atrociously wicked cruelty, that we are not now, nor have ever been, violators of law,

That we desire the peace, prosperity and happiness of the whole country, the North, the South, the East, the West; and this desire has led us to bear up under wrongs and injustice that no other set of men ever would have borne;

That we shall hereafter hold every one of you accountable for the murders and atrocities that any of your party may commit;

That if Union men cannot live in peace and quiet where you are in the majority, you cannot enjoy peace and quiet here. We want you to fully understand the situation. We deprecate the causes which have made this step necessary, but know you that we cannot, we will not, see our Union brethren who have perilled their lives in the defence of Liberty, Justice, and good government endangered by a traitorous set of hell-hounds, whom you pat on the backs, without avenging their blood.

That the matter is in your hands, and you will please take notice that bitter experience has taught us to prepare, and we are ready for any emergency which you may bring upon us. The mine is laid in sixty counties of this State, and if you spring it we will burst you into atoms, and give you a little by way of interest on the old score. Remember 1862; be warned, and control the viciousness of your fiendish party, or death and desolation will follow the L. & U. A. Avengers.

Done by Order
    GRAND COUNCIL,
      Of L. & U. A. A. State of Missouri
Approved by
LEADER-IN-CHIEF, Dist. of Mo.

<small>Civil War Collection, Missouri Historical Society, St. Louis.</small>

W. R. DYER FEARS THAT THE COUNTRY
IS DRIFTING INTO CIVIL WAR AGAIN

After Lincoln's assassination in 1865, Vice President Andrew Johnson assumed the office of president. Many young Republicans who had fought on the side of Union resented Johnson's conciliatory policies toward former rebels and his repeated attacks on the cabinet he had inherited from Lincoln. W. R. Dyer, a carpenter who made his living in St. Louis, evidently detested Johnson's conservative politics. In his description of a speech Johnson gave in St. Louis in 1866, Dyer refers to Republican senator Charles Sumner from Massachusetts, Pennsylvania congressman Thaddeus Stevens, and Wendell Phillips, an ardent abolitionist. All three men were well-known radicals who advocated harsh policies toward former rebels and thus had earned Johnson's enmity. Dyer probably served with the Thirty-second Missouri Infantry.

To Mr. Freeman Hall
Matinicus, Maine
St. Louis
Sept 9th 1866.

Mr. Hall
Dear Sir

I have long been intending to fulfil my promise made last winter to write to you and believe I will now do so. . . . We have been stopping in St. Louis since we arrived last Feb. I have been following my avocation of carpentering. Business has been quite good with wages three and a half dollars per day but so great is the expense of living here that even with the most rigid economy one can make but little headway working by the day. A stranger here or nearly so I have worked by the day thus far but if I should continue to stop here I hope to get into a good business myself. I am strongly debating in my mind however the propriety of going into some smaller place. . . .

Though the west is a great farming country we have here in the city but little chance to know or learn much of it. I have occasionally talked with a farmer and found that farming out here is a much easier and more interesting business than in the east. There the necessity of manuring the soil and of thoroughly hoeing and tilling every crop makes the farmers life a very laborious one and limits the amount tilled to a very small quantity. I was brought up on a farm and believe it the most natural, most independent, most healthy, interesting and happy kind of life that human beings can live and often wish I was well situated on a good farm out here. . . .

We had a great time here yesterday. Business suspended. The cause the arrival of President Johnson. I went to see him from curiosity. Sec. Seward, Wells, Gen. Grant, and Admiral Farragut were with him. The president seems to me to make a great mistake in assuming that all who flock to see him in the places he visits are supporters of his policy. They go from curiosity . . . As president of the U. S. his speeches ought to be of a national and not of a partizan character. But he looses all pretensions to dignity and talks like a pothouse politician, denouncing congress a coordinate branch of the government as a nest of traitors even asking the people as he did here yesterday why they dont hang Sumner Stephens and Philips. In his harangue here yesterday he set all right and justice as well as common sense at defiance. . . . I fear that our country is fast drifting into civil war again. For thirty years the South ruled by threats and already the game has again commenced, and even Mr. Johnson is its mouthpiece and even asks the people if they want more bloodshed intimating that if the country dont adopt his policy another revolution will follow. I hold to doing *right* regardless of threats and if another war must come why then I can volunteer again. But my sheet is full. Please write me

Yours in friendship and esteem

W. R. Dyer

W. R. Dyer, Western Historical Manuscripts Collection, University of Missouri, Columbia.

JOHN MERCER LANGSTON DEMANDS EQUALITY BEFORE THE LAW

Black abolitionist John Mercer Langston earned bachelor's and master's degrees from Oberlin College and later studied law in Ohio. He became active in the antislavery movement in the mid-1850s, distinguishing himself as an orator. During the Civil War, he helped recruit black men for the Union army and later served as inspector general for the Freedmen's Bureau. A year after the war ended, Langston spoke to the Missouri House of Representatives, pleading for equal rights for black people.

A SPEECH ON "EQUALITY BEFORE THE LAW" DELIVERED BY J. MERCER LANGSTON, IN THE HALL OF REPRESENTATIVES, IN THE CAPITOL OF MISSOURI, ON THE EVENING OF THE 9TH DAY OF JANUARY, 1866.

... It has always been our fortune to be held to a full discharge of all the obligations and duties which citizenship imposes, while it has ever been our misfortune to be denied well-nigh all the privileges, advantages, and rights, it naturally confers. We have been taxed, and denied representation. We have paid to the Government the full debt of our allegiance; and then we have been denied the protection due its defenders. No plea of color or race, urged on our behalf against these exactions of the Government, would avail us aught. No peculiarity in the texture of our hair, the color of our countenance, or our extraction, could shield us against the demands of the tax-gatherer. Against the black man, as against the white man, his demands have ever been inexorable. We are told that taxation and representation are inseparable. We are told that allegiance is due the Government, and protection due the subject; and that these are not to be sundered. In the application of these sentiments, to the colored American as well as to the white, we ask that what God, in his wisdom, has joined together, let not man put asunder.

The heroic deeds of our fathers and sons, in the wars of this country, are indeed most honorable, and we may well plead them in claiming equality before American law. These deeds are forever garnered up in the immortal records of those wars, as written in our National history; and our statesmen, orators, and poets have immortalized their gallant conduct in their beautiful periods. Indeed, Crispus Attucks, and Peter Salem, and Salem Poor, have erected to their memories, in the letters of our land, monuments which shall endure when those which are built of stones and granite and brass shall molder and decay. We not only furnished, however, heroes in the Revolutionary struggle, but at a later date in our National history the colored American gave full demonstration of his gallantry, his heroism, and devotion. ...

Our behavior in the late rebellion, which cost the nation so many millions of treasure and so many thousands of precious lives, is familiar to you all. At the call of the country, colored Americans came from the hills of New England, from the prairies of the West, from the plantations of the South, from all parts of our vast land, offering their brave hearts and strong arms in its defense. How bravely they fought, how heroically they died, you know full well, Our loyalty and devotion, however, were not only displayed on the battle-field, but in the kind, tender treatment which we gave your sons, brothers, and fathers, when, naked, starving, and wandering, in their flight from the foul and loathsome prison-houses of the South—from Libby and Andersonville—we fed them, clothed them, and guided them on their way to the lines of the American army. From your own State came nine thousand black men, brave and true, giving their stalwart bodies to the service of the country. Many of those men, having been honorably discharged, are again among you. They return, however, bringing the scars received in many hotly-contested battles. These scars are the strong, unanswerable argument which they make to you in favor of a full recognition of their equality before the law.

In the name of our citizenship; in the name of the American axiom that taxation and representation are inseparable; in the name of the sentiment that allegiance and protection are mutually obligatory, the one upon the Government and the other upon the subject; and in the name of our loyalty and devotion to the country, as demonstrated in the wars of the country, we demand the enjoyment of all the rights of unrestricted and impartial suffrage.

But to all this the reply is made that we are ignorant and unfit to vote. It is not denied that many of us are ignorant. And yet it is not true, as some would have us believe, that colored men in this country enjoy a monopoly of ignorance. Indeed, if they were instantly blotted out, by a fiat of Almighty Power, ignorance would still remain. It will not be denied that many very ignorant white men vote in this country. If one class is to be excluded from the voting privilege, because of ignorance, let the other be also. If, in your wisdom, you think it well to establish an intelligence qualification for voters in your State, we wilt make no objection, provided you make it applicable alike to white men and black. What we ask is impartiality in the regulation of suffrage.

Colored men are not, however, so ignorant as many suppose. They have made laudable advancement in all things that belong to a well-ordered and dignified life. We have already established among us, in this very State, many well-conducted churches and colleges; and we have supplied our school-rooms and our pulpits with teachers and preachers of our own complexion. And many of our teachers and preachers are men of no inconsiderable attainment. Topics of general interest are becoming among us subjects of general and common thought, conversation, and debate. Indeed, it would be a very unusual thing now to enter the family of any ordinary colored man in your cities and villages, and not find there the newspapers commonly read in your State. In St. Louis, Hannibal, Macon City, Chillicothe, St. Joseph, and Kansas City, as well as here in the Capital of the State, I found many colored men who read and write very well, and who possess all the qualifications necessary to make them good and successful business men.

These men read, understand, and converse about all the discussions held in your Legislative halls and in our National Congress. In one word, the intellectual and moral being of your colored population is greatly ameliorated. . . .

I would utter no word, in this connection, in favor of suffrage founded upon a property qualification, for I believe that the right to exercise the elective franchise is an essential and inseparable part of self-government, and stands conspicuous among our inherent rights; nor can any man native to the soil, who is qualified by age and residence, justly be deprived of this right. But should you see fit to adopt the rule requiring colored residents of your State to own a certain amount of property: on which they shall pay an annual tax in order to vote, we will urge no objection to it, provided you will make it apply alike to all classes, white as well as black. We ask no special favors; we object to all class legislation which springs out of anti-democratic discriminations. . . .

While we can tolerate the test of intelligence or property in regard to suffrage, we enter our earnest protest against that standard which rests upon the tint of our skin. It is not only unreasonable and absurd, but utterly impracticable. What the word "white" means in our country to-day, and what class of persons it includes, no man can tell. It does not include simply those who possess no other than Anglo-Saxon blood. They tell us it includes some persons who possess in large measure even negro blood. In Ohio, where I live, this belief has crystalized into law; and there persons who are of African descent, and yet who possess more Anglo-Saxon blood than negro, are citizens, and entitled to all the rights and privileges, social and political, that attach to any and all others. . . .

In the reconstruction of your State legislation we beseech you, in the name of our humanity and our manhood—in the name of all the sacred elements that constitute the body of that law whose "soul is its reasonableness"—to recognize no such rule and tolerate no such practice under your Constitution and laws.

We urge the erasure of the word "white" from your Constitution also; because so long as it remains we are incapable of acting as jurors, being denied the qualifications of electors; nor are we tried, when accused of crime, by a jury of our political and legal equals; nor do we enjoy such a jury trial, in suits at common law, as the Constitution of the United States guarantees to every citizen. . . .

Three things are essential to our elevation in life. The first is Education. We ourselves, as well as our children, are to be educated; and by our education we are to remove forever the charge of ignorance, so often brought against us by our enemies. The second thing is Property. Industrious, economical habits of life will bring this into our possession; and, once secured, we may use it as a moral lever to lift us out of degradation, and as an incontestable argument in refutation of the foul aspersion, so often made against us, that we are wanting in thrift, energy, and enterprise. The third thing is Character; and herein is found all truthfulness and trustworthiness. Let us but make for ourselves character, and none will ever again charge us with being unfaithful and unreliable. Then our word will be pronounced good, our contracts sure of performance; and all will seek, will covet, our patronage. . . .

I am not insensible to the fact that you have already made commendable progress in this work. Indeed, what you have already done gives the gratifying earnest

of the glad and glorious success which, at no distant day, will bless and crown our
efforts. God help the Right!

African American Pamphlet Collection, Library of Congress.

THIS GREAT PROBLEM OF RECONSTRUCTION

This editorial appeared in the Daily Missouri Democrat *(later known as the*
St. Louis Globe-Democrat*), a Republican newspaper that always took a firm
pro-Union stance. The editorial focuses on the magnitude of the efforts and trials
the state had endured, and expresses anxiety about the state's future, but without
harking back to divisive language or political rhetoric. The author may have been
J. F. Wright.*

RECONSTRUCTION.

The problem of reconstruction presents the all engrossing subject of the day.
Therefore, . . . we . . . keep it before the people, that the work of reconstruction
is a legislative and political labor, not a simple, executive work. It belongs to the
thinking, not the acting department of the government. We have emerged from a
war, not merely from a rebellion. We have not put down an insurrection, but have
overthrown a government—a government with President, Congress, judiciary
and organized military power, that reared its horrid front in the full panoply of
war. It was in one sense a foreign government; it drew off a third part of the states
from their allegiance—withdrew them as political powers from the Union, and
though still on the territory of the United Sates, spurned and defied its power. . . .

The question is not simply whether the military power of the late Confederate
government is broken, but is the nation safe? Are the elements of war and discord
so far subdued that it will be safe to restore our late enemies to their former political powers? Does the spirit to injure remain? Is the snake killed and scotched? Do
they desire the perpetuity of the United States? Are they willing to bear their share
of the national debt? Do they extend equal rights to the citizens of all States? . . .
Or do they still desire the establishment of a separate Confederacy with slavery
for its cornerstone, and stand ready to use such political power as they may obtain
in re-establishing slavery and a slave empire on the territories of the Union? Do
not the frequent murders and massacres, and the tone of the legislative assemblies
indicate a hostile feeling, slumbering like the fires of a volcano in the bosom of the
South, and only wanting opportunity to break out?

Now, whether these things are so or not, whether the South looks on the North
as the victor in an aggressive war begun by the North and carried on by them
against an inoffensive and harmless people that has been merely struggling to re-

main in the Union and under the Constitution, or not, is not the present question. The question is, "shall these matters be determined by the legislative and judicial departments of our government, or by the executive." . . .

We do not intend now to say whether Congress does right or wrong in submitting terms, upon which they may be readmitted; or whether or not the president is too willing and ready to admit the former rebels to power. Congress may be too lenient, or too strict. It matters not for the present. All that we maintain now is that to the government only belongs to the power to restore the enjoyment of political privileges upon a fair consideration of national duty and expediency.

We do not exclude the President from exercising his power and influence. In his legitimate department, nor would we allow the Congress or Judiciary to be excluded from theirs. Let all work together harmoniously if possible to solve this great problem of reconstruction in such a manner as may best [serve] the welfare of the nation, and to restore wandering stars to their proper orbit, that we may again enjoy the music of the spheres in harmony, peace, and prosperity,

J. W. F.

Daily Missouri Democrat, January 12, 1867.

FREEDMAN'S BANK RECORDS

The following documents are applications from free black people in Missouri to open savings accounts in the Freedman's Bank. The microfilmed rolls from the National Archives and Records Administration contain hundreds of applications, dating from shortly after the end of the war until the bank lost all its funds in 1873. Some of the depositors were individuals; others were corporations or organizations—primarily black churches. Rev. Simon Peter Anderson served as pastor of the Second African Baptist Church of St. Louis from 1869 to 1880. He was the son of Rev. John Richard Anderson and the first and only pastor to serve the flock twice as its shepherd. He formed the Samaritan Relief Society in 1874 to help the aged, poor, and sick of the church as well as to provide burial services for its members. Reverend Anderson championed the cause of public education for blacks in the city of St. Louis. In 1877, he served as a member of the first and only African American board of education in the city.

Record for George William Barnes
Date, and No. of Application: Sept 30, 1866, 415
Name of Master   John W. Clark
Name of Mistress   Agnes W.
Plantation
Height and Complexion   5 ft. 6 in. high Brown

Father or Mother? Married? [line crossed out]
Name of Children,
Regiment and Company,   Private
Place of Birth   St. Louis Mo.
Residence   Washington D. C.
Occupation   Was private servant to Maj. General Grant
      Signature, George William Barnes

No. 286 Record for Greer Young
Date of Application: June 23rd, 1869
Where born,   Fairfield District, S. C.
Where brought up,   "   "   "
Residence,   Barnfield Station, Mo.
Age,   Thirty (about)
Complexion,   Black
Occupation,   Baggage Car
Works for
Wife   Silva
Children   Tom, Moses, Creesy, Budd, infant not yet named
                                  one month old
Father   Sam Young
Mother   Judy
Brothers   None
Sisters   Two–Eliza, Sevelle
      Signature, (cannot write)

No. 316 Record for Benjamin Price
Date of Application,   August 9th 1869
Where born,   Chester dist S. C.
Where brought up,   "   "   "   & in Tenn.
Residence,   St. Louis, Mo.
Age,   about Twenty one
Complexion,   quite dark
Occupation,   Barber
Works for
Wife   Single
Children
Father   Robt. Price
Mother   Sarah
Brothers   Thomas. Andrew Samuel—

Sisters   Adaline—Sarah Mary—
    Signature, (Cannot write)

No. 321 Record for Ladies Ch Aid Society 2^d Bap Ch

Date of Application,	August 13th 1869
Where born,	/
Where brought up,	/
Residence,	
Age,	
Complexion,	
Occupation,	
Works for	Rev S P Anderson Teas
Wife	
Children	
Father	
Mother	
Brothers	
Sisters	

    Signature, Simon P. Anderson, Treasurer.

Registers of Signatures of Depositors in Branches of the Freedman's Savings and Trust Company, 1865–1874 (Washington, D.C.: National Archives and Records Administration, 1970), micropublication M816, 27 rolls.

MARTYRDOM IN MISSOURI

The new Missouri Constitution of 1865 required "test oaths" of all citizens, who had to swear that they had always been loyal to the Union. Several Protestant ministers and Catholic priests were removed from the pulpit when they refused to sign the oaths (what the author refers to as "non-juring"). When the Liberal Republican Party came to power in Missouri, the legislature ratified amendments to the constitution that abolished the test oath. After Rev. Samuel B. McPheeters, pastor of the Pine Street Presbyterian Church in St. Louis, was banished for baptizing a child with the name "Sterling Price Robbins" in 1863, President Lincoln rescinded the banishment order and restored Reverend McPheeters. This pamphlet was published after the test oath law was revoked in 1870. (See "A St. Louis 'She-Devil'," chap. 5.)

. . . The authors of the New Constitution can not plume themselves upon the originality of its "test oath," however much they may merit distinction in other respects. . . .

[T]he State of Missouri, in both her civil and military departments, was not a whit behind her sister States in devising, concocting, inventing, framing, prescribing, requiring, enforcing and filing "test oaths," and "oaths of allegiance," so called, during and since the war. And in no State or country, perhaps, have civil and military oaths been so often changed, revised, altered, amended and reconstructed; and this, too, by military commanders, State conventions, legislatures, civil courts, military courts-martial, provost-marshals, post commanders, scout captains, squad lieutenants, orderly sergeants, civil magistrates, notaries public and common soldiers, almost at pleasure and indiscriminately. . . .

A refusal to "take the oath" was assumed to be evidence of guilt of some kind, and no protestations of innocence or qualms of conscience could shield the victim. A provost guard, a filthy prison, upon the roughest fare, for months and years; the forfeiture of all the rights of citizenship, expatriation, the confiscation of all property, real and personal—all, and much more, could not atone for such an offense. Thousands of good men, with many ministers of the gospel, went to prison, or into exile and many of them from prison cells and prison hospitals to their graves, for *no other offense* than that of refusing to take the oath. Old men, who were too infirm to bear arms, were arrested by rough soldiers, torn from their homes and families, and "thrust into the inner prison" with common felons, from which some of them were brought out only to be buried, for no cause under heaven but refusing to take an oath from some shoulder-strapped tyrant who desired to vaunt his little brief authority and support his vanity and loyalty by cold, savage inhumanity.

This oath business in Missouri made a remarkable history, and was made the pretext for unnumbered and nameless wrongs and outrages upon the non-combatant population. By it men were deprived of property, liberty and life. . . .

The statement has frequently been made that ministers of the M. E. Church, South, through the greater, were not the only sufferers during the dark days of persecution in Missouri. Some of the best men and brightest lights in the Presbyterian pulpit were the victims of arbitrary power and military malice.

The Rev. Dr. McPheeters, of St. Louis . . . [was] conspicuous amongst the living martyrs of that period of general persecution . . . and many of them bore a conspicuous part in the great struggle between Church and State under the "test oath" of the New Constitution after the war closed.

No ministers in the State were more fearless and outspoken in defense of the integrity of the Church of Jesus Christ, the purity of the gospel ministry and the rightly kingship of Christ as the unchallenged Head of the Church than the non-juring ministers of the Presbyterian Church. The noble stand taken by the Rev. Drs. Brookes, Anderson, McPheeters, Farris, Yantis and others against the arbitrary usurpation of ecclesiastical authority by military commanders and provost-marshals, and the sacrilegious intermeddling with the kingdom of Christ by State conventions and civil functionaries, inspired courage and confidence in the

Church and ministry throughout the State, and supplied very largely the moral power that finally broke the bands of proscription, paralyzed the arm of persecution, scattered the forces of the enemy, and lodged in the public mind the most complete vindication of the purity and integrity of the church of Jesus Christ. . . .

William M. Leftwich, *Martyrdom in Missouri; a history of religious proscription, the seizure of churches, and the persecution of ministers of the gospel, in the state of Missouri during the late civil war, and under the "test oath" of the new constitution* (Saint Louis: Southwestern Book, 1870).

AN EX-CONFEDERATE SOLDIER APPLIES FOR A PENSION

In 1913, the Missouri state legislature passed a law providing for pensions and care for Confederate veterans. According to this law, the men had to prove not only that they had served but also that they had been honorably discharged and were of sound mind. Enoch B. Gill served with the Sixth Missouri Independents. He suffered a broken leg at the battle of Port Gibson on May 1, 1863.

PENSION FOR EX-CONFEDERATE SOLDIERS

Application for the purpose of certifying those entitled to obtain pension under the terms of C. S. H. B. 465, 47th General Assembly, State of Missouri.

———

I DO SOLEMNLY SWEAR TO THE FOLLOWING FACTS:

1. That I am a bona fide resident of Missouri, and have been for two years preceding April 23, 1913, and am at present residing at *Dallas, Jackson County*— Missouri;

2. That I am an Ex-Confederate soldier and served for not less than six months in the army of the Confederate States of America in the late Civil War as per my record given below;

3. That I was honorably discharged therefrom and, as evidence, will submit my discharge papers to the Adjutant General of Missouri; *I received no discharge.*

4. That I am not an inmate of the Confederate Home at Higginsville, or any other similar institution, but that

(a) on account of wounds received (state nature of wound) *on the 1ˢᵗ day of May 1863, near Port Gibson Miss. my left leg was amputated just below the knee.*

(b) or on account of disease contracted (state nature of disease)

(c) and on account of old age (state age) *73 years, Dec. 14ᵗʰ 1912.*

I am incapacitated to labor, and have no business or profession or property from which I may derive an income, and no means sufficient to my support. (State if applicant has any property in wife's name, or if he has children or any other relations who should support him.)

I own a little store at the village of Dallas Junction Jackson Co. Mo. about $300 but have been unable to attend to it the last 5 yrs. My wife is becoming feeble and cannot attend it any longer. I am Justice of the Peace and Notary Public which yields an income of from 25.00 to 50.00 per year for both.

Enoch B. Gill

(Signature of Applicant)

Subscribed and sworn to before me this 24th day of *June* 1913.

G. T. Limbaugh

Notary Public.

My commission expires *April 1st 1915.*

We, citizens of *Jackson County Missouri,* certify that we know the above *Enoch B. Gill* to be a man of reliability, and that the declaration above as made by him is correctly and truthfully stated. *We were in the service with him, and know them to be facts.*

> *Sterling Watts*
>
> *S. N. Pilcher*
>
> (To be signed by two citizens of city
> or county where applicant resides.)

Timeline

1820

March   President James Monroe approves the Missouri Enabling Act, which authorized the Missouri Territory to form a state constitution and government.

July   Missouri's first state constitution is adopted.

October   Thomas Hart Benton is elected as Missouri's first senator; although he could attend Senate sessions, he had no vote.

1821

August   Missouri comes into the Union as a slave state.

September   William Becknell, a Missouri trader, opens the Santa Fe Trail at Council Grove.

December   Jefferson City is chosen as the first capital of Missouri; St. Charles remains the capital from 1821 to 1826.

1824

December   The Missouri Assembly passes the freedom law, which provides that persons illegally held in slavery may sue for their freedom.

1831

July   Mormon leader Joseph Smith brings his followers to Independence, Missouri, which he claims is the place for building the temple and awaiting the second coming of Jesus Christ.

1837

November   Abolitionist and St. Louis newspaper editor Elijah Lovejoy is murdered by a mob in Alton, Illinois.

1838

October   Governor Lilburn Boggs issues an executive order driving all Mormons from Missouri.

1846

April   Dred and Harriet Scott initiate a suit for freedom in St. Louis, claim-
             ing that because they had resided in Wisconsin, a free territory, they
             were entitled to their liberty.

1847

February   The Missouri Assembly passes legislation prohibiting free black
             people from settling in the state and forbidding the establishment of
             schools for free black people.

December   First trans-Mississippi telegraph connection reaches St. Louis.

1848

March   After the discovery of gold in California, the cities of St. Louis, St.
             Joseph, and Independence, Missouri, become jumping-off points for
             western emigrants.

August   Liberty Party organizes in opposition to the extension of slavery
             into territories gained from the war with Mexico.

1849

January–   A cholera epidemic in St. Louis leaves more than four thousand
September   people dead.

1850

January   Senator Henry Clay introduces various compromise provisions in
             Congress in an effort to settle the dispute over the entry of Califor-
             nia into the Union.

September   President Millard Fillmore signs the Fugitive Slave Act.

1851

July   St. Louis celebrates the groundbreaking for the Pacific Railroad
             from St. Louis to Jefferson City.

1852

March   Harriet Beecher Stowe's serialized story *Uncle Tom's Cabin* is pub-
             lished in book form and soon becomes a national best seller.

1854

January   Illinois senator Stephen A. Douglas introduces the Kansas-Nebraska Act in Congress, providing for "popular sovereignty" and threatening to overturn the Missouri Compromise.

May   President Franklin Pierce signs the Kansas-Nebraska Act, setting off years of border violence between Kansas and Missouri.

1855

September   Steamboat *Arabia* sinks at Westport Landing, Missouri.

December   In Kansas, the antislavery Topeka Constitution is ratified but is later rejected by Congress.

1856

November   Republican John C. Frémont runs for president against Democrat James Buchanan, who wins the election.

1857

March   *Dred Scott* case reaches the U.S. Supreme Court, where Chief Justice Roger B. Taney hands down a decision declaring that Scott is not free and that black people are not citizens of the United States.

December   In Kansas, the proslavery Lecompton Constitution passes (fraudulently).

1858

May   In Kansas, the Leavenworth Constitution is ratified but is later rejected by Congress.

1859

October   In Kansas, the Wyandotte Constitution is ratified.

November   John Brown's raid at Harpers Ferry, Virginia.

1860

April   The Pony Express begins its first run from St. Joseph, Missouri, to Sacramento, California.

May   Missouri Democrats endorse Stephen A. Douglas for president.

               The Democratic Party splits into three factions supporting three different candidates for the November presidential election.

November   Abraham Lincoln is elected sixteenth president of the United States.

December   South Carolina secedes from the Union.

               Kentucky senator John Crittenden proposes the "Crittenden Compromise," extending the 36°30' line to the Pacific and offering compensation for escaped slaves.

1861

January   Kansas enters the Union as a free state.

               Alabama, Florida, Georgia, Louisiana, and Mississippi secede from the Union.

               A crowd of young men prevents the sale of seven slaves on the courthouse steps by disrupting the auction. This will be the last slave auction in St. Louis.

February   Confederate States of America is established, with President Jefferson Davis, of Mississippi, and Vice-President Alexander Stephens, of Georgia, at the helm.

               Texas secedes from the Union.

March   Abraham Lincoln is inaugurated.

               The Missouri State Convention moves from Jefferson City to the Mercantile Library in St. Louis, establishes the Board of Police Commissioners, and elects former supreme court justice Hamilton R. Gamble as chair.

April   Bombardment and surrender of Ft. Sumter. Lincoln calls for seventy-five thousand three-month volunteers, blockades Southern ports, and suspends the writ of habeas corpus in Maryland.

May   Arkansas, North Carolina, and Virginia join the Confederacy.

               General Nathaniel Lyon captures Camp Jackson in St. Louis, resulting in the deaths of more than civilians.

June   Tennessee secedes from the Union.

June	Battle of Boonville. Lyon raises the Union flag at Jefferson City.
July	Engagement at Carthage in southwest Missouri.

General George B. McClellan becomes general in chief of the Union army.

Congress authorizes Lincoln to accept five hundred thousand three-year volunteers.

Lincoln holds second conference with border state politicians regarding voluntary emancipation.

Confederate forces defeat Union army at Bull Run in Virginia.

Missouri State Convention elects Unionist Gamble as governor; Claiborne F. Jackson goes into exile.

August   Battle at Athens, Missouri, results in defeat of pro-Southern Missouri State Guard.

Battle of Wilson's Creek results in Union retreat and the death of Lyon.

General John C. Frémont proclaims martial law in St. Louis.

The Confederate Congress officially allies the Confederacy with Missouri and recognizes the state's rebel government; federals win a skirmish at Klapsford, Missouri.

Frémont seeks to emancipate slaves in Missouri and confiscate the property of rebels in arms.

September   Skirmishing near Fort Scott, Kansas.

Lincoln asks Frémont to rescind his proclamation.

Confederates under General Sterling Price begin their siege of Lexington, Missouri, defended by Colonel James Mulligan.

Frémont orders the arrest of Frank Blair.

Mulligan surrenders Lexington to Price.

October   Union troops recapture Lexington, Missouri.

Major Charles Zagonyi, commanding Frémont's cavalry regiment, captures Springfield, Missouri.

Missouri's exiled pro-Southern legislature at Neosho, Missouri, votes to secede from the Union and to join the Confederacy.

November   Frémont removed from command of the Western Department; Major General David Hunter temporarily replaces him. Major General Henry W. Halleck assumes command of the Department of the Missouri in St. Louis on November 19.

Missouri is officially admitted to the Confederacy.

December   Congress reconvenes in its regular session.

1862

February   General Ulysses S. Grant captures forts Henry and Donelson on the Tennessee River.

March   Battle of Pea Ridge, Arkansas, ends Confederate military threat in Missouri.

Union victory at New Madrid, Missouri.

April   Union victory at battle of Shiloh; Confederates surrender Island No. 10 in Missouri.

May   Homestead Act passes in Congress, allocated 160-acre parcels to heads of household more than twenty-one years of age.

June   Congress passes a law prohibiting slavery in the territories.

The battles known as "Seven Days" begin in Virginia.

The Missouri Convention rejects a gradual emancipation plan, as well as congressionally compensated emancipation.

July   Major General Henry W. Halleck assumes command of the armies of the United States.

August   Confederate victory at the second battle of Bull Run, Virginia.

September   General George McClellan restored to full command of the Union armies.

Union victory at Antietam, Maryland.

President Abraham Lincoln announces the Preliminary Emancipation Proclamation.

October   Battle of Corinth, Mississippi.

November	Democrats elect Horatio Seymour as governor of New York; Democrats win political victories in Illinois, New Jersey, and Wisconsin.
	Major General Ambrose Burnside assumes command of the Army of the Potomac.
December	Battle of Fredericksburg, Virginia.

1863

January	The Emancipation Proclamation goes into effect.
	Major General Joseph Hooker replaces Major General Ambrose Burnside.
March	President Abraham Lincoln signs the Conscription Act.
April	A civilian mob plunders wagons and shops during the Richmond, Virginia, bread riot.
	Brigadier General John Sappington Marmaduke begins his raid out of Arkansas into Missouri.
May	Confederate victory at Chancellorsville, Virginia.
	Siege of Vicksburg, Mississippi, begins.
June	Major General George Gordon Meade replaces Hooker as commander of the Army of the Potomac.
July	Union victory at Gettysburg, Pennsylvania.
	General Ulysses S. Grant's siege at Vicksburg ends with Confederate surrender.
	Draft riots in New York and other northern cities.
	Federal assault on Battery Wagner, South Carolina.
August	William Clarke Quantrill and his raiders sack the city of Lawrence, Kansas, murdering nearly 150 men and boys.
	Brigadier General Thomas Ewing issues General Order No. 11, evacuating civilians from western counties in Missouri.
September	Battle at Chickamauga.
November	Lincoln gives his famous address at Gettysburg.

December   Thirty-eighth Congress convenes in Washington, D.C.

               Lincoln issues Proclamation of Amnesty and Reconstruction.

1864

January   Missouri senator John B. Henderson proposes the Thirteenth
               Amendment to the federal Constitution to abolish slavery through-
               out the United States.

May   General William T. Sherman begins his march on Atlanta.

August   The Democratic Party nominates General George B. McClellan for
               president.

September   Sherman captures Atlanta.

October   General Sterling Price's army is defeated at Westport, Missouri; last
               battle in Missouri.

November   Abraham Lincoln is elected to serve a second term, with Andrew
               Johnson, of Tennessee, as vice president.

               Sherman leaves Atlanta and begins his March to the Sea.

December   Sherman captures Savannah.

1865

January   Missouri constitutional convention meets in St. Louis and abolishes
               slavery. Missouri's Drake Constitution includes a provision for an
               "ironclad oath" that disfranchises traitors.

March   Creation of Bureau of Refugees, Freedmen, and Abandoned
               Lands.

April   General Ulysses S. Grant captures Richmond.

               General Robert E. Lee surrenders the Army of Northern Virginia to
               General Ulysses S. Grant at Appomattox, Virginia.

               John Wilkes Booth assassinates President Abraham Lincoln.

               Lincoln dies; Vice President Andrew Johnson takes the oath of office.

               Joseph E. Johnston surrenders to General William T. Sherman at
               Durham Station, North Carolina.

               Booth captured.

May   Johnson declares armed resistance to the United States govern-
                ment at an end.

                Johnson grants general amnesty to rebels.

July   Lincoln assassination conspirators are executed in Washington, D.C.

December   Thirteenth Amendment is ratified.

1866

April   The U.S. Supreme Court rules in *Ex parte Milligan* that use of mili-
                tary tribunals to try citizens when civilian courts are still operating
                is unconstitutional.

                The Ku Klux Klan is established in Tennessee and employs vio-
                lence and intimidation to prevent black suffrage.

June   Congress passes the Fourteenth Amendment to the federal Consti-
                tution; President Andrew Johnson vetoes the First Reconstruction
                Act.

1867

March   Congress passes the Military Reconstruction Act, placing former
                Confederate states in five military districts and making ratification
                of the Fourteenth Amendment and the drafting of state constitu-
                tions that provide for black suffrage conditions of readmission.

1868

February–May   Impeachment of President Andrew Johnson.

July   Fourteenth Amendment ratified.

1869

February   Fifteenth Amendment passed.

1870

February   Fifteenth Amendment ratified.

1873

September   Susan Blow opens the first public kindergarten in the United States
                in St. Louis.

Discussion Questions

CHAPTER 1: SLAVERY IN MISSOURI

1. Consider what you know about slaves living on large plantations in the Cotton South and compare their situation with that of slaves living in Missouri.

2. In your view, what was the most difficult challenge confronting Missouri's slaves?

3. Why did Dred Scott fail in his bid for freedom when so many other slaves, including Rachel, who sued for their liberty under the 1824 freedom statute succeeded?

4. What do you make of the proslavery arguments contained in some of the documents in this book (for example, A. A. Edwards's letter to his uncle Lewis G. Harvey)? What do these attitudes tell you about Missourians' relationship with their slaves?

CHAPTER 2: MISSOURI DIVIDES

1. Why did Missouri's admission to the Union become such a controversial issue? What was at stake for each side in the debate?

2. In your opinion, were the compromises that settled these difficulties a reasonable solution? Why or why not?

3. How do you understand the role of a western state like Missouri in the national conflict between North and South?

4. Why was Kansas statehood such an explosive issue? Why did violence break out there?

5. Why did Stephen A. Douglas (rather than one of the other Democratic candidates) win Missouri's popular vote in the 1860 presidential election? Did that outcome surprise you? Why or why not?

6. Consider Governor Claiborne Jackson's activities during the first year of the Civil War. In your view, was he a competent political leader? Why or why not? What could he or should he have done differently?

CHAPTER 3: MISSOURIANS CONFRONT WAR

1. How likely was it that the state of Missouri could have joined the Confederacy? In your view, was it a close decision? Or was the state's loyalty a foregone conclusion?

2. Who were the key players in the battle for Missouri? In your view, who was the most powerful figure in the conflict over secession?

3. Consider what you know about the Democratic and Republican parties during the Civil War. You might make a chart listing their key beliefs, values, and platforms. Which party do you believe was ultimately more important in keeping Missouri in the Union?

4. What was the role of ethnic divisions in determining the outcome of the secession crisis in Missouri?

CHAPTER 4: MISSOURI'S BATTLES

1. Why did the Camp Jackson incident become such a disaster? What was the main cause of the tragedy?

2. List the three most important military engagements in Missouri. Justify your choices, describing casualties, outcomes, and tactical advantages.

3. Why was St. Louis (and not Jefferson City) such a crucial objective for both sides?

4. What was the significance of the battle at Wilson's Creek in Missouri's decision to remain loyal?

5. What was the greatest problem Union commanders faced in their attempt to control Missouri? What about Confederate commanders?

6. What was role did military battles play in Missouri's wartime politics?

7. In your opinion, what were the greatest challenges confronting Confederate and Union soldiers from Missouri?

CHAPTER 5: CIVILIANS COPE WITH WAR

1. How were civilians able to help the war effort (on either side)?

2. Describe refugee relief efforts. Who had the greatest responsibility for caring for refugees?

3. How would you explain the attitudes of women like Lucy Thurman? Why would she encourage a Confederate soldier to take the oath of loyalty?

4. Why would soldiers have become so callous toward civilians?

CHAPTER 6: BUSHWHACKERS, JAYHAWKERS, AND PRISONERS

1. Why was guerrilla fighting such a significant issue in Missouri, as opposed to other border states? What do you think accounts for the viciousness along the border?

2. In your view, was General Thomas Ewing's General Order No. 11 a necessary and wise move? Why or why not? How else could Ewing have handled the situation?

3. Discuss loyalty oaths in Missouri. Were they effective in controlling civilian unrest? Did they help restore peace, or did they contribute to the problems of dissent?

4. Describe the refugee problem in wartime Missouri. What were some of their most serious hardships?

CHAPTER 7: FIRST STEPS TOWARD EMANCIPATION

1. Draw up a timeline of the process of emancipation in Missouri. You may want to consider the effects of earlier events, such as the passage of the 1824 freedom statute, the *Dred Scott* decision, and military activities within the state.

2. Why did white Missouri residents began to change their minds about slavery, while some of their representatives in Washington remained stubbornly opposed to emancipation?

3. Which of these three groups had the greatest impact on emancipation: Missouri's slaves, radical politicians, or the U.S. Army?

4. Why did nonslaveholding Missourians fear emancipation?

5. How did enslaved Missourians cope with the transition to freedom?

CHAPTER 8: RECONCILIATION AND PROMISES

1. Summarize and assess Provisional Governor Hamilton Gamble's career. How effective was he as a wartime political leader?

2. Given the radical Republican presence in Missouri politics, why was it so difficult for free black people to attain political rights?

3. Do you believe that Reconstruction in Missouri was a success? A failure?

4. Were the political shifts toward radicalism helpful to other groups seeking to gain greater rights and opportunities?

5. Why did Missouri's economy recover so quickly after the war?

Notes

PREFACE

1. *Missouri Republican*, November 10, 1861.

INTRODUCTION

1. *St. Louis Globe-Democrat*, January 19, 1856.

2. Perry McCandless, *A History of Missouri*, vol. 2, *1820 to 1860* (Columbia: University of Missouri Press, 2000), 31.

3. William E. Parrish, Charles T. Jones Jr., and Lawrence O. Christensen, *Missouri: The Heart of the Nation* (St. Louis: Forum Press, 1980), 55.

4. Diane Mutti Burke, "On Slavery's Borders: Slavery and Slaveholding on Missouri's Farms, 1821–1865" (PhD diss., Emory University, 2004).

5. R. Douglas Hurt, *Agriculture and Slavery in Missouri's Little Dixie* (Columbia: University of Missouri Press, 1992), 273–78.

CHAPTER 1: SLAVERY IN MISSOURI

1. R. Douglas Hurt, *Agriculture and Slavery in Missouri's Little Dixie* (Columbia: University of Missouri Press, 1992), 2–6, 290; Diane Mutti Burke, "On Slavery's Borders: Slavery and Slaveholding on Missouri's Farms, 1821–1865" (PhD diss., Emory University, 2004).

2. *Annals of the Congress of the United States*, 16th Cong., 1st sess., 1462.

3. Perry McCandless, *A History of Missouri*, vol. 2, *1820 to 1860* (Columbia: University of Missouri Press, 1973), 14–16.

4. Hurt, *Little Dixie*, 67.

5. For a discussion of the Missouri Compromise, see Floyd Calvin Shoemaker, *Missouri's Struggle for Statehood, 1804–1821* (Jefferson City, Mo.: Hugh Stevens Printing, 1916; repr., New York: Russell and Russell, 1969).

6. McCandless, *History of Missouri*, 2:6.

7. Burke, "On Slavery's Borders," chap. 2.

8. Don Fehrenbacher, *Slavery, Law, and Politics: The Dred Scott Case in Historical Perspective* (New York: Oxford University Press, 1981).

9. Cyprian Clamorgan, *The Colored Aristocracy of St. Louis*, ed. with an introduction by Julie Winch (Columbia: University of Missouri Press, 1999); William E. Parrish, Charles T. Jones Jr., and Lawrence O. Christensen, *Missouri: The Heart of the Nation* (St. Louis: Forum Press, 1980), 144–45.

10. Hurt, *Little Dixie*, 231, 261.

CHAPTER 2: MISSOURI DIVIDES

1. William E. Parrish, Charles T. Jones Jr., and Lawrence O. Christensen, *Missouri: The Heart of the Nation* (St. Louis: Forum Press, 1980), 149–50.

2. Paul C. Nagel, *Missouri, A Bicentennial History* (New York: Norton, 1977), 77.

3. R. Douglas Hurt, *Agriculture and Slavery in Missouri's Little Dixie* (Columbia: University of Missouri Press, 1992), 280.

4. Nicole Etcheson, *Bleeding Kansas: Contested Liberty in the Civil War Era* (Lawrence: University Press of Kansas, 2004).

5. Robert W. Johannsen, *Stephen A. Douglas* (Urbana: University of Illinois Press, 1997), 474.

6. Edward E. Leslie, *The Devil Knows How to Ride: The True Story of William Clarke Quantrill and His Confederate Raiders* (New York: Da Capo, 1998), 15–16.

7. John Greenleaf Whitter, "Le Marais du Cygne," *Atlantic Monthly* 2, no. 8 (1858): 429.

8. *Dred Scott v. Sandford*, 60 U.S. 393, 407 (1856).

9. Christopher Phillips, *Missouri's Confederate: Claiborne F. Jackson and the Creation of Southern Identity in the Border West* (Columbia: University of Missouri Press, 2000), 229–31.

10. William E. Parrish, *Turbulent Partnership: Missouri and the Union, 1861–1865* (Columbia: University of Missouri Press, 1963), 1–2, 4–6.

11. Dennis Boman, *Lincoln's Resolute Unionist: Hamilton Gamble, Dred Scott Dissenter and Missouri's Civil War Governor* (Baton Rouge: Louisiana State University Press, 2006), 99–100. For an excellent discussion of St. Louis during the secession crisis, see Louis S. Gerteis, *Civil War St. Louis* (Lawrence: University Press of Kansas, 2001).

CHAPTER 3: MISSOURIANS CONFRONT WAR

1. Robert J. Rombauer, *The Union Cause in St. Louis in 1861* (St. Louis: St. Louis Centennial Year, 1909). Nearly 80 percent of the votes for delegates seated pro-Union candidates. See Christopher Phillips, *Missouri's Confederate: Claiborne F. Jackson and the Creation of Southern Identity in the Border West* (Columbia: University of Missouri Press, 2000), 236.

2. Phil Gottschalk, *In Deadly Earnest: The History of the First Missouri Brigade, CSA* (Columbia, Mo.: Missouri River Press, 1991). See also Leslie Anders, *The Eighteenth Missouri* (Indianapolis, Ind.: Bobbs-Merrill, 1968).

3. Blair eventually asked his Wide Awakes as well as the German *Schwarzjäger* (Black Marksmen) to enlist in the federal army and placed them under General Nathaniel Lyon.

4. Phillips, *Missouri's Confederate*, 235–36.

5. William E. Parrish, *Turbulent Partnership: Missouri and the Union, 1861–1865* (Columbia: University of Missouri Press, 1963), 20.

6. For a description of the Camp Jackson incident and continuing problems in St. Louis, see Louis S. Gerteis, *Civil War St. Louis* (Lawrence: University Press of Kansas, 2001).

7. Phillips, *Missouri's Confederate*, 268.

8. William E. Parrish, *A History of Missouri*, vol. 3, *1860 to 1875* (Columbia: University of Missouri Press, 1973). For a discussion of the rival legislature, see pages 49–51.

9. For Gamble's wartime contributions, see Dennis Boman, *Lincoln's Resolute Unionist: Hamilton Gamble, Dred Scott Dissenter and Missouri's Civil War Governor* (Baton Rouge: Louisiana State University Press, 2006).

10. Parrish, *History of Missouri*, 3:59.

11. For the Twenty-first Missouri, see Leslie Anders, *The Twenty-first Missouri: From Home Guard to Union Regiment* (Westport, Conn.: Greenwood, 1975.)

CHAPTER 4: MISSOURI'S BATTLES

1. Christopher Phillips, *Missouri's Confederate: Claiborne F. Jackson and the Creation of Southern Identity in the Border West* (Columbia: University of Missouri Press, 2000), 260–61.

2. Ibid., 156; William E. Parrish, *A History of Missouri*, vol. 3, *1860 to 1875* (Columbia: University of Missouri Press, 1973), 105.

3. Parrish, *History of Missouri*, 3:46–50.

4. Christopher Phillips, *Damned Yankee: The Life of General Nathaniel Lyon* (Columbia: University of Missouri Press, 1990).

5. Douglas L. Gifford, *Lexington Battlefield Guide* (Winfield, Mo.: Douglas L. Gifford, 2004), 5–6.

CHAPTER 5: CIVILIANS COPE WITH WAR

1. *The War of the Rebellion: A Compilation of the Official Records of the Union and Confederate Armies*, ser. 1, vol. 3 (Washington, D.C.: Government Printing Office, 1881), 423.

2. Perry McCandless, *A History of Missouri*, vol. 2, *1820 to 1860* (Columbia: University of Missouri Press, 2001), 59–60; William E. Parrish, *Turbulent Partnership: Missouri and the Union, 1861–1865* (Columbia: University of Missouri Press, 1963), 53.

3. *Official Records*, ser. 1, vol. 3, 529–30.

4. William E. Parrish, *Missouri under Radical Rule, 1865–1870* (Columbia: University of Missouri Press, 1965), 4–5.

5. Parrish, *Turbulent Partnership*, 99.

6. Michael Fellman, *Inside War: The Guerrilla Conflict in Missouri during the American Civil War* (New York: Oxford University Press, 1989), xix, 98.

7. See Rosemary Hopkins, "Tried in the Furnace of Affliction" (PhD diss., Saint Louis University, 2004).

8. Parrish, *Turbulent Partnership*, 78.

9. For home front efforts during the Civil War, see J. Matthew Gallman, *The North Fights the Civil War: The Home Front* (Chicago: I. R. Dee, 1994).

10. Hopkins, *Tried in the Furnace*, 152–54.

11. Mary Denis Maher, *To Bind Up the Wounds: Catholic Sister Nurses in the U.S. Civil War* (New York: Greenwood, 1989), 37–38.

12. Mark E. Neely Jr., *The Fate of Liberty: Abraham Lincoln and Civil Liberties* (New York: Oxford University Press, 1991), 128–29.

13. Dennis K. Boman, *Lincoln's Resolute Unionist: Hamilton Gamble, Dred Scott Dissenter and Missouri's Civil War Governor* (Baton Rouge: Louisiana State University Press, 2006).

14. *The War of the Rebellion: A Compilation of the Official Records of the Union and Confederate Armies*, ser. 1, vol. 35, pt. 2 (Washington, D.C.: Government Printing Office, 1891).

15. According to historian Howard V. Canan, the Paw Paw Militia was composed of the Eighty-first and Eighty-second regiments of the Enrolled Missouri Militia under the command of Colonel John Scott and Colonel James H. Moss. Canan, *Missouri Historical Review* 4, no. 62 (1968): 431–88.

CHAPTER 6: BUSHWHACKERS, JAYHAWKERS, AND PRISONERS

1. Michael Fellman, *Inside War: The Guerrilla Conflict in Missouri during the American Civil War* (New York: Oxford University Press, 1990), 254–55.

2. Jay Monaghan, *Civil War on the Western Border, 1854–1865* (Boston: Little, Brown, 1955), 289.

3. For an in-depth discussion of the painting and Bingham's politics, see Barbara Groseclose, "Painting, Politics, and George Caleb Bingham," *American Art Journal* 10 (November 1978): 4–19.

4. Michael Fellman, *Inside War: The Guerrilla Conflict in Missouri during the American Civil War* (New York: Oxford University Press, 1989), 211.

5. William E. Parrish, Charles T. Jones Jr., and Lawrence O. Christensen, *Missouri: The Heart of the Nation* (St. Louis: Forum Press, 1980), 187.

6. Edward E. Leslie, *The Devil Knows How to Ride: The True Story of William Clarke Quantrill and His Confederate Raiders* (New York: Da Capo, 1998), 365; Fellman, *Inside War,* 232–33.

7. For more information on Russell's experiences, see Cyrus A. Peterson and Joseph Mills Hanson, *Pilot Knob: The Thermopylae of the West* (New York: Neale, 1914), 185–96.

8. I am indebted to Hank Trent for this explanation.

CHAPTER 7: FIRST STEPS TOWARD EMANCIPATION

1. R. Douglas Hurt, *Agriculture and Slavery in Missouri's Little Dixie* (Columbia: University of Missouri Press, 1992), 123.

2. Vernon Volpe, "The Frémonts and Emancipation in Missouri," *Historian* 56, no. 2 (1994): 336–54.

3. Dennis K. Boman, *Lincoln's Resolute Unionist: Hamilton Gamble, Dred Scott Dissenter and Missouri's Civil War Governor* (Baton Rouge: Louisiana State University Press, 2006.)

4. Allen C. Guelzo, *Lincoln's Emancipation Proclamation: The End of Slavery in America* (New York: Simon and Schuster, 2004).

5. William E. Gienapp, "Abraham Lincoln and the Border States," *Journal of the Abraham Lincoln Association* 13 (1992): 13–46.

6. Ira Berlin, Barbara J. Fields, Steven Fr. Miller, Joseph P. Reidy, and Leslie S. Rowland, *The Wartime Genesis of Free Labor: The Upper South,* Freedom: A Documentary History of Emancipation, ser. 1, vol. 2 (New York: Cambridge University Press, 1993), 551–57.

7. Boman, *Gamble,* 209–10.

8. William E. Parrish, *A History of Missouri,* vol. 3, *1860 to 1875* (Columbia: University of Missouri Press, 1973), 147, 182.

CHAPTER 8: RECONCILIATION AND PROMISES

1. William E. Parrish, Charles T. Jones Jr., and Lawrence O. Christensen, *Missouri: The Heart of the Nation* (St. Louis: Forum Press, 1980), 185.

2. Floyd Calvin Shoemaker, *Missouri's Struggle for Statehood, 1804–1821* (Jefferson City, Mo.: Hugh Stevens Printing, 1916; repr., New York: Russell and Russell, 1969), 943–44.

3. Perry McCandless, *A History of Missouri*, vol. 2, *1820 to 1860* (Columbia: University of Missouri Press, 2001), 195, and William E. Parrish, *Turbulent Partnership: Missouri and the Union, 1861–1865* (Columbia: University of Missouri Press, 1963), 78.

4. C. D. Drake's speech at Louisville was recorded in William Barclay Napton's diary on February 22, 1864, quoted in Barclay, *The Union on Trial: The Political Journals of William Barclay Napton, 1829–1883*, ed. Christopher Phillips and Jason Pendleton (Columbia: University of Missouri Press, 2005), 242–43.

5. *Rolla Express*, September 5, 1865.

6. David D. March, "Charles D. Drake and the Constitutional Convention of 1865," *Missouri Historical Review* 47 (January 1953): 110–23.

7. Duane G. Meyer, *The Heritage of Missouri*, 3rd ed. (St. Louis: River City, 1982), 507.

8. William E. Parrish, "Reconstruction Politics in Missouri, 1865–1870," in *Radicalism, Racism, and Party Realignment: The Border States during Reconstruction*, ed. Richard O. Curry (Baltimore, Md.: Johns Hopkins Press, 1969), 1–36.

9. Quoted in Parrish, *History of Missouri*, 3:156.

10. Ibid., 3:201.

11. See Christopher Phillips and Jason L. Pendleton, *The Union on Trial: The Political Journals of Judge William Barclay Napton, 1829–1883* (Columbia: University of Missouri Press, 2005).

Selected Bibliography

INTRODUCTION

Anderson, Galusha. *The Story of a Border City during the Civil War*. Boston: Little, Brown, 1908.

Bannon, John F. "Missouri, a Borderland." *Missouri Historical Review* 63 (January 1969): 227–40.

Donald, David Herbert, Jean Harvey Baker, and Michael F. Holt. *The Civil War and Reconstruction*. New York: Norton, 2001.

Levine, Bruce. *Half Slave and Half Free: The Roots of the Civil War*. New York: Hill and Wang, 1992.

McCandless, Perry. *A History of Missouri*. Vol. 2, *1820 to 1860*. Columbia: University of Missouri Press, 2000.

McPherson, James M. *Battle Cry of Freedom: The Civil War Era*. New York: Oxford University Press, 1988.

McPherson, James M., and William J. Cooper Jr., eds. *Writing the Civil War: The Quest to Understand*. Columbia: University of South Carolina Press, 1998.

Paludan, Phillip Shaw. *A People's Contest: The Union and Civil War, 1861–1865*. 2nd ed. Lawrence: University Press of Kansas, 1996.

Parrish, William E. *A History of Missouri*. Vol. 3, *1860 to 1875*. Columbia: University of Missouri Press, 1973, 2001.

CHAPTER 1: SLAVERY IN MISSOURI

Bellamy, Donnie D. "Free Blacks in Antebellum Missouri, 1820–1860." *Missouri Historical Review* 67 (January 1973): 198–226.

Berwanger, Eugene H. *The Frontier against Slavery*. Urbana: University of Illinois Press, 1971.

Blassingame, John W. *The Slave Community: Plantation Life in the Antebellum South*. New York: Oxford University Press, 1979.

Burke, Diane Mutti. "On Slavery's Borders: Slavery and Slaveholding on Missouri's Farms, 1821–1865." PhD diss., Emory University, 2004.

Fehrenbacher, Don E. *Slavery, Law, and Politics: The Dred Scott Case in Historical Perspective*. New York: Oxford University Press, 1981.

Gerteis, Louis S. *From Contraband to Freedman: Federal Policy toward Southern Blacks, 1861–1865*. Westport, Conn.: Greenwood, 1973.

Hermann, Janet S. "The McIntosh Affair." *Missouri Historical Society Bulletin* 26 (January 1970): 123–43.

Hurt, R. Douglas. *Agriculture and Slavery in Missouri's Little Dixie*. Columbia: University of Missouri Press, 1992.

McLaurin, Melton A. *Celia, a Slave*. Athens: University of Georgia Press, 1999.

Morrison, Michael A. *Slavery and the American West: The Eclipse of Manifest Destiny and the Coming of the Civil War*. Chapel Hill: University of North Carolina Press, 1997.

Trexler, Harrison. *Slavery in Missouri, 1804–1865*. Baltimore, Md.: Johns Hopkins Press, 1914.

Voegeli, V. Jacque. *Free but Not Equal: The Midwest and the Negro during the Civil War.* Chicago: University of Chicago Press, 1967.

CHAPTER 2: MISSOURI DIVIDES

Baker, Jean H. *Affairs of Party: The Political Culture of Northern Democrats in the Mid-nineteenth Century.* New York: Fordham University Press, 1998.

Bartlett, Ruhl Jacob. *John C. Frémont and the Republican Party.* New York: Da Capo, 1970.

Bates, Edward. *The Diary of Edward Bates, 1859–1866.* Edited by Howard K. Beale. Washington, D.C.: Government Printing Office, 1933.

Boman, Dennis K. *Abiel Leonard, Yankee Slaveholder, Eminent Jurist, and Passionate Unionist.* Lewiston, N.Y.: Edwin Mellen, 2002.

———. *Lincoln's Resolute Unionist: Hamilton Gamble, Dred Scott Dissenter and Missouri's Civil War Governor.* Baton Rouge: Louisiana State University Press, 2006.

Britton, Wiley. *The Civil War on the Border, 1861–1862.* New York: G. P. Putnam's Sons, 1899.

Brugioni, Dino A. *The Civil War in Missouri as Seen from the Capital City.* Jefferson City, Mo.: Summers, 1987.

Cain, Marvin R. *Lincoln's Attorney General: Edward Bates of Missouri.* Columbia: University of Missouri Press, 1965.

Etcheson, Nicole. *Bleeding Kansas: Contested Liberty in the Civil War Era.* Lawrence: University Press of Kansas, 2004.

Foner, Eric. *Free Soil, Free Labor, Free Men: The Ideology of the Republican Party before the Civil War.* New York: Oxford University Press, 1970.

Levine, Bruce. *The Spirit of 1848: German Immigrants, Labor Conflict, and the Coming of the Civil War.* Urbana: University of Illinois Press, 1992.

Mering, John Vollmer. *The Whig Party in Missouri.* Columbia: University of Missouri Press, 1983.

Neely, Jeremy. *The Border between Them: Violence and Reconciliation on the Kansas-Missouri Line.* Columbia: University of Missouri Press, 2007.

Parrish, William E. *David Rice Atchison of Missouri: Border Politician.* Columbia: University of Missouri Press, 1961.

———. *Frank Blair: Lincoln's Conservative.* Columbia: University of Missouri Press, 1998.

———. *Turbulent Partnership: Missouri and the Union, 1861–1865.* Columbia: University of Missouri Press, 1963.

Phillips, Christopher. "'The Crime against Missouri': Slavery, Kansas, and the Cant of Southernness in the Border West." *Civil War History* 48 (March 2002): 60–81.

———. *Missouri's Confederate: Claiborne F. Jackson and the Creation of Southern Identity in the Border West.* Columbia: University of Missouri Press, 2000.

CHAPTER 3: MISSOURIANS CONFRONT WAR

Anderson, Galusha. *The Story of a Border City during the Civil War.* Boston: Little, Brown, 1908.

Attie, Jeanie. *Patriotic Toil: Northern Women and the American Civil War.* Ithaca, N.Y.: Cornell University Press, 1998.

Burnett, Robyn, and Ken Luebbering. *Immigrant Women in the Settlement of Missouri.* Columbia: University of Missouri Press, 2005.

Corbett, Katharine T. *In Her Place: A Guide to St. Louis Women's History.* St. Louis: Missouri Historical Society, 1999.

Gerteis, Louis S. *Civil War St. Louis.* Lawrence: University Press of Kansas, 2001.

Gienapp, William E. "Abraham Lincoln and the Border States." *Journal of the Abraham Lincoln Association* 13 (1992): 13–46.

Hyde, William, and Howard L. Conrad. *Encyclopedia of the History of St. Louis: A Compendium of History and Biography for Ready Reference.* New York: Southern History, 1899.

Kirschten, Ernest. *Catfish and Crystal.* Garden City, N.Y.: Doubleday, 1960.

Krug, Mark M., ed. *Mrs. Hill's Journal: Civil War Reminiscences.* Chicago: Lakeside, 1980.

Monaghan, Jay. *Civil War on the Western Border, 1854–1865.* Boston: Little, Brown, 1955.

Peterson, Norma L. *Freedom and Franchise: The Political Career of B. Gratz Brown.* Columbia: University of Missouri Press, 1965.

Phillips, Christopher, and Jason L. Pendleton, eds. *The Union on Trial: The Political Journals of Judge William Barclay Napton, 1829–1883.* Columbia: University of Missouri Press, 2005.

Primm, James Neal. *Lion of the Valley: St. Louis, Missouri.* St. Louis: Missouri Historical Society, 1998.

Rombauer, Robert J. *The Union Cause in St. Louis in 1861.* St. Louis: St. Louis Centennial Year, 1909.

Rowan, Steven, and James Neal Primm, eds. *Germans for a Free Missouri: Translations from the St. Louis Radical Press, 1857–1862.* Columbia: University of Missouri Press, 1983.

Scharf, J. Thomas. *History of St. Louis City and County.* 4 vols. Philadelphia: Louis H. Everts, 1883.

Stampp, Kenneth. *And the War Came: The North and the Secession Crisis, 1860–1861.* Baton Rouge: Louisiana State University Press, 1970.

Winter, William C. *The Civil War in St. Louis: A Guided Tour.* St. Louis: Missouri Historical Society, 1994.

CHAPTER 4: MISSOURI'S BATTLES

Adamson, Hans C. *Rebellion in Missouri, 1861: Nathaniel Lyon and His Army of the West.* Philadelphia: Chilton, 1961.

Anders, Leslie. *The Eighteenth Missouri.* Indianapolis, Ind.: Bobbs-Merrill, 1968.

———. *The Twenty-first Missouri: From Home Guard to Union Regiment.* Westport, Conn.: Greenwood, 1975.

Bartels, Carolyn M. *The Civil War in Missouri Day by Day, 1861–1865.* Shawnee Mission, Kans.: Two Trails, 1992.

Bearss, Edwin C. *The Battle of Wilson's Creek.* Bozeman, Mont.: Aircraft Printers, 1975.

Castel, Albert. *General Sterling Price and the Civil War in the West.* Baton Rouge: Louisiana State University, 1968.

———. "A New View of the Battle of Pea Ridge." *Missouri Historical Review* 62 (January 1968): 136–51.

Connelly, Donald B. *John M. Schofield and the Politics of Generalship.* Chapel Hill: University of North Carolina Press, 2006.

Gifford, Douglas L. *The Battle of Pilot Knob: Staff Ride and Battlefield Tour Guide.* Winfield, Mo.: Douglas L. Gifford, 2003.

———. *Lexington Battlefield Guide.* Winfield, Mo.: Douglas L. Gifford, 2004.

Hinze, David C., and Karen Farnham. *The Battle of Carthage: Border War in Southwest Missouri, July 5, 1861.* Campbell, Calif.: Savas, 1997.

Peckham, James. *General Nathaniel Lyon and Missouri in 1861: A Monograph of the Great Rebellion.* New York: American News, 1866.

Peterson, Cyrus A., and Joseph Mills Hanson. *Pilot Knob: The Thermopylae of the West.* New York: Neale, 1914.

Peterson, Richard C., James E. McGhee, Kip A. Lindberg, and Keith I. Doleen. *Sterling Price's Lieutenants: A Guide to the Officers and Organization of the Missouri State Guard, 1861–1865.* Shawnee Mission, Kans.: Two Trails, 1995.

Phillips, Christopher. *Damned Yankee: The Life of General Nathaniel Lyon.* Columbia: University of Missouri Press, 1990.

Piston, William Garrett, and Richard W. Hatter III. *Wilson's Creek: The Second Battle of the Civil War and the Men Who Fought It.* Chapel Hill: University of North Carolina Press, 2000.

Schofield, John M. *Forty-six Years in the Army.* New York: Century, 1897.

Shalhope, Robert E. *Sterling Price: Portrait of a Southerner.* Columbia: University of Missouri Press, 1971.

CHAPTER 5: CIVILIANS COPE WITH WAR

Bradbury, John F., Jr. "Buckwheat Cake Philanthropy: Refugees and the Union Army in the Ozarks." *Arkansas Historical Quarterly* 57 (Autumn 1998): 233–54.

Forman, Jacob Gilbert. *The Western Sanitary Commission: A Sketch of Its Origin, History, Labors for the Sick and Wounded of the Western Armies, and Aid Given to Freedmen and Union Refugees, with Incidents of Hospital Life.* St. Louis: Mississippi Valley Sanitary Fair, 1864.

Frémont, Jessie. *The Letters of Jessie Benton Frémont.* Edited by Pamela Herr and Mary Lee Spence. Urbana: University of Illinois Press, 1993.

Hyman, Harold Melvin. *Era of the Oath: Northern Loyalty Tests during the Civil War and Reconstruction.* Philadelphia: University of Pennsylvania Press, 1954.

Massey, Mary Elizabeth. *Refugee Life in the Confederacy.* Baton Rouge: Louisiana State University Press, 1964.

CHAPTER 6: BUSHWHACKERS, JAYHAWKERS, AND PRISONERS

Breihan, Carl W. *Sam Hildebrand, Guerrilla.* Wauwatosa, Wis.: Leatherstocking Books, 1984.

Brownlee, Richard S. *Gray Ghosts of the Confederacy.* Baton Rouge: Louisiana State University Press, 1958.

Castel, Albert. "A New View of the Battle of Pea Ridge." *Missouri Historical Review* 62 (January 1968): 136–51.

————. "Order No. 11 and the Civil War on the Border." *Missouri Historical Review* 57 (July 1963): 357–86.

Castel, Albert, and Thomas Goodrich. *Bloody Bill Anderson: The Short, Savage Life of a Civil War Guerrilla.* Mechanicsburg, Pa.: Stackpole Books, 1998.

Cornish, Dudley T. *The Sable Arm: Negro Troops in the Union Army, 1861–1865.* New York: Russell and Russell, 1953. Reprint, New York: Norton, 1966.

Fellman, Michael. *Inside War: The Guerrilla Conflict in Missouri during the American Civil War.* New York: Oxford University Press, 1989.

Gambill, Edward L. *Conservative Ordeal: Northern Democrats and Reconstruction, 1865–1868.* Ames: Iowa State University Press, 1981.

Glatthaar, Joseph T. *Forged in Battle: The Civil War Alliance of Black Soldiers and White Officers.* New York: Free Press, 1990.

Gottschalk, Phil. *In Deadly Earnest: The History of the First Missouri Brigade, CSA.* Columbia, Mo.: Missouri River Press, 1991.

Irwin, Ray W., ed. "Missouri in Crisis: The Journal of Captain Albert Tracy, 1861." Pts. 1 and 2. *Missouri Historical Review* 51 (October 1956): 8–21; 51 (January 1957): 151–64.

Johnson, Robert Underwood, and Howard L. Conrad, eds. *Battles and Leaders of the Civil War.* New York: Thomas Yoseloff, 1956.

Klement, Frank L. *Copperheads in the Middle West.* Chicago: University of Chicago Press, 1960.

Leslie, Edward E. *The Devil Knows How to Ride: The True Story of William Clarke Quantrill and His Confederate Raiders.* New York: Da Capo, 1998.

Neely, Mark E., Jr. *The Fate of Liberty: Abraham Lincoln and Civil Liberties.* New York: Oxford University Press, 1991.

Nichols, Bruce. *Guerrilla Warfare in Civil War Missouri.* Vols. 1 and 2. Jefferson, N.C.: McFarland, 2004 and 2007.

Weber, Jennifer L. *Copperheads: The Rise and Fall of Lincoln's Opponents in the North.* New York: Oxford University Press, 2006.

CHAPTER 7: FIRST STEPS TOWARD EMANCIPATION

Berlin, Ira, Barbara J. Fields, Steven Fr. Miller, Joseph P. Reidy, and Leslie S. Rowland, eds. *Free At Last: A Documentary History of Slavery, Freedom, and the Civil War.* New York: New Press, 1992.

Foner, Eric, and Joshua Brown. *Forever Free: The Story of Emancipation and Reconstruction.* New York: Knopf, 2005.

Guelzo, Allen C. *Lincoln's Emancipation Proclamation: The End of Slavery in America.* New York: Simon and Schuster, 2005.

Richardson, Joe M. "The American Missionary Association and Black Education in Civil War Missouri." *Missouri Historical Review* 69 (July 1971): 433–48.

Volpe, Vernon. "The Frémonts and Emancipation in Missouri." *Historian* 56 (Winter 1994): 339–54.

Washington, Versalle F. *Eagles on Their Buttons: A Black Infantry Regiment in the Civil War.* Columbia: University of Missouri Press, 1999.

CHAPTER 8: RECONCILIATION AND PROMISES

Apperson, George M. "Presbyterians and Radical Republicans: President Lincoln, Dr. McPheeters, and Civil War in Missouri." *American Presbyterians* 73 (Winter 1995): 239–50.

Blight, David. *Race and Reunion: The Civil War in American Memory.* Cambridge, Mass.: Belknap Press, 2001.

Foner, Eric. *Reconstruction: America's Unfinished Revolution, 1863–1877.* New York: Harper, 2002.

Parrish, William E. *Missouri under Radical Rule, 1865–1870.* Columbia: University of Missouri Press, 1965.

Richardson, Heather Cox. *The Death of Reconstruction.* Cambridge, Mass.: Harvard University Press, 2001.

————. *West of Appomattox: The Reconstruction of America after the Civil War.* New Haven, Conn.: Yale University Press, 2007.

Vorenberg, Michael. *Final Freedom: The Civil War, the Abolition of Slavery, and the Thirteenth Amendment.* Cambridge: Cambridge University Press, 2001.

Wang, Xi. *The Trial of Democracy: Black Suffrage and Northern Republicans, 1860–1910.* Athens: University of Georgia Press, 1997.

Index